CLUNY MACPHERSON is professor in the School of Social and Cultural Studies at Massey University, Albany. He is an author of the textbook *Oceania: an Introduction to the Cultures and Identities of Pacific Islanders* (2001), editor of a number of collections, and author of numerous book chapters and journal articles. He gave the 2007 Macmillan Brown lectures on the subject of this book.

LA'AVASA MACPHERSON is a research associate at Oceania Inc. and co-author with Cluny of *Sāmoan Medical Beliefs and Practices* (AUP, 1990).

The Warm Winds of Change

GLOBALISATION IN CONTEMPORARY SĀMOA

Cluny and La'avasa Macpherson

AUCKLAND UNIVERSITY PRESS

First published 2009

Auckland University Press
University of Auckland
Private Bag 92019
Auckland 1142
New Zealand
www.auckland.ac.nz/aup

© Cluny and La'avasa Macpherson 2009

ISBN 978 1 86940 445 1

National Library of New Zealand Cataloguing-in-Publication Data
Macpherson, Cluny.
The warm winds of change : globalisation and contemporary
Samoa / Cluny and La'avasa Macpherson.
Includes bibliographical references and index.
ISBN 978-1-86940-445-1
1. Globalization—Social aspects—Samoa. 2. Globalization—
Economic aspects—Samoa. 3. Samoa—Social conditions.
I. Macpherson, La'avasa. II. Title.
303.48299614 —dc 22

This book is copyright. Apart from fair dealing for the purpose of private study, research, criticism or review, as permitted under the Copyright Act, no part may be reproduced by any process without prior permission of the publisher.

Printed by Printlink Ltd, Wellington

Mo le fanau peleina
Tahamoana, Penina and Christina

Contents

Acknowledgements *ix*
Introduction 1
1. Warm winds of change 7
2. A brief history of Sāmoa's engagement with global forces 25
3. Migration and social transformation 59
4. Ideas and social transformation 99
5. Technology and social transformation 149
6. Warm winds of change or gathering storm? 185
Notes 194
Bibliography 201
Index 207

Acknowledgements

This is a book about the ways in which Sāmoa has changed and is changing. It identifies a range of forces that have transformed and are transforming the worldview and lifestyle of contemporary Sāmoa. It is the end-product of many conversations with family and friends both in New Zealand and during many visits to Sāmoa over a long period of time. Without the friendship, stories, reflections, insights, frankness, advice and patience of our family and friends, the ideas in this book might never have formed and this book would probably not have been written. We hope that the book fairly reflects the views that were shared with us, but we accept full responsibility where it does not. *Faʻafetai tele, tele lava ia te outou uma, mo lo outou agalelei, ma le fesoasoani, aʻo maua taumafai mo suʻesuʻega ma le tusiaina o lenei tusi.*

We thank our very good friend and long-time colleague, Professor Karen Nero, Director of the Macmillan Brown Centre, and the Centre's Board of Trustees, for the invitation to present the 2007 Macmillan Brown Lectures at the University of Canterbury. That invitation gave us reason to organise our thoughts about contemporary Sāmoa, and it is from this process of organisation and distillation that the idea for the book arose. We wish to thank Karen Nero, David Gegeo and Moana Matthes for their generosity and hospitality during visits to the Centre and for their untiring efforts in arranging the lectures.

The lectures might then have remained a series of downloadable podcasts, but encouragement and support from those who attended the lectures, people who heard the broadcasts, and colleagues who made comments and asked questions propelled our thinking in new and productive directions. However, it was a distinguished colleague, Professor Kerry Howe, who pushed us, as only he can, to write something more. We are grateful to Sam Elworthy for entertaining the possibility that there might be a book in this, to readers who made some helpful suggestions, and again to Sam and Vani Sripathy at AUP for their interest and encouragement throughout the process, and to Ginny Sullivan for her fastidious editing, unlimited patience and unfailing good humour.

Amongst those who listened to the broadcast lectures were our adult children, Tahamoana and Penina, who spent periods of their childhood in Sāmoa and were interested in the changes outlined in the lectures and in the processes that had produced them. They too encouraged us to develop this work and this book is for them. It is an attempt to explain to them how the Sāmoa that they knew and enjoyed as children has changed and why.

Introduction

Books are born and grow. This one grew out of the 2007 Macmillan Brown Lecture series, *The Warm Winds of Change in the Contemporary Pacific*. The lectures, and now this book, drew heavily on findings from a 40-year research partnership that developed out of our interest in Sāmoans in both Sāmoa and abroad. This started in the early 1970s when we carried out fieldwork for the first comprehensive study of Sāmoan migrants in New Zealand (Pitt and Macpherson 1974) and has, since then, led us into such disparate areas as the social correlates of youth suicide (Macpherson and Macpherson 1987), medical knowledge and practice (Macpherson and Macpherson 1990), dependency and sovereignty (Macpherson and Macpherson 1998), changing contours of migrant kinship (Macpherson and Macpherson 1999), ethnic diversity in migrant populations (Macpherson and Macpherson 2000), evangelical religion among migrants (Macpherson and Macpherson 2001), fine mats and the valuation of social honour (Macpherson and Macpherson 2005), social dimensions of the Pacific labour migration process (Macpherson and Macpherson 2006a), the nature and limits of traditional dispute resolution (Macpherson and Macpherson 2006b), and the experiences of migrants' children who have returned to the islands (Macpherson and Macpherson 2009). This book provides an opportunity to acknowledge our partnership in a way that the lectures could not: neither of us could, or would, have produced this work alone. The project has given us a chance to bring together a number of ideas and conversations, and is, we hope, more valuable because of the range of research and experience on which it draws, and the complementary skills we have brought to it.

The series emerged from a growing awareness of the impact of global forces on daily life in the village in which we live during annual stays in

Sāmoa. Evidence of their pervasive, and often almost imperceptible, influence is everywhere, and the series provided both reason and opportunity to outline some changes in village life over the past 40 years and to discuss the forces that have produced them. Since we began to think about these issues over an evening meal, the evening itself provides a convenient illustration of both the changes and the processes that are producing them.

Evenings, in the 1960s and 1970s, were typically quiet times spent with family. In the early evening, when the locust chorus began, adults stopped work, returned to their homes, bathed and chatted. Around the house, children talked as they did chores and played games. When the village church bell rang, the family gathered inside for evening devotions and shared a meal interrupted only by adult conversation and laughter. Dinner, prepared over a fire in a small outdoor cook house, included breadfruit and talo from the family gardens, some fresh fish and a crab caught earlier in the day, washed down with tea made from the leaves of the orange tree behind the house, or with cocoa made from beans from the family cocoa plantation. The meal was served from large, smoke-stained aluminium stockpots and eaten from banana leaves on woven mats, and a few enamel plates and mugs; the tea was made in a large, battered aluminium teapot. After dinner children played outside until it became dark and they went inside where, in the dim glow cast by a single light bulb, adults played animated games of cards and draughts, swapped gossip, discussed the day's events, planned the following day and, occasionally, speculated on the religious significance of particular local and national events. News of the world beyond the village was of limited interest, and only those who made the nightly trip to the pastor's house to listen to the news from Apia on the government radio station 2AP, and a very few people who owned shortwave radios, ever heard it.

Evenings in 2008 are very different. On our first evening in Sāmoa that year, we ate a meal of tinned herrings from Malaysia, rice and noodles from China, washed down with instant coffee from the US, sugar from Fiji and powdered milk from New Zealand. The meal was cooked over gas and in a microwave, and water was boiled in an electric jug in the kitchen. Dessert, a new item on the menu, was ice-cream, which had been kept in the fridge. The meal was served from stainless steel pots and eaten from a floral-patterned Chinese dinner set with matching bowls; the tea was made in a china teapot. With dinner over, we settled down to the Television One news from New Zealand with our family. Adults and children alike watched with great interest and in silence, punctuated only by incoming cellphone calls and text messages. The news was followed by animated discussions over everything from the selection of the latest All Black squad, New Zealand's prospects in the Bledisloe Cup, the wisdom of becoming involved in the Iraq war, Barack Obama's prospects in the US presidential elections and the Labour party's prospects in the forthcoming New Zealand election. The conversation ended with a debate about possible causes of simultaneous floods in England and Bangladesh: were they the consequence of global political inaction on climate change or divine intervention in the biblical tradition? The family spent the rest of the evening watching world news, a BBC documentary on global warming, an Indian television movie and a televised rugby match from Sydney. From time to time people flicked between the Samoan Broadcasting Service channel and the new Chinese channel, CCTV, which offers a broad range of English-language programming.

In a relatively short time, the world beyond the village, as seen on TV, has become for many families in Sāmoa the focal point of the evening. Families even move meals and evening devotions, previously the high point of the day, to accommodate the evening news in both English and Sāmoan. This change reflects the growing interest in events beyond the village and, indeed, beyond Sāmoa. Discussion of these events reflects a new knowledge of the outside world and a growing awareness of its influence on their daily lives.

The 'global' economy has a direct and obvious impact on 'local' daily life, controlling the market for the village's main cash crop, copra; demand for labour from the village both in and beyond Sāmoa; and the prosperity of expatriate relatives. These factors in turn influence opportunities for local employment and the level of remittances received from expatriate relatives, which then determine whether or not people can pay school fees, extend their homes, renovate the village school and buy new uniforms for the village rugby team. World food shortages now translate into rises in prices of new 'staples' such as flour, rice and sugar, and impact in new ways on household economies, which were once almost self-sufficient. Shifts in world currency exchange rates impact on how much foreign currency will be worth and how much wages and remittances from relatives abroad will buy in Sāmoa on any given day. Rice, at one time a luxury, is now such a staple that the cost of a sack, which is influenced by both currency exchange rates and world food supply, has become the new index of the cost of living in the village.

These 'global' influences are changing the rules of social, political and economic organisation in ways that neither of us anticipated even ten years ago, and the pace of change seems to increase each year. The lecture series and now this book provided reason and opportunity to discuss changes in village life over the past 35 years and the forces that produced these changes. The book has given us an opportunity to expand and develop our ideas, and invariably led us back to the growing impact of three factors on both the village and the nation: the movement of people, the introduction of ideas and ideologies, and the development and spread of technologies. These themes framed the lectures and now frame this book.

One of the risks inherent in such projects is the tendency to romanticise a society's past and to lament its passing. This is particularly true where a society's 'tradition' is fundamental to its national identity and leads, in many cases, to 'explanations' that place responsibility for change on external agencies bent on remaking smaller, less powerful societies in their image. While not disputing the significance of the power of large states and international agencies, the risks inherent in such explanations are that they often understate the active role small societies play in embracing and shaping the direction of social change. Explanations that require external agencies, such as the World Bank, to explain change ignore, or at least understate, the significance of internal agency and the fact that social transformation is a continuous process that occurs where external forces meet internal ones.

We have tried to avoid this in three ways: by identifying the role of both external and internal agency, by avoiding passing judgments on the desirability of changes and by placing contemporary change in historical context. Rather than depicting change as 'loss of tradition', we have focused instead on the 'dynamism' inherent in social organisation, and on how and why change is embraced and shaped by people in the village. We have refrained from judgements of whether change is 'good' or 'bad' for the village: change happens and is the consequence of people making decisions about what is 'good' or 'bad' for them. We have tried to contextualise contemporary transformation: the changes outlined here, and the forces producing them, are simply the most recent manifestations of a process of transformation that has been occurring since people settled in these islands some 3000 years ago. In the end, it will be the reader who decides whether we have succeeded.

While this book focuses on Sāmoa, it may have more general significance. Many Pacific states have similar ecosystems, and demographic, social, political and economic profiles. Most confront similar external agencies, expatriate populations, patron states, international financial organisations and global non-governmental organisations (NGOs), all of which constrain their development options. While the importance of each of these factors, and the ways in which they interact, may vary from one location to another, there are likely to be significant similarities in the processes, options and outcomes throughout the region. Factors that impact on contemporary Sāmoa are, for the reasons outlined above, also occurring elsewhere in the contemporary Pacific, albeit at different rates. In concentrating on processes at work in a society with which we are familiar, we hope to identify factors that may throw light on the dynamics of transformation as it occurs elsewhere in the region. However, the way each state reacts to these combinations of circumstances will also be unique, for cultural, historical and political reasons, and the reader is warned that broad generalisations about a region as diverse as the Pacific often founder on the rocks of complex reality.

Churches dominate the landscape and yet they are rarely thought of as evidence of earlier transformations. Christianity has transformed the Samoan worldview and lifestyle in significant ways.

Young village people periodically visit relatives in enclaves as far apart as Auckland, Los Angeles, Sydney and are much more familiar with the world beyond the village than their parents were.

1.

Warm winds of change

Sāmoa is a small, independent state in the southwest Pacific Ocean. Its 185,000 citizens,[1] descendants of Austronesian explorers who settled in the islands some 3000 years ago (Irwin 2006: 64), live in two port towns and some 360 villages on two large, well-endowed high islands and eight smaller islands with a total land area of 2934 square kilometres. Only 23 per cent of the population live in urban areas; the remainder live in mainly coastal villages. Situated in the central Pacific, between 171° and 172° west longitude and 13° and 14° south latitude, and some 1200 km from Suva, 2890 km from Auckland, 4400 km from Sydney and 8400 km from Los Angeles, Sāmoa is relatively geographically isolated. Yet despite its distance from other land masses, Sāmoa is not, and has not been, as isolated as one might expect.

Since the Sāmoans' ancestors settled in the archipelago, influences from beyond their shores have periodically reshaped Sāmoan society. These were, initially, the consequences of linkages within the Pacific regional system and, more recently, Sāmoa's incorporation into the global political economy. This process commenced with contact with agents of the west over 200 years ago, gained momentum in the latter part of the nineteenth and the first half of the twentieth centuries, and has intensified over the 47 years since independence on 1 January 1962. Sāmoa has become increasingly integrated into the international community. Successive Sāmoan governments have taken the country into 34 international organisations,[2] and have made it a party to a number of significant international agreements[3] that now influence Sāmoa in various ways. Sāmoa also plays an increasingly active role in Pacific regional politics and in the politics of the ACP bloc.

Over the same period, the population of Sāmoa has become increasingly dispersed. Significant Sāmoan enclaves are now well-established in New Zealand, Hawai'i and the US west coast, Australia, American Sāmoa and Fiji. Smaller Sāmoan populations are now growing in cities throughout the world (Sutter 1995). This process seems set to continue: each year Sāmoa is estimated to lose some 8.81 persons per 1000 to other countries, and Sāmoans routinely move between and beyond enclaves. Over 200,000 people of Sāmoan descent are believed to live outside Sāmoa, with 131,100 in New Zealand alone. Those emigrants and their children move freely between their homes and Sāmoa, bringing with them ideas, capital and technology, and making up a significant part of Sāmoa's 122,000 visitors each year.

Sāmoa's small open economy has also become increasingly integrated with the global economy. The pace of change increased after independence as migrants left to work abroad and their remittances flowed back into the domestic economy, and has intensified since the 1990s as the government has pursued a comprehensive programme of macroeconomic reform that has led to the opening and restructuring of the Sāmoan economy. At independence, Sāmoa exported small amounts of mainly primary production and was almost solely dependent on export income. Its economy is now more complex, and while it continues to rely on exports of primary and some manufactured products, it is increasingly dependent on revenue from provision of services including offshore banking, remittances from migrants, assistance from development partners and tourism. These parallel processes, diversification of the domestic economy and integration into the global economy, have, as we will argue, been a significant force in the transformation of Sāmoan society.

While Sāmoan society has confronted, and engaged with, significant external influences, it has not passively accepted all the external forces to which it has been exposed, even when these were wielded by much larger and more powerful agencies. In incorporating some of these influences while resisting others, Sāmoan society has sought to 'manage' the impact of the movement of people, ideas and technologies over time. In the early twentieth century, a European administrator, frustrated by his inability to bring about social change in Sāmoa, likened the resistance of Sāmoan society to external forces to the ability of bamboo to withstand high winds. In each case, a combination of inherent strength and flexibility makes it possible for significant forces to be resisted without serious damage to the structural integrity of the entity subject to those forces.

This book explores contemporary Sāmoan engagement with, and reaction to, three rapidly intensifying globalising forces: the increasing movement of people to and from Sāmoa, the influence of new ideas and ideologies, and the impact of a range of new technologies. While acknowledging the power and pervasiveness of external forces, this account resists the tendency to depict global influences as large and compelling 'new' forces that must inevitably remake the lives of those exposed to them. Instead, Sāmoa is presented as a site where global forces confront local ones, and Sāmoans are assumed to be active agents in the transformation of their society in the early twenty-first century.

Earlier responses to the influences of the outside world are compared with contemporary ones to establish whether, and how, these differ. The comparisons are used to illustrate and explain differences in the capacity and willingness of Sāmoan society to manage innovation at different times in its history, and have led us to the conclusion that the elements of Sāmoan social organisation that allowed it to engage with and manage external influences in the past have lost some of their resilience and flexibility. This conclusion rests on two observations: the range of globalising forces is increasing and their influence is intensifying, while at the same time Sāmoan society is becoming increasingly plural and less able, or willing, to agree on how to confront and manage these forces. It is our contention that a combination of intensifying winds of change and fundamental shifts in the organisation of contemporary Sāmoan society has reduced its capacity to resist the external forces as effectively as it once did.

In the following chapters, we explore how the movement of people, ideas and technologies has transformed Sāmoan society throughout history, and how each of these movements has changed, and is changing, life on a daily basis for families and villages in Sāmoa. The winds of change that Sāmoans have managed for centuries are intensifying and it remains to be seen whether they will develop into a storm that will transform Sāmoa more radically than ever before. Before we do this, it may be helpful to explain two key methodological decisions – to focus on process rather than trends and to focus on the village rather than the nation – that frame our discussion and analysis.

Methodology

The focus on process

Studies of global influences on the organisation of societies often focus on national 'indices of change' that are used to 'measure' and 'quantify' these 'impacts' in 'objective' ways that allow 'cross-national comparisons'. Studies of the impact of globalisation typically begin with reviews of selected 'indices of globalisation' that reflect levels of 'global connectedness' such as migration flows, international trade volumes and patterns, telecommunications and internet usage. The data and indices from a number of nations are then collated to create models that allow their modellers to compare the differential impacts of globalisation on societies. Since this account concentrates instead on the processes that produce these indices, and focuses on the 'local' rather than 'national' manifestations of globalisation, we owe the reader an explanation of our preference for this approach.

The value of an approach based on indices that can be clearly defined, measured, collated and used to chart the progress of nations in ways that allow both nations and international agencies to compare their development trajectories is not disputed. The apparently 'scientific' and 'objective' nature of the 'measures' may, however, mask a number of problems with these approaches. Indices are reflections of the results of globalisation processes and offer little insight into the social processes that produce them. Declines in the numbers of children born to women in any society are readily measured and compared, but they cannot tell us whether this trend is the consequence of higher levels of education, conscious decisions by women to limit family size, access to better family planning facilities, or falling standards of living resulting in declining standards of women's health and a reduced capacity to conceive. The indices that point to the same trend in two nations may reflect very different processes.

But there are also often problems that stem from the national data on which indices rest. Firstly, the national statistics from which indices are derived are not, despite their apparent quantitative authority, always reliable. They are as likely to reflect the cultural and logistical difficulties of collecting them as clearly as they reflect trends in the society. Suicide in Sāmoa, for instance, is under-reported for cultural reasons (Macpherson and Macpherson 1987), and yet it is routinely used as an 'index' of social transformation in ways that ignore this reality. With limited human and financial resources available for data collection, governments are often not in a position to consider, or control for, the social processes that may influence the quality of the data gathered, or, in this particular case, the implications for the accuracy of the incidence and rates of suicide derived from them. It is sufficient to calculate a 'national' rate based on 'reported' cases. The national data, which may understate both the real incidence and rates of suicide, are provided to regional and international health agencies and are then incorporated in a series of regional and international data sets. The consolidated datasets, which may now contain similarly flawed data from a number of nations, are then used to derive age-specific rates of suicide, to compare rates of youth suicide and to develop models that relate these to other indices of development.

Secondly, in an attempt to create indices for which cross-national data are available, the measures conflate apparently similar activities where closer examination would show that they are quite different. The resulting 'indices' reflect the desire to construct indices more clearly than they reflect the social reality that underlies them. In the case of suicide, it is presented, in many studies, as if it were a singular phenomenon and a consequence of the anomie that is supposed to accompany social transformation. In fact, only some suicides in Sāmoa are anomic and reflect the influences of social transformation; others are altruistic and reflect cultural values that relate to the protection of the reputation of the collectivity (Macpherson and Macpherson 1987). Indices that cannot or do not make these distinctions create elaborate, superficially attractive and authoritative 'measures' that rest ultimately on defective foundations.

Thirdly, the choice of indices, and the ways in which they are used, often reflect narrow disciplinary interests. Economists have, for instance, selected and combined a number of economic indices to demonstrate connections between the pursuit of structural adjustment programmes and Samoa's recent economic growth. These economic models use economic indices selectively to draw attention to economic patterns. Repeated use and citation of these disciplinary formulae and models eventually create the appearance of authority. But, like all disciplinary models, they draw attention to selected relationships and away from other equally significant ones between, for example, economic and social trends. A more critical inter-disciplinary approach to modelling would combine a wider range of indices to explore both the 'benefits' and the 'costs' of growth strategies. A more comprehensive approach may well demonstrate that 'economic' benefits are offset by parallel 'social' and 'environmental' costs.

Finally, these problems are compounded where data sets are used, by people who have little or no understanding of their limitations, to build increasingly elaborate models that produce still further indices of relationships between indices. The apparent clarity and 'authority' of indices lead readers and researchers to overlook some important shortcomings and either to ignore, or conflate, significant differences. The cross-national models cannot tell us whether, for instance, similar trends in different places are produced by the same social processes.

This study focuses instead on the processes that lie behind such indices. It seeks to link observed changes by showing how global forces are seen and embraced, and how their consequences, both intended and unintended, are then 'managed' by people in villages. If this study does nothing but clarify some of the benefits of focusing on the social processes that produce indices of change, and the risks of depending entirely on crude numerical indices, it will have served a useful purpose.

The focus on family and village

There are both substantive and strategic reasons for placing family and village at the centre in this account:[4] they are the principle and overlapping sources of social identity in Sāmoan society. Family and village frame and define people's social worlds, and their lives and identities. They are also the sites where processes of globalisation and change become apparent before they are reflected in national indices.

Family, or *āiga*, is a foundation of Sāmoan society. Extended families, *āiga potopoto*, comprise a series of households,[5] *fuaifale*, that act independently in some matters and collectively in others. Within families, children learn to understand and model the relationships that constitute the social universe Sāmoans refer to as the *va fealoa'i*. For instance, children in families learn how a number of central principles of Sāmoan society – gerontocracy, kinship, respect, reciprocity, order, power and authority – are embodied in social life. These principles are encapsulated and reflected in a series of social roles that are central to each person's ability to function in the family and in Sāmoan society more generally. Families are also political entities in which children learn the fundamental elements of political power and authority and the processes and roles in which these are embodied. Families are headed by one or more chiefs, or *matai*, who have traditionally been elected to the position on the basis of demonstrated energy, ability and service, *tautua*, to the family. The family discussions that precede these appointments clarify and restate the linkages between these attributes and power. *Matai* articulate and represent the family's interests in various political forums. Families are also micro-economies that hold and manage the family estate, which typically comprises agricultural land and house sites in a village, and periodically raise and invest funds usually in sociopolitical activity on behalf of their members. Within the family, children thus learn how the principles of social and political life apply in and structure economic activity and relations.

Villages, or *nu'u*, are also fundamental elements of Sāmoa's social, political (Va'ai 1999) and economic organisation (Pitt 1970; Lockwood 1971), and important sources of individual social identity. Social life is lived in the many social entities that comprise the village and through which individuals pass in the course of their lives.[6] Secular education for most Sāmoans occurs within schools built and maintained by the village, while religious and moral education and life occur in and around the village church to which villagers go throughout their lives. Political education is also imparted within the *nu'u* as people come to understand the sources of authority and the dynamics of power within the village polity. The *matai* of the village families meet regularly in council, as the *fono a matai*, to deliberate on and regulate a range of moral, political and economic matters within the village. The council's authority over these activities derives from a period when villages were autonomous polities with exclusive jurisdiction over all activities within their boundaries. This authority has been confirmed more recently by the Sāmoan government in the Village Fono Act (1990) that, while curtailing some rights formerly exercised by the village polity, has confirmed its powers to act in a number of matters on the basis of 'tradition and usage'. This legislation acknowledged the historical reality and recognised the significant role that villages play in the maintenance of law and order, the management of community development, the provision of secular education and the organisation of primary production within the nation.

Families and villages are vitally connected: villages comprise between five and 15 extended families of varying sizes that have lived in the village, often for many generations, and hold rights to house sites, agricultural land and marine resources that comprise the village estate (Va'ai 1999: 42–47). Families identify, and are identified, with the villages within which they hold such rights. Members of each *āiga* typically reside together in a part of the village in which the family's house sites are found, and are inextricably linked with villages with which their *āiga* are associated. Families' chiefly titles, *suafa matai*, have their origins in particular villages and are included in their polities' political hierarchies or *fa'alupega* (Gilson 1967: 17). Titleholders sit in the village council, *fono a matai*, with which their titles are connected and regulate that village's affairs. *Matai* manage the family's social, political and economic activity and represent its interests within the village polity (Va'ai 1999: 42–43).

Villages periodically engage in major capital works such as church building, school rebuilding, the construction of access roads to plantations and smaller projects such as village beautification (Lockwood 1971). These corporate activities unite and celebrate the village both for those who live in it and those who live around it. These projects also provide opportunities for village families to compete with one another for social and political influence and, in the process, to enhance their social and political standing within the village. The successful performance of these corporate activities restates and reinforces both the villages' and the families' collective identities and, indirectly, their co-dependence.

By comparison, the 'nation' is, for many, a much less significant entity in daily life. Individuals engage only occasionally with the 'nation', when they need a birth certificate, a passport, a licence to operate a taxi, or a permit to buy and apply herbicide. Engagement with the nation is more likely to occur at village level: the government has appointed salaried village mayors, or *pulenu'u*, who liaise with government agencies on policy formulation. These mayors convey the government's legislative intentions to their constituents, and gather and relay the latter group's views to government. Sāmoans do, of course, identify with the 'nation' when national sports teams go abroad and succeed; when Sāmoans come to prominence on the global scene; when Sāmoa hosts other nations, for instance, during the South Pacific Games; or when they go overseas and are labelled 'Sāmoans' by others. Outside of these occasions, Sāmoans tend to identify primarily on the basis of family and village.

There are also strategic reasons for selecting family and village as sites for a study of social transformation: these entities are the front-lines in the confrontation between Sāmoan society and globalising forces. Villages are relatively small, comprising between 200 and 1000 people, and compact. They tend to lie on the coastal fringe, with houses along the roads, and certain community buildings such as churches, the pastor's house, the meeting house, primary schools and women's committee houses near their physical centre. The agricultural lands associated with villages are located between the coast and the mountains and vary in size for historical reasons. Public discussion about the actual and potential impact of innovation, and the need to regulate it, takes place in a range of formal and informal settings within the family and the village, and is inevitably relatively open.

Discussions that occur within families are typically strategic, and focus on the social and economic costs and benefits of innovations, and on how any given option might enhance the family's social, economic and political interests and status within the village. Discussions about innovations also occur in a range of informal forums within the village, such as in religious settings that tend to focus on the moral impact of innovations. Lay leaders, often with guidance from ordained clergy, consider the latent impacts of innovations for the moral well-being of the parish. If and when leaders formulate religious positions on innovations, these are communicated to various bodies in the village parish by lay leaders and from the village church's pulpit by pastors.

After a period of informal discussion, matters are taken to regular meetings of the village council, or *fono a matai*, in which all village families are represented by their chiefs. Village leaders, influenced by the families whom they represent and by the positions taken by the churches to which they belong, debate the potential secular impact of an innovation and the need to mitigate this impact. Where a view clearly becomes dominant, the council may move to formulate its response and to manage the impact of an innovation within the village. This generally involves the proclamation of local regulations, *tulāfono*, which prescribe permitted uses, and of penalties, *sala*, for violation of these.

For example, families debated the social, political and economic merits of pooling their resources to purchase larger, outboard-powered, aluminium twin-hulled fishing vessels (*'alia*) when these first became available. When a portable chainsaw sawmill was first used in the village, a number of men gathered at various times over several days to watch it and to talk about the relative risks, costs and benefits of the new technology. In several villages, sessions debated the need to ban video players on the grounds that they could be used to show pornographic material, and in one case, the council decided not to ban video players in the village but to make it an offence to play pornographic material instead.

The debates that occur in and around these forums provide an interesting insight into people's analyses of the social and economic ramifications, and costs and benefits of innovations, and the tests that are applied to determine whether and how to manage their impacts. These debates expose, often in considerable detail, the ways in which people model their society, worldview and lifestyle; and define and weigh the risks posed by innovations. They also reveal the rationale people use when they seek to manage outside forces, and thus give us an indication of the social processes underlying acceptance, rejection or mitigation of these influences. The language in which these analyses are framed, the contexts in which they are canvassed, the status of those who lead the discussions, the intensity of the feelings aroused and the urgency that surrounds them, provide important insights into the process of social transformation. Monitoring the discussion of, and engagement with, a range of innovations over time clarifies the nature and process of the interaction between local and external agency and the influence of each, both singly and in concert, on village social organisation.

'Family' and 'village'

To have confined this account to a particular 'family' or 'village' would have raised a series of issues about how 'typical' these were of all Sāmoan families and villages. While we started from the personal experiences of the processes in a particular family and village, these were supplemented with material from other families and villages that expanded and refined our understanding of these processes. The family and the village referred to in this book are thus composites constructed from a range of experiences and conversations about what is happening in families and villages throughout Sāmoa. Composites are constructed to focus attention on units of analysis and on processes, rather than on a particular family or village or place. These composites also allow us to introduce and discuss variations in processes within families and villages and to produce a more nuanced account of how these are changing.

This book simply could not be confined to one village or family. This was not a deliberately conceived and executed 'research project' that involved the gathering of ethnographic data designed to answer a pre-selected set of theoretical questions about a particular place. The questions at the centre of this book were rather the product of growing curiosity about what we were seeing around us, and the answers arose from incidental and casual conversations with a range of people with whom we had everyday contact. By the time we decided to bring the material together in this account, our experience and understanding of how villages and families were changing was no longer derived from a particular family or village or place. It was the consequence of a process of unconscious, and largely unstructured, accretion of information that came to us in the course of daily life.

A brief example of how this process of accretion and accumulation worked to expand and refine our account may be useful for readers unused to such unstructured approaches. Over a number of years we have been repairing and refurbishing our family home in Sāmoa. Over this time we have met a number of people who passed comment on what we were doing, and told us how and why they were approaching similar tasks. Those people asked us questions about why we were doing things in a particular way, and then reflected on the ways in which what we said compared with their own experiences. Those who know Sāmoa will appreciate that these conversations reflect a genuine interest in others. For those who do not, it may be helpful to describe how this process worked by showing the ways by which ordinary conversations expanded and elaborated on what we knew.

We had engaged a builder who sent a number of carpenters and labourers from different villages for varying lengths of time to work on our house. In Sāmoa, one feeds the workforce as a gesture of respect for their skill, and because it creates goodwill that ensures that the job will be done well (Hiroa 1930: 88–89). Our builders generally arrived in time for breakfast, worked during the morning, came in to share lunch with us, worked again during the afternoon and joined us for a cup of coffee and a snack before leaving. Out of a sense of respect we ate and talked with the builders on most days. Conversation ranged over many topics over the course of a month, but typically started with a question about what we were doing and why, or what a neighbour was doing and why. Our answers almost inevitably generated conversations about whether such a course of action was wise and whether it would be contemplated in their families or villages. Most present felt compelled to explain how and why things were done in their families and villages. On other occasions, conversation focused on something that had happened in someone's village or on what someone had heard on the news, and ranged over issue after issue until the foreman sent the men back to work or sent us to Apia to order more material.

The taxi driver who took us into Apia to order our building supplies asked us what we needed them for, and how and why we had engaged our builders, and then proceeded to tell us why it would have been better to have engaged relatives to do the job. The assistant in the building supplies store wanted to know what we were doing and then proceeded to tell us that, on the basis of his long experience with local builders, we would have been better to bring a builder from New Zealand and why. The taxi driver who took us home asked us where we had been, how and why we had engaged our builders, and then told us we were wise to engage builders who were not relatives!

Each day our relations, who are also our neighbours, came to 'inspect' the job and talk about their day. One would explain how lucky we were to live in this village or family because things were done with more dignity than they were in their spouse's family or village. By way of explanation, they would compare the two situations that had led them to this view in considerable detail. Another would arrive for the 'inspection' and complain that things in this village or family were unnecessarily complicated and that their spouse's family and village had a much simpler way of doing things. By way of explanation, the person would tell us in some detail how they had formed this judgement. When a visitor arrived mid-way through the conversation, you could be almost certain that they too would have a view that was worth airing and would provide yet another useful comparison.

These conversations simply happened because we live in the place. The topics were not usually of our choosing and went in directions that we could not and did not wish to control. There was no way we could have removed ourselves from this 'society' without appearing extremely ill-mannered. In the end there was, quite simply, no way of limiting our knowledge or experience to our family or village. Life in Sāmoa is not that simple or simply managed. Any discussion of our experience of village and family was an invitation for others to explain how theirs differed and why. But, in each conversation, like it or not, we discovered how our family and village differed from others, and more importantly, how these things could be 'known'!

Nor were the conversations confined to our stays in Sāmoa. We have a large kin group in New Zealand and people from the village visit regularly on a range of missions for everything from education to medical treatment. Visiting these visitors and taking them gifts is a part of *fa'asāmoa*: it acknowledges and reaffirms relationships and shared history. It is simply something that well-mannered people do. After formal pleasantries on these occasions, the first order of the day is relaying news of family and village, and hours are typically spent catching up with the latest family and village developments. Now, in a break with the past, some of this information has already reached us because the falling cost of telecommunications means that people are in touch more regularly than was the case until quite recently. The value of personally-delivered news, however, is that it can be imparted slowly and with detailed descriptions of what happened; and where, when and who was involved. These conversations allow a range of interpretations and descriptions to be canvassed in more depth, and shared explanations to be constructed.

One final, and unexpectedly interesting, source of the information and ideas that have found a place in this book was the increasingly popular Sāmoan-language radio talkback shows. At first we listened to them in Sāmoa, either because radios around us were playing them and we could not ignore them, or because our builders asked us to turn on the radio so they could listen in. Over some weeks we realised that the shows were creating a new and unique 'social space'. People can call anonymously and put a point of view that they might not feel able to express in other social contexts where cultural etiquette determines who can say what to whom, and where some views simply cannot be entertained.

Unlike New Zealand English-language talkback, on which views are often expressed with a great deal of force and very little tact, Sāmoan talkback is governed by formal conversational etiquette and is marked by politeness, mutual respect and, occasionally, wonderful humour. Thus, while some content may be contentious, it is delivered and mediated with a degree of formality and respect: speakers are typically courteous to other contributors even when they may be strongly opposed to their views, and hosts are rather more patient. Discussions on a range of contentious topics occurred regularly and provided a useful insight into views that are presently expressed in private contexts but that may become more significant as they find their way into the public arena. Along with broadcasts of Sāmoan parliamentary debates, which also provide an interesting insight into Sāmoan worldview and philosophy, talkback became another source of 'background noise' that needs to be acknowledged here.

Beyond 'family' and 'village'

While family and village provide a useful starting point and the focus for our study of the process of social transformation in Sāmoa, families and villages exist within a modern state and are increasingly subject to its authority. The national government must also form a view of the impact of innovation on village life and of the need to regulate such impacts in the nation's interest. The government may, necessarily, use different criteria from those used in the village to make these assessments, and to decide to what extent new influences need to be mitigated. It is possible and indeed probable that village and national polities, using different tests and criteria, will arrive at various and sometimes opposing assessments of the need for regulation and that, from time to time, representatives of the bodies involved will find themselves at odds over how to engage with globalising forces.

These debates occur in formal bodies such as the government-sponsored council of village mayors and in parliament, and are also matters of public record. In addition, the debates are routinely aired in Sāmoa's increasingly open mass media. Sāmoa has several TV channels, some controlled in Sāmoa and some controlled from elsewhere. The government television station periodically assembles panels to explore issues of public interest. Sāmoa has a number of AM and FM radio stations, some government-controlled and some privately-owned, that regularly canvass public issues on talkback radio and on public information programmes. Sāmoa has a well-regarded daily newspaper, *Samoa Observer*,[7] and a number of weekly newspapers that fluctuate from year to year as some fail and new ones spring up in their place. The government's official position on public issues is set out in the government newspaper *Sāvali*, and the privately-owned newspapers explore public views in editorials and letters to the editor. Beside these mainstream mass media, there are a number of sidestream media including on-line news journals, such as *Talamua*, and journals published by NGOs and religious organisations that canvass issues of public interest. These debates are also increasingly aired on websites and in internet-based chat rooms by kin and interest groups. Some are embodied in song and performance and are staged in public venues to large audiences on occasions such as the annual independence celebrations in June and the Teuila Festival in September.

We have, over time, drawn together views from all of these sources and have become aware of an increasing divergence of opinion. Once, there seemed to be a single view that was apparently reproduced, with only minor variations, at each level of public discourse. The convergence of opinion and the apparent consensus were as striking as was the absence of any critical public commentary on many issues. Now this has changed and there is much more divergent, and critical, public commentary on a much wider range of issues. We have drawn on discussions at each of these levels to capture the range of views that is reflected in and reflects Sāmoan society. This increasing pluralism, we will show, may be the force that now constrains Sāmoa's ability to engage with and manage the steadily intensifying forces from beyond its shores.

In summarising both these views and the influences that are producing them, we have tended to concentrate on the evidence of shifts rather than the evidence of what apparently remains unchanged. This is an inevitable consequence of focusing on factors and processes that are beginning to produce changes in people's worldviews and lifestyles. Some will read cases outlined here and say that what we have described has not happened and could not happen in their family or village. That would be to miss the point.

We are not suggesting that these changes have taken place in every family or village in Sāmoa: indeed, we know they have not. There is considerable variety in the ways in which villages respond to all sorts of phenomena: there is a saying in Sāmoa that each village has its own procedures and practices, *ua tofu le nu'u ma le aganu'u*.

We are, however, suggesting that sooner or later these forces and processes will produce changes of the type we have described, or very similar ones, in families and villages throughout Sāmoa. No family or village can stop its people coming or going: most benefit in various ways from migration and would not want to limit their movement. But the experience of migration changes people in many different ways and few who migrate return unchanged. Nor can any family or village prevent ideas entering conversation, and later, ways of seeing, and later still, ways of acting. They may be able to ban debate in public spaces and to banish bearers of the most unacceptable of these ideas, but there are a growing number of 'sites' that cannot be policed and managed in the way that the public sphere can, and in which new ideas and practices can gain traction. Nor can any family or village exclude the use of new technologies, and since many benefit from these, few would seek to. But even those technologies that people do not wish to embrace now will eventually find their way into the country because their benefits will be seen to outweigh their potential costs.

Before we confront the contemporary winds of change, we need to understand something of the history of Sāmoan engagement with various earlier external forces, the ways in which Sāmoan society sought to manage these and the factors that made it possible. Since any such account will depend on the quality of the historical scholarship that is available to reconstruct the past, it is useful to visit this issue briefly. We are fortunate that Sāmoa has been the subject of much interest from scholars and writers from a number of backgrounds who have produced comprehensive and reliable coverage of Sāmoan history. The earliest changes that resulted from visits by neighbours from islands within the Pacific region have been documented by archaeologists such as Clark (1996), Green (2002b and 2007), Barnes and Hunt (2005), and Barnes and Green (2008); and historians such as Gunson (1993) and Tuimaleali'ifano (1990).

After 1800, Sāmoa's exposure to the global political economy increased and a wider range of influences produced more significant changes in Sāmoan society. Their impacts have been conscientiously documented by missionaries (Stair 1983; Turner 1983); historians (Davidson 1967; Gilson 1970; Meleisea 1987b and 1992; Meleisea and Schoeffel 1987; So'o 2000 and 2007; Tuimaleai'ifano 2006b); anthropologists (Shankman 1976; Yamamoto 1990 and 1994; Le Tagaloa 1992; O'Meara 1995); administrators (Rowe 1930; Gratton 1948; McKay 1957); sociologists (Pitt 1970; Macpherson 1988; Macpherson and Macpherson 1990); economists (Stace and Lauterbach 1963; Lockwood 1971; Fairbairn 1985); and writers (Wendt, 1973, 1974, 1977, 1986). Since these works were published, some of the forces that the various authors described have intensified and new ones have emerged. Sāmoan society is more exposed now than ever before to an increasing range of social, political and economic forces that could not have been anticipated by the authors of earlier studies. The following chapter uses information from these and other sources to outline the ways in which Sāmoan society has engaged with the various external forces to which it has been exposed since its settlement.

2.

A brief history of Sāmoa's engagement with global forces

Studies of globalisation tend to focus on the impacts of new technologies on the fabric of contemporary life in a society (Steger 2002), and to present globalisation as a phenomenon that commenced with growing global interdependence and the technologies that facilitated this unprecedented level of interconnectedness (Castells 1996). But most societies have long histories of steadily increasing contact with other societies that have changed them in ways that are at least as significant as the impact of computers, the internet and cellphones. While we accept that new technologies are transforming societies in dramatic ways, the range of reactions to any given technology suggests that social context is at least as significant as the technologies themselves. Societies' reactions to global influences are shaped by their histories, cultures and social organisation. For that reason, a society's reactions to earlier periods of 'globalisation' may provide insights into the ways in which it might react to current forms.

Sāmoa's relative geographical isolation; its regular depiction as a place of deserted beaches, endless horizons and scenes of 'traditional' village life; and its linkage with marketing slogans such as 'Sāmoa: the islands that time forgot' and 'Sāmoa: the lost paradise' lead some to assume that globalising forces have only recently begun to reach its shores. Even more historically informed discussions of Sāmoa assume that globalisation commenced with the establishment of regular air services and increased emigration after World War ll. Sāmoa has, of course, been exposed to external forces for much longer and, as Gilson notes, some of the most significant social changes occurred in the nineteenth century during an earlier period of globalisation (Gilson 1970: 31–75). Before turning to the impact of global forces on contemporary Sāmoa, it is useful to place these in an historical context, if only to see whether the way Sāmoan society has responded to earlier forces might provide clues as to how it might respond to new ones. This chapter summarises the history of external forces on Sāmoan society and Sāmoan responses to them.

The settlement of Sāmoa

The exploration and settlement of Oceania began in Asia some 40,000 years ago. The eastward movement of Austronesian explorers into Oceania commenced about 8000 years ago and ended with settlement of the outer reaches of Polynesia some 900 years ago. The ancestors of the modern Sāmoans, bearers of the Lapita culture and an Austronesian language, arrived in the Sāmoan archipelago, from Melanesia, some 3000 years ago (Irwin 2006: 64). For reasons that remain unclear, they remained in those well-endowed islands for about 1000 years and established the foundations of contemporary Sāmoan culture, social organisation and language. Then, for reasons that are equally unclear, some of the early settlers' descendants left Sāmoa on a series of epic eastward journeys during which they found and eventually settled the furthest reaches of the Pacific: Rapanui or Easter Island in the east,[1] the Hawai'ian Islands in the north, and Aotearoa or New Zealand in the south, around 700 years ago (Irwin 2006: 89). Throughout this period of exploration, a core population remained in the Sāmoan archipelago.

This is the population that we identify as the first Sāmoans, and they, like their descendants, were exposed to the influences of external forces. Oral history and genealogy provide evidence of contact between Sāmoans and peoples of the islands of Fiji, Tonga, Tuvalu and Niue (Tuimaleai'ifano 1990: 16–36) during what has been called the golden age of Pacific voyaging that ended around 1500 AD (Irwin 2006: 91). Archaeologists who have studied early Sāmoan culture, such as Barnes and Hunt (2005), Clark (1996) and Green (2002a and b and 2007), have suggested that contact with visiting populations may have resulted in the relocation of Sāmoan settlements from inland areas, where houses were spread out along clearly defined pathways, to the coastal fringes, in what are now widely regarded as 'traditional' settlement patterns, and in the design of fortified structures found on ridgetops. These early visits may also have led to abandonment of large inland built structures, such as the Pulemelei, or Seu Tia, in Vailoa, Savai'i (Martinsson-Wallin 2007), that were apparently associated with earlier forms of religion and had fallen into disuse before European contact commenced in the late eighteenth century.

One current difficulty of reconstructing the impact of the pre-European visits is that much of the evidence has been submerged as sea levels have risen and sea floors have sunk, but advances in submarine archaeological research, which revealed the Lapita association, may yet tell us more of the story of this period. Oral history has also preserved some fragments of this past. Anthropologists believe that incantations offered to the gods in the early evening, enjoining them to keep the 'sailing gods' from landing on Sāmoan shores and causing illness, reflect an historical memory of an early visit that brought an epidemic to Sāmoan shores and left Sāmoans cautious about contact with people from the outside (Rowe 1930).

The impact of Sāmoa's exposure to these early visits and exchanges is likely to have been limited for several reasons. Visitors during this period came in relatively small numbers, from island societies with similar ecosystems, social systems and technologies (Krämer 1994: 51–52). With the exception of the Tongans, who exerted considerable influence in Sāmoa for a period around 900 years ago (Gunson 1993; Krämer 1994: 11), none of the visiting groups was in a position to impose innovations on the Sāmoan population by force, even if they had been inclined to do so. Finally, these contacts were not continuous and ended around 1500 AD as various populations involved became more established in particular locations, and the range and frequency of regular inter-island voyaging declined (Irwin 2006: 64).

World empires and Sāmoa

Sāmoa's isolation did protect it from exposure to the first truly global systems. The early world empires were founded when China, Persia and Rome set about incorporating isolated and formerly autonomous populations into empires to establish and maintain access to luxury goods and revenues from taxation. The processes by which the economies and polities of formerly autonomous 'nations' were transformed in fundamental ways to establish imperial control and to ensure a reliable flow of goods and taxes to the centres of the empires have been outlined by world-systems theorists (Shannon 1996).

Those world empires were inefficient and expensive entities. The costs of incorporating new domains, usually by force, were high and the expense of making reluctant populations produce surpluses from which they derived no benefit was considerable. Even higher were the costs of maintaining the military dominance necessary to extract taxes and ensure production. Periodic rebellions by reluctant subjects further increased the cost of imperial dominance, and imperial powers inevitably became stretched and more vulnerable to attacks from other aspiring powers. As empires grew in size and complexity, the marginal benefits of imperial dominance declined and the costs of maintaining empires eventually exceeded the benefits derived from them. While isolation protected Sāmoa from the predatory attentions of those early imperial powers, it could not protect it from the next phase of globalisation that gained momentum in the mid-sixteenth century.

Capitalism, colonialism and christianity

Crises in the feudal mode of production in western Europe gave rise to a new mode of production, capitalism, that displaced feudalism throughout Europe from the mid-sixteenth century on (Shannon 1996). Capitalism depended on access to territories beyond those in which it evolved, for both raw materials and markets for its manufactured production. The growing wealth and influence of capitalists in emerging western European nation states was, at least in part, behind the creation of colonial empires by these powers from the seventeenth century onwards. The continued growth of colonial empires was also driven, in part, by the requirements of increasingly influential capitalists who sought new sites in which to invest their surplus capital, new markets for their existing manufactured production and new sources of raw material for their expanding industrial activities (Wallerstein 1974).

Colonial powers incorporated formerly isolated autonomous societies into what has been called a 'world-system' and 'world-economy' in ways that ensured that capitalism had access to their labour and raw materials at the lowest possible prices, and access to markets into which to sell goods and services (Wallerstein 1974). In this process, formerly autonomous polities and economies were transformed in ways that made sure the interests of colonial capital could be advanced predictably and consistently, and that basic property rights – fundamental to profitable capitalism – were established and maintained.

Imperial expansion was also driven, in part, by missionary activity. The commitment of Christian churches to saving the souls of newly discovered peoples led to the expansion of missionary activity into the new world. Missions from both Europe and America fanned out across the recently discovered world, seeking to save new souls, and in the process, created new missionary empires. While missions could, and in places did, operate without the support of colonial governments or commerce, they benefited indirectly from the establishment of colonial government and infrastructure.

A symbiotic relationship between the three developed: missions produced peace in which capitalism could operate more predictably, and commerce produced civil and physical infrastructure that allowed missions to function more effectively. Colonial empires provided the geopolitical frameworks within which capitalism, commerce, Christian evangelism and exotic diseases flourished, and in which societies exposed to them were transformed, often dramatically and with tragic consequences for their citizens (Kunitz 1994: 22–81). These impacts were soon felt within the Pacific.

The progressive incorporation of Pacific societies into commercial, colonial and religious empires, from 1552 on, had profound effects on their worldviews and lifestyles. When Spanish explorers entered the Pacific, it was inevitable that eventually all Pacific societies and cultures would be exposed to the impact of these outside forces. The north-westerly courses that Spanish ships sailed as they entered the Pacific from the east protected Sāmoa for some 200 years, but finally, and inevitably, a Dutch explorer, Jacob Roggeveen,[2] in 1722, and a French captain, Bougainville, in 1768, rediscovered Sāmoa in fleeting encounters at sea (Tcherkezoff 2004: 15–27). From that point on, Sāmoa's exposure to the globalising forces of capitalism, colonialism and Christianity, as well as the incursions of disease and epidemics, was only a matter of time and extent.

Sāmoans and early Europeans

The first recorded on-shore encounter between Sāmoans and Europeans occurred in December 1787 when two ships commanded by the French explorer, Lapérouse,[3] visited Asu in eastern Sāmoa in search of water and supplies. The visit, as with so many early encounters, was marred by cultural misunderstanding and loss of life. When a curious Sāmoan visited the ships, he was hung by his thumbs from the rigging, and the Sāmoans, offended by his treatment, then attacked and killed a scientist and 11 of Lapérouse's marines. This tragic incident was reported in maritime circles and established Sāmoa as a destination to be avoided, postponing further interest in the archipelago for another 30 years.

After these early, fleeting encounters, a few Europeans, only deserters and escaped convicts 'who were desperate enough to try their luck among a reputedly hostile people' (Gilson 1970: 68), established themselves in Sāmoa. They were kept for their technical skills and as intermediaries in trade, and had only limited influence in Sāmoan society. As Gilson notes:

> . . . none of these emerges as the 'white chief' of romantic fiction. A few tried to dominate the Samoans by acts of terror, but they were

killed. Others fell in with local factions and gained influence by supporting the projects and aspirations of the chiefs with whom they lived; but they probably exerted little power in their own right. There is no evidence that any of them seriously affected the course of Samoan politics, or acquired any land, or for that matter, that the introduction of a few firearms caused any change in the system of warfare prior to 1840. (Gilson 1970: 68)

Some gained limited influence as Sāmoan interest in the potential benefits of the gospel grew: some of the beachcombers exploited this interest by offering their services as 'spiritual leaders' and others were pressed into service by their Sāmoan hosts (Meleisea 1992: 52–53).

Sāmoans and missionaries

Missionary interest in the people of Oceania, fuelled by rapid and comprehensive conversions in the island groups now known as French Polynesia and the Cook Islands (Buzacott 1866) and steady progress in the Tongan group, was growing. It was inevitable that the well-endowed islands of the Sāmoan archipelago would eventually attract the interest of the missions active in the area. Sāmoan converts living in Tonga in the 1820s encouraged the Methodist Mission to establish a mission in their home islands, but when the Reverend Peter Turner visited Sāmoa in 1828 he decided against it. Sāmoans visiting Wallis and Futuna had encouraged the Roman Catholic Church to send priests and teachers to Sāmoa from 1839 (Hamilton 2005: 97–99). The London Missionary Society (LMS), which was particularly successful in the islands to the east, began to take an active interest in Sāmoa after approaches from Sāmoans living in Tonga. On a visit to Tonga, an LMS missionary, the Reverend John Williams, met an expatriate Sāmoan chief named Faueā who encouraged Williams to establish a mission in Sāmoa, a country that he claimed was ripe for conversion. Faueā offered to accompany Williams' party and smooth the path of the mission in Sāmoa by introducing Williams to influential chiefs to whom he was related and whom he claimed would protect them (Moyle 1984: 54–55, 67–68).

While all of the missions remained interested in Sāmoa, the London Missionary Society was the first to establish itself there, in Savai'i under the protection of Malietoa Vaiinupō in July 1830. The Methodists led by Peter Turner founded short-lived missions on Manono and Savai'i in 1835;[4] and the Roman Catholic Church commenced work when two Marist priests, Gilbert Roudaire and Théodore Violette, a Marist brother, Jacques Peloux, and two Sāmoan teachers, Constantin and Joachim,[5] landed in Savai'i and, despite resistance from English settlers, won influential converts and began to grow (Hamilton 2005: 100–3). After a false start, the Church of Jesus Christ of Latter-day Saints established a presence in Sāmoa in 1888 and was rather slower to take root (Meleisea and Schoeffel 1987: 65–67; Douglas 2005: 258–9). The missions would become the most significant forces for change in Sāmoa.

It is important to understand that Sāmoan interest in Christianity stemmed not from some spiritual void or a deep dissatisfaction with Sāmoan life and society. Sāmoans already had a comprehensive body of religious belief and a large hierarchy of gods and spirits who shaped and controlled their lives (Turner 1983: 16–77). Their interest in the new religion arose from the spiritual, political and material benefits that might accrue to those who embraced it. From the very earliest contact with the mission, when Faueā explained that if they accepted the new religion in the institutional guise of the mission they would enjoy peace and that, 'in its wake would come vessels carrying an abundance of goods, which must prove that Jehovah was indeed the most powerful of gods' (Gilson 1970: 69), the material benefits were central in discussions of the merits of the new religion.

Indeed, comparisons between the different churches, and between Christianity and the indigenous religion, focused on the material and technical benefits rather than the fine points of religious difference. Williams noted in his journal that Faueā's comparisons of the Sāmoan religion and the new *lotu* drew attention to its technical and material benefits (Moyle 1984: 68); and Gilson comments that these comparisons were repeated in other debates about the merits of the new religion, based on the idea that any superiority attributed to Jehovah seemed to be connected with his ability to enrich his followers (Gilson 1970: 72–73). Accounts of early contact suggest that Sāmoans were prepared to regard the missionaries as equals who might provide access to certain goods; they certainly did not feel overwhelmed by the missionaries and were able, for example, politely to decline various of John Williams' requests. It was not necessarily the 'good news' alone that interested Sāmoans. The historian Malama Meleisea (Meleisea 1992: 21) notes that Sāmoans claimed that the new religion legitimated, rather than challenged, *matai* authority, and cites a popular song which asserted that –

Ua tofia nei e le Atua Sāmoa, ina ia pulea e matai
Aua[6] o lona suafa ua vaelua i ai
God has willed that Sāmoa be controlled by matai
because he has shared his authority with them . . .

Even if missionaries believed that their lifestyle and religion were superior, they were not in a position to impose their views on the Sāmoans because they depended heavily on both chiefs and villages for support and protection in what was, basically, an asymmetrical relationship in which the missions had relatively little power (Macpherson 1997: 19–24). John Williams was well aware that Sāmoans were not solely or even predominantly drawn to the spiritual benefits of Christianity and that they held expectations of the material advantages that might follow conversion. Gilson notes that Williams realised that 'a people drawn to Christianity by a desire for worldly gain must not be subjected immediately to sweeping condemnations of their behaviour "lest they take a total dislike to a religion that prohibited that in which their whole life and comfort consisted"' (Gilson 1970: 74).

Initially, the London Missionary Society mission, on the advice of Faueā, made conversion relatively straightforward (Gilson 1970: 74), and the Wesleyans followed suit. They attempted to ban only a few selected Sāmoan customs and practices, such as warfare and the performance of 'obscene' songs and dances, to avoid alienating the chiefs on whom they depended for protection (Macpherson 1997: 19–24). But as the missions became more established, the missionaries' attempts to proscribe practices considered contrary to Christian teaching increased (Gilson 1970: 75–78). Scripture was invoked repeatedly, with varying degrees of success, to ban warfare, for example, a focus of missionary zeal since first contact but something not halted until the Sāmoans tired of it themselves. Other practices were frowned upon and attempts made to modify them, for example, family organisation, clothing standards and domestic activity (Pritchard 1863–64 and 1866; Lundie 1846: 18, 195, 280; Meleisea and Schoeffel 1987: 59–60).

The early influence of the missions on Sāmoan politics was limited by their small numbers, lack of understanding of Sāmoan language and society, and the dynamics of their relationships with the Sāmoans. Most Sāmoans, for instance, refused to leave their villages for the mission stations that were set up to make the most efficient use of limited missionary resources; instead, the local people sought instruction in their villages (Gilson 1970: 98). Their reluctance to move to mission stations where a small number of European missionaries could provide teaching and preaching services for large numbers of converts meant that more personnel were required to meet the growing interest in the gospel, which in turn had further political, social and spiritual impacts upon Sāmoa.

The mission became increasingly dependent on Sāmoan teachers to spread the gospel message in the villages and they in turn were dependent on the goodwill of the village leadership for their continued presence. This relationship conferred considerable power on the Sāmoans and placed significant constraints on what missions could do because, as Gilson notes, 'the teacher, with his limited functions and powers, could not prevent its being organised and run on Sāmoan lines, even if he had wanted to . . . . This meant, in effect, that he was subject to the will of the chiefs of his congregation, or of the village council, regardless of who belonged to his church' (Gilson 1970: 101). Similarly, in their attempts to outlaw war, the success of the missions varied significantly and, after an apparent early victory in their prohibitions and proselytising, the missions, despite wielding punishments that included the expulsion of converts who became involved in wars, were powerless to stop them (Gilson 1970: 120–5).

But while these prohibitions may have met with only limited success, and the influence of the missionaries in Sāmoan politics was fairly limited, Christian teachings and missionary activity began to transform Sāmoan culture and society. Within ten years, the LMS and the Wesleyans had large numbers of converts throughout Sāmoa. In contrast to its cautious beginnings, the mission grew and its impact on the Sāmoan worldview and lifestyle expanded and eventually became unassailable. Arguably, the most profound of the changes wrought by the missions was the replacement of the polytheistic religion of the Sāmoans with a monotheistic one (Turner 1983: 17–77), which fundamentally altered the relations between humans, nature and supernature in a relatively short time (Hamilton 2005: 187–205; Schmidt 2005: 42–65). Some practices signalled these transitions in highly public and heavily symbolic ways: significant members of families were invited to eat or otherwise desecrate their family's protective totem and to await retribution. Where none was forthcoming, the chief accepted the new religion on behalf of his family, the members of which then, at his direction, typically converted en masse.

But if some missionary strategies were highly public and laden with symbolism, others such as literacy, numeracy, and the teaching and advocacy of social values and practices were less dramatic and had more far-reaching effects on Sāmoan social organisation (Gilson 1970: 95–114). One of these was the decline in the power of the 'sacred priests', *ali'i pa'ia*, whose political authority had rested on 'sacred power', which was transferred to the missionaries and later to the Sāmoan ministers (Meleisea 1992: 21). These powers were further constrained by the subjection of the sacred priests to the same rules as commoners within the new communities of faith. Part of their power had traditionally come from completing a series of strategic marriages that established political alliances and extended their political influence. The missionary proscription of polygamy reduced their ability to extend influence by this means (Meleisea 1992: 21–22). At the same time, commoners who participated actively and wholeheartedly in the life of the church could gain new social status from their familiarity with the new sacred teachings. Christianity, in short, transformed social hierarchy by mitigating its extremes.

The requirement of literacy, which became a prerequisite for church membership for all but the blind and the aged, was a key to the change because it not only opened the way to an understanding of the Bible but also of other texts. Missionary introduction of new public health practices, agricultural crops and technical innovations, and the creation of surpluses for sale and engagement in trade also had profound effects on the organisation of the social, political and economic lives of church converts. The Catholic missions had, in fact, already joined with French mercantile interests and established a combined mission-trading enterprise, La Société Française de l'Océanie, which established a trading base on land obtained by Roudaire for the church (Gilson 1970: 171–4). The establishment of this trading station that offered its converts lower prices than those available at other European businesses led to tensions with missions that were losing converts to the Marists. Later, other missions became involved in trading to ensure that their converts did not trade for forbidden commodities such as alcohol and firearms, and used the profits from the trade to develop the mission field into the western Pacific. Missionary influence extended to providing information and advice to Sāmoans on engagement with and management of innovations. Missions, for example, used scripture to encourage particular approaches to production, and to the use of 'profits' from agricultural activity.

This process of transformation was documented by some missionaries who began recording changes in the societies to which they ministered in the latter half of the nineteenth century. Those who managed to set aside the prejudices of the time produced detailed accounts of the transformation that followed the move from a polytheistic worldview (Stair 1983: 210–41) to a monotheistic one and the social changes that ensued within a relatively short period (Pritchard 1866; Moyle 1984: 95–173). Missionary linguists, such as the redoubtable George Pratt, provided early and comprehensive lexicons of Sāmoan that can be used to track the entry of new ideas and technologies into the Sāmoan language (Pratt 1911). Missionary botanists, such as George Powell, produced early collections of Sāmoan flora and fauna that can be used to follow the entry of new plants and animals into the Sāmoan ecosystem (Powell 1868 and 1886).

In addition, three remarkable secular reports of Sāmoan society provide important baseline information and insights into the process of social transformation in the nineteenth century. These are the accounts of the US Naval Expedition, under the control of Commodore Wilkes (Wilkes 1845) that visited Sāmoa in the late 1830s, and documented the natural and human resources of Sāmoa; that of Dr Oscar Stuebel, the German consul in Apia between 1884 and 1894 (Stuebel 1897); and the later but extraordinarily comprehensive report by the German naval physician, Dr Augustin Krämer that was first published in 1902 (Krämer 1994). Krämer's remarkable book, entitled, *The Samoan Islands*, published in both German and Sāmoan, remains the most thorough and best documented study of 'classical' Sāmoan society.

Sāmoans and commercial settlement

The missionaries' 'success' in Sāmoa, publicised during their fund-raising trips to Britain and elsewhere and in published records of their activity, encouraged European commercial interests to believe that Sāmoa was ripe for the introduction of commerce. Encouraging wholesale settlement and commerce was not the missionaries' intention: they found many consequences of European settlement and trade elsewhere – such as the trade in liquor, and the introduction of gambling, prostitution and firearms – repugnant. Nevertheless, increasing linkages through settlement and commerce were an inevitable consequence of their reporting of their achievements and of accounts by secular supporters such as Commodore Wilkes of the US Exploring Expedition (Gilson 1970: 186–7).

The arrival of larger numbers of European or *papālagi* settlers from Britain, the United States, Germany and elsewhere in the Pacific, in search of cheap land and labour, was the second force to have a profound effect on Sāmoan culture and society.[7] Their presence generated a demand for the 'commodification' of land and labour and the establishment of 'market' values for land and labour that had previously had only 'use' values. They soon encountered problems in both areas. Settlers expected to be able to purchase inexpensive land on which to produce and process commodities such as copra and cotton more cheaply than producers elsewhere. But Sāmoan land was vested in families and held in perpetuity for the use of *āiga* members. It was centrally connected with collective identity and was not a commodity owned by individuals that could be 'bought' or 'sold'. Sāmoans had no reason to sell land: social identity was connected with particular lands, social standing was linked to the scale of landholdings, and their physical and social needs were well met within existing arrangements.

Land could under certain exceptional circumstances be alienated, usually as a gift or form of lease. While small tracts of land around Apia were leased and sold to European settlers 'whose presence and enterprise seemed to them likely to prove congenial and rewarding' (Gilson 1970: 161), Sāmoans were generally reluctant to alienate large tracts of agricultural land on a permanent basis early. Frustrated settlers had to wait until the funding requirements of wars and church activities caused Sāmoans to give up land. After 1860, a combination of circumstances led Sāmoans to alienate larger areas of land and intensified European interest in the law and order necessary to guarantee the security of their title and economic activity (Hempenstall and Rutherford 1984: 21). In time, the idea of commodification of land, along with acceptance of land surveys and the registration of transactions, gained traction and transformed the conception and nature of wealth.

Settlers also expected to be able to secure cheap Sāmoan labour to undercut the costs of production. Here, too, they encountered problems. Labour power was not, for the Sāmoans, a commodity that could be 'bought' and 'sold' by individuals for their personal benefit. Labour power was provided within and 'employed' by collectivities to extend their social and political influence within the Sāmoan polity: it was exchanged within kinship matrixes and the proceeds of labour accrued to families. Unlike landless populations elsewhere, Sāmoans were able to meet their needs within their existing economic arrangements, and widespread land alienation never created a pool of landless labour that was forced to enter the labour market on a permanent basis (Gilson 1970: 182–3). This economic reality was reflected in the high prices that Sāmoans were able to demand for their labour (Gilson 1970: 181–2). Sāmoans who found themselves with insufficient land in one place could invoke kinship connections in another and transfer their allegiance to kin groups with more land (Macpherson 1999: 71–95). After 1860, the costs of funding church-building and wars led more Sāmoans to offer labour for sale, and the emergence of the new 'labour market' extended the range of revenue sources and economic options for Sāmoans at a time when they needed immediate additional income for particular short periods. It provided an adjunct to, rather than a replacement for, traditional relations of production.

While the settlers may not have been able to secure either as much labour or land as they had anticipated or wanted, the establishment of 'markets' for land and labour transformed social and economic relations in Sāmoa in fundamental ways. Settler capitalism was a new model of economic activity that would significantly alter Sāmoan society. Sāmoan economic activity had traditionally provided a subsistence living, the outputs of which were consumed by the producers and their families. The Sāmoan economy could and did produce surpluses that were used to create sociopolitical capital for families and villages. However, the idea of deliberate production of a surplus for 'sale' for 'cash' in a 'market' was foreign. By contrast, settler capitalism, which focused on production of commodities for sale and on accumulation and retention of economic profits by individuals for their exclusive use, was an entirely unprecedented rationale and provided an alternative model of economic organisation and activity. The arrival of settler capitalism created a new framework for conceptualising objectives for planning outputs, and fresh options for investment of the outputs of production.

Sāmoans and the consuls

The attempts by European consular representatives to assert political 'rights' and to transform Sāmoan political organisation[8] was the third major force to change Sāmoan society. The settlers and their consuls, many of whom had chequered careers, stood outside the recognised polity and had no 'traditional' rights to power or authority, but nevertheless sought to challenge the integrity of Sāmoan political power and polity. Consuls invoked 'international conventions', the 'authority of foreign powers' and the 'accepted standards of European civilisation' as the basis of claims to levy taxes, promulgate codes of social and commercial conduct, and establish courts to try and punish those who violated their codes. In the process they sought to limit the rights of the Sāmoans and to impose political obligations on their leaders.

At first, their interests were confined to the right to manage the area round Apia Bay where European settlement and interests were concentrated (Gilson 1970: 162–87; Hempenstall and Rutherford 1984: 21). But this ambition, fuelled by the appointment of three consuls, acting for Britain, Germany and the United States respectively, eventually expanded to the protection of the interests of European settlers throughout Sāmoa. Attempts to extend their influence in the governance of Sāmoa gained momentum in the 1860s as European settlers claimed ownership of more land and consolidated their commercial interests (Hempenstall and Rutherford 1984: 21). The consuls' early efforts to exert influence served to demonstrate the extent of their misunderstanding of Sāmoan society and their inability to set their various national interests aside and to work together to impose their aspirations on Sāmoa.

These external agents also sought to advance their interests by influencing Sāmoan political organisation, which they did not understand well, at times by the use or threat of force, and at other times by interventions in the political system. In an ill-fated attempt to set up a unified kingship that they hoped they could use to establish and maintain order and predictability (Hempenstall and Rutherford 1984: 21–23), they sought, unsuccessfully, to remove the source of dynamic tension between the major factions by installing one as 'leader' over the other. To gain influence in the new government, the various consuls backed different Sāmoan factions in their struggle to secure the 'leadership'. All they achieved was to ensure that the two major factions were able to play the 'great powers' off against each other until the late 1880s (Hempenstall and Rutherford 1984: 23–25).

Frustrated, the three powers convened in Berlin in 1889 to resolve this situation. The 1889 Berlin Act, negotiated without Sāmoan input by the German, British and US colonial powers, and signed only later by the Sāmoan 'king', provided for a condominium designed to extend the powers and to advance the interests of the three foreign powers and to open up Sāmoa. Gilson notes that, 'In contemplating how Sāmoa should be governed, the Berlin conference took for its orientation the political and economic problems of Europeans, leaving the Sāmoans' affairs largely out of account, except in so far as they impinged on foreign concerns' (Gilson 1970: 397). The colonial powers' efforts at resolution were singularly unsuccessful for, as Gilson comments, 'the conference actually aggravated the jurisdictional tangle, creating institutions and laying down procedures so cumbersome and often so ill-defined, that the result almost defies description' (Gilson 1970: 397).

Predictably enough, the arrangements led to a new round of conflict and to civil war that the foreign powers, with complex and competing aspirations, were unable to head off. Faced with another crisis in 1899, the three powers appointed a commission that arrived in Sāmoa and promptly determined that, since the 'king' had resigned his office, the powers of the kingship should be henceforth assumed by the consuls, who then worked toward a proposal to partition the archipelago. Despite a lack of consultation, the proposal was eventually signed off by the Sāmoans who were by now tired of some 30 years of war and the intrigues of the colonial powers. A tripartite convention formalising arrangements under which Germany assumed control of the islands west of 170°, the US the administration of the eastern islands, and Britain abandoned claims in Sāmoa in favour of recognition of her interests in Tonga, was signed in December 1900 (Gilson 1970: 425–33; Hempenstall and Rutherford 1984: 23–24).

Sāmoans and the German administration

The pace of change increased in the twentieth century. The transfer of power in what became known as 'Western Sāmoa' to Germany in 1899 installed a more organised and determined colonial presence with the intellectual and economic resources and the power to impose its will on Sāmoan society. German administrators, notably the redoubtable Dr Solf and later Dr Erich Schultz, were demonstrably more successful than the consuls had been in bringing about changes in Sāmoan political organisation between 1900 and 1914 (Hempenstall and Rutherford 1984: 24–32). Dr Solf, the first governor, found that settlers were demanding a solution to the 'labour problem' caused by the fact that Sāmoans were reluctant to provide labour within the master–servant relationship the Germans envisaged. Solf was not keen to force Sāmoans to provide labour and 'resolved' the issue by allowing the recruitment of plantation workers from elsewhere.

This involved increasing the number of Melanesian labourers the German company Deutsche Handels und Plantagens Gesellschaft der Südsee Inseln (DHPG) had started to bring to Sāmoa from the Duke of York Islands after 1882. These labourers signed on for three years and were paid in cloth, lamps, axes, knives and, until 1900, liquor and firearms. Only DHPG was allowed to recruit in this area and, between 1895 and the early 1900s, more than 7000 workers were taken from Bougainville and Malaita in the Solomons and from the Bismarck Islands in what is now Papua New Guinea. These workers were kept in barracks on DHPG plantations around the edges of Apia and, because they were deliberately segregated from local populations, found it difficult to form relationships with the Sāmoans. The history of the life and exploitation of Melanesian labour in Sāmoa is dealt with in detail in Meleisea's 1980 book *O Tama Uli: Melanesians in Samoa*. Their harsh treatment compared unfavourably with the way the Sāmoans were treated by the Germans that may well have given the Sāmoans an insight into the nature of European racism. The Sāmoans soon adopted the German view that Melanesians were an 'inferior race' and became active advocates of policies of continued segregation between Melanesians and Sāmoans (Munro and Firth 1990: 3–29). But while this arrangement resolved the labour problem for DHPG, it did little for other planters who were prevented by Solf from forcing Sāmoans to work in plantations.

To solve this problem, Solf agreed, at the urging of Richard Deeken, the proprietor of Deutsche Samoa-Gesellschaft, to explore the possibility of employing indentured Chinese labour. He reluctantly agreed to this plan, and the first 289 recruits arrived in Sāmoa from southern China in March 1903. Six further drafts, all on three-year contracts, arrived before 1913 (O'Connor 1968: 11). Despite warnings against mistreating their new labourers, the settlers were harsh employers and they initially had difficulty recruiting new workers. As conditions in China worsened, however, recruitment again became easier. By 1914, there were 2184 Chinese labourers in Sāmoa at a time when the Sāmoan population was around 36,000 (Field 1984: 30–31). This presence had a profound effect on Sāmoa: despite German attempts to preserve 'ethnic purity' by keeping the Sāmoans and Chinese apart, the Sāmoans over time formed a range of relationships with the Chinese (Field 1984: 31–33). Some of these relationships were marital, and the Chinese consul estimated that there were 100 Sino-Sāmoan couples living on plantations; some were medical and we recorded a number of medicines that were given to Sāmoan healers by Chinese; some were based on trade where Chinese bought or traded eggs from Sāmoans and resold them at a profit.[9] Despite ordinances forbidding marriage between Sāmoans and Chinese, 'cohabitation continued relatively unchecked' (Willson, Moore and Munro 1990: 97). The relationships that developed with the Chinese gave Sāmoans an early insight into another people and their worldview, and produced a certain grudging respect for their commercial talents.

The Germans then turned their attention to undermining elements of Sāmoan culture and, in particular, to those who used it to unite Sāmoans in challenges to German authority. Solf confronted his nemesis in the person of Namulau'ulu Lauaki Mamoe, an experienced politician, articulate political negotiator and active advocate of Sāmoan independence (Meleisea 1980: 117). Solf's first challenge came in 1904 when the price of copra was reduced by 44 per cent, and a part-Sāmoan named Pullack encouraged Sāmoans to form an enterprise to buy and sell Sāmoan growers' copra in competition with German companies. Lauaki became the public advocate of this expression of sovereignty and levied Sāmoan chiefs and orators to form a Sāmoan company, Oloa Kamupanī, to break the German monopoly of the copra market. Solf, determined to put down this Sāmoan challenge to

German commercial domination, managed to undermine Lauaki's project but alienated Sāmoans in the process.

Lauaki again challenged Solf in 1905 when he asserted that the Tumua and Pule were the rulers of Sāmoa. Solf set out to weaken his position by forming a Sāmoan advisory group, Fono a Faipule, and co-opting Lauaki to the body. When Lauaki refused to accept German authority and instead formed a resistance movement called Mau a le Pule, Solf exiled Lauaki, his supporters and their families to Saipan in the Marianas. With Lauaki's influence effectively neutralised, the Germans were free to continue with their colonial project, albeit with some ongoing resistance (Field 1984: 30).

Some of their difficulty lay in the dynamic character of Sāmoan politics that was in part a product of the fact that Sāmoa's most powerful families attempted to secure all four of the so-called *pāpā* titles and the office of *tafa'ifā*. The 1899 Commission had noted that contests around the *pāpā* and *tafa'ifā* were principal causes of the instability in Sāmoan society and recommended their abolition. Between 1900 and 1914, the Germans set about reducing the influence of the *pāpā* and *tafa'ifā* by promoting and supporting an alternative Sāmoan polity, based around other families and titles and known as the *tama a āiga*, that they believed would be more stable and amenable to their influence (Tuimaleali'ifano 2006b: 36–37). In so doing, they redistributed Sāmoan political power and transformed a central dynamic of Sāmoan politics. They might, with more time to consolidate their initial gains, have been more successful, but their project ended when New Zealand, acting for the British government, seized German assets and assumed control of Western Sāmoa in October 1914.

Sāmoans and the New Zealand administration

The transfer of colonial power was confirmed in a League of Nations mandate, granted in 1920, that was converted to a United Nations trusteeship after World War II in 1946 (Gratton 1948: 8–9). New Zealand, despite its worthy intentions, proved a singularly inept administrator and was unable to produce the social and political change it had planned in Sāmoan society. It did, however, bring about some significant social changes by accident. The earliest of these focused on economic development and the creation of a public service that was supposed to protect the 'common people' until they could be gradually led into the dynamic world of the west. In these aims, New Zealand administrators were largely frustrated, which raises the question of why a programme designed to improve standards of living met such resistance among Sāmoans.

The lack of success was in part because New Zealand administrations under-estimated the Sāmoans' political sophistication and their by then considerable experience in dealing with Europeans. These difficulties were compounded by the limited abilities of New Zealand administrators, many of whom were chosen for their military records rather than for their experience in government. Several of them were also overtly racist and found no need, or reason, to try to understand the society that they sought to govern and, in time, to change. If they had, they might have realised that Sāmoans could live well within their existing social and economic arrangements and had no reason to accept the wholesale changes, in such central areas as land reform and governance, proposed by the New Zealanders.

The administrators might also have realised that the Sāmoans considered their society at least equal and in many respects superior to that of the New Zealanders, and saw no reason to adopt the culture and values promoted by New Zealand. Had New Zealand administrators understood Sāmoan society better, it might also have occurred to them that their patronising approach to, and lack of respect for, the Sāmoans would immediately alienate the latter who placed great importance on dignity and decorum (Gratton 1948: 10–24). They were, after all, the original and natural rulers of Sāmoa. The Maori doctor and anthropologist Sir Peter Buck, Te Rangi Hiroa, who studied Sāmoa in the late 1920s, recounted a story that exemplified this view:

> This attitude of the mass of the people is expressed in the reply of
> a talking chief to myself after I had sketched the migration of the

Polynesians from the mainland of Asia to the remote isles of the Pacific. 'We thank you for your address,' he said. 'The rest of the Polynesians may have come from Asia, but the Sāmoans – No. The Sāmoans originated in Sāmoa'. (Hiroa 1930: 5)

Finally, a series of ill-conceived moves by administrators alienated the Sāmoans even further and provided causes around which they could rally. The first of these was a proclamation on 31 August 1914 by Colonel Robert Logan, the first New Zealand administrator, in which, without any consultation with the Sāmoans, he summarily placed a series of restrictions on them. Sāmoans were directed to obey any order by a military officer; subjected to a 10 pm to 6 am curfew; banned from changing residence; forbidden to use any boat or canoe, which restricted their ability to travel; prohibited from holding public meetings, and printing or distributing written material; forbidden to manufacture or consume alcohol without government consent; and required to surrender cars, horses and carts, and firearms (Meleisea and Schoeffel 1987: 127–8).

While these restrictions may, to Logan at least, have seemed eminently reasonable precautions in wartime, the Sāmoans resented the high-handed unilateral imposition of limits to their freedom without explanation or consultation. This signalled a lack of respect for and acknowledgement of the Sāmoan role in governing the country when it was under German control. New Zealand did not have the experience or the personnel to back up this early and apparently decisive act, and the Sāmoans found room to manoeuvre as the new administration sought to control the Germans and to expropriate their property. They were able, Meleisea notes, to resume a number of activities that the Germans had banned and to re-establish the traditional Sāmoan government of Tumua ma Pule (Meleisea and Schoeffel 1987: 129).

The second ill-considered move by the New Zealand administration was the decision to allow the *SS Talune*, which was carrying the Spanish influenza, to land at Apia in 1918, leading to the rapid spread of flu throughout the Sāmoan population. This decision, exacerbated by the administration's refusal to allow European medical practitioners to attend to rural Sāmoans, resulted in the loss of some 8000 people, or between 22 and 24 per cent of the Sāmoan population (Tomkins 1992: 181–97). It completely alienated the Sāmoans. The epidemic itself also had profound effects on the highly gerontocratic Sāmoan society.

In a gerontocracy, the loss of many older people carries with it the prospect of social instability and of radical change, because the knowledge that guarantees the stability of the society is lost before it can be transmitted to the succeeding generation. This is what happened when many older and highly influential Sāmoans died from influenza. The epidemic took the lives of all of the senior pastors of the London Missionary Society and many of their assistants, and left the church leaderless. The ranks of senior chiefs and orators who had represented Sāmoans in their relationships with the colonial consuls, the German administration after 1900 and the New Zealand administrator after 1914, were also decimated: between 24 and 31 members of the Sāmoan government were killed by the flu. In this case, the numbers were less significant than the calibre of those who died.

The changes that were wrought by the epidemic have been characterised as 'a watershed' that 'accelerated the transition of political leadership from the elites of "Old Sāmoa" to younger, twentieth century men ... all associated with later political rebelliousness' (Hempenstall and Rutherford 1984: 33). These younger leaders were arguably better equipped to engage with Europeans on their own terms: a number of them had obtained a good understanding of European society and had already established influence within the colonial elite. Many of them were of mixed Sāmoan and European descent and had privileged insights into both cultures, which gave them an advantage over the European administrators who did not. Furthermore, a number of these *'afakasi* were the offspring of marriages between traders and Sāmoan women and were engaged in, and familiar with, commerce; they not only had skills but also financial resources that were not available to some of the leaders whom they succeeded (Cyclopedia of Samoa 1907: 95–109). Indeed, some of those younger leaders, including O. F. Nelson, would play a significant role in the next incident that would rally the Sāmoans against the New Zealand administrators.

The passage of the Samoan Constitution Order in 1920, and the confirmation of the Mandate by the League of Nations in 1921, conferred on New Zealand both the right to govern and the responsibility to develop Sāmoa. But the New Zealand administration's incompetent and callous handling of the influenza epidemic, and revelations that Sāmoa's future was to be determined by the League of Nations and New Zealand, and without consultation with the Sāmoans, led to growing dissatisfaction within both Sāmoan and settler communities. While their respective interests differed, they each found themselves ignored by Logan and the New Zealand government (Meleisea and Schoeffel 1987: 132–4). In the Sāmoan case, the dissatisfaction arose from New Zealand's determination to limit Sāmoans' participation in the new government while proscribing Sāmoan leaders' zealously guarded powers to control their villages and districts:

> It was not that Sāmoans did not want peace, good health and prosperity. They did, but they felt strongly that they should have a voice in planning and policy-making. Village authorities throughout Sāmoa deeply resented the imposition of rules and regulations to which they had been unable to make any contribution. (Meleisea and Schoeffel 1987: 132–3)

The situation was not helped by successive administrators' patronising attitudes to the Sāmoans and their unswerving belief that Sāmoans could, with their guidance, live like Europeans and that this was what they wanted to do. While Sāmoans did indeed want some new technical skills, they were, in other respects, quite satisfied with their own lives and society. Their complaints to the administrator and to visiting New Zealand dignitaries were largely ignored, and by 1926 local dissatisfaction led to the formation of a joint Sāmoan–settler organisation, the Sāmoan League, O le Mau, to represent local interests to the administration (Field 1984). The movement adopted the slogan 'Sāmoa mo Sāmoa' or 'Sāmoa for the Sāmoans' that provoked an immediate response from the administrator who banned the Mau and deported two of its leaders to Apolima.

This move in turn produced widespread support for the movement through Sāmoa, involving,

> ... a peaceful, orderly programme of non-cooperation with the New Zealand administration. Committees and councils established by the Administration stopped meeting, villages ignored visiting New Zealand officials, courts of law were avoided by disputing parties, children were withdrawn from government schools, and officially-promoted copra and banana projects were abandoned. In many districts, all New Zealand imposed village regulations, even those which promoted public health, were disregarded, and, instead of paying taxes, money was raised and collected for the Mau. (Meleisea and Schoeffel 1987: 135)

The Mau protest could not be ignored, and a Royal Commission was established in 1927 to investigate complaints presented by the Mau. In the event, the Commissioners held the Sāmoans responsible for the issues and deported one of its key strategists, a highly successful part-Sāmoan businessman Taisi O. F. Nelson, and two local Europeans, E. W. Gurr and A. G. Smyth, whom they believed were orchestrating protests against the government. The Mau continued to hold protests but, without its leaders, was losing momentum. It might have lost even more but for New Zealand's handling of a Mau parade in December 1929 to welcome Gurr and Smyth back to Sāmoa that resulted in serious escalation of the dispute.

A dispute between some young Sāmoans and the military police early in the day led to the death of a policeman, raised the level of tension in Apia and increased the determination of the New Zealand authorities to exercise arrest warrants on some of the movement's leaders during the protest. As police attempted to seize the Mau's secretary, there was a fracas, and police fired on the protestors killing Tupua Tamasese Lealofi lll and injuring two other senior *matai*, Tuimaleali'ifano and Faumuinā, who were attempting to restore order. When the confrontation ended, a total of 11 Sāmoans had died from wounds (Field 2006). This confrontation, which became known as 'Black Saturday', led to renewed determination on the part of New Zealand to assert its authority, and to a Mau declaration of their desire for self-government and independence from New Zealand.

A period of intensified conflict ensued as New Zealand marines attempted to undermine the Mau, which had by this time been designated a seditious organisation. Marines attempted to break the movement by pursuing men into the hills and intimidating their supporters in the villages with varying degrees of success (Field 1984: 170–82). With its men forced into the bush, a women's Mau, led by its leaders' wives and widows, arose and maintained pressure on the administration for accommodation of the Mau's goals over several years. But the movement was also suffering from disagreement within its ranks on the direction of the organisation. A change of government in New Zealand in 1936 brought about a different approach to Sāmoa and some concessions to the Mau, including the withdrawal of its designation as a seditious organisation, the freeing of O. F. Nelson to return to Sāmoa, and dispatching a goodwill mission that, over a month in Sāmoa, agreed to a more consultative style of government. But just as quickly as issues of governance in Western Sāmoa had finally attracted more sympathetic attention in New Zealand, it waned as New Zealand was drawn into the Second World War.

Sāmoa had, by 1939, confronted two colonial powers each of which had been bent on its transformation, albeit in different ways and for different ends. New Zealand had taken over just as the Germans seemed to be having greater success, but were in the end no more successful in remaking Sāmoa in its image. Sāmoans had shown themselves capable to resisting external forces and changes in which it had not been consulted. Summarising the impact of the New Zealand administration on Sāmoan society, Michael Field observes that:

> New Zealanders could not, or would not, accept that the Samoan point of view was a valid one. Their attitude clashed directly with the fundamental Samoan pride in country and culture. They did not need legal justification for their claims that they were entitled to govern their own destiny. Samoans believed very simply that Samoa was their country and that anyone else in it was a guest, welcome or otherwise. And they looked back on a 3000 year civilisation as ample evidence that they were capable of looking after themselves. (Field 1984: 135)

The Second World War and Sāmoa

The Second World War brought Sāmoa face to face with another population and, briefly, opened the door for significant change. In March 1942, the first US forces arrived in Western Sāmoa to 'protect' the Pacific from Japanese invasion. By the end of 1942, there were several thousand marines in the country and that number had grown to 12,000 by the end of 1943. The physical impact of the presence of marines and naval construction battalions was significant: they extended and improved the country's road network, built an airport and fortifications, and established new infrastructure. While these changes altered patterns of movement and, indeed, villages were relocated to accommodate this new activity, the more significant impact was on Sāmoan culture and social organisation. The demand for labour saw some 2000 young men drawn into well-paid labour on US construction projects, and large numbers of women employed in the provision of laundry services and entertainment. The demand for food produced a significant cash market for Sāmoan farmers. The new wealth available during the brief period between 1942 and 1943, when the bulk of the US forces moved on, also provided opportunities for some local entrepreneurs. These outsiders, called *maligi amelika* by the Sāmoans, were clearly unlike any they had encountered to date.

With the war over, the Western Sāmoans hoped that the Labour government in New Zealand would again focus on its desire for self-government. Under a United Nations trusteeship, New Zealand assumed responsibility for preparing Sāmoa for independence. A United Nations mission was sent to Sāmoa in 1947 to determine the direction for change. While it received an enthusiastic reception, it was presented with divergent plans by the Sāmoans and by the Citizens' Committee that represented primarily the interests of Europeans and part-Europeans based in Apia. Certain compromises were made and in 1948 a new form of government, in which Sāmoans had significantly more power than in previous administrations, was established to begin to move the country towards independence (Davidson 1967: 163–233).

This was to be achieved through parallel processes of consultation, negotiation and constitution-making and revealed the selective approach of Sāmoans toward change: the new constitution and government embodied principles of Sāmoan society, or *fa'asāmoa*, and the models offered to it by those who guided the process of decolonisation.[10] While the consultation process reflected great degrees of agreement among Sāmoans on some issues and principles, such as the desire to retain key elements of both traditional political power and land tenure, it also reflected increasing divergence among them on others that were to prove increasingly significant.

Independence and migration

Western Sāmoa[11] attained independence on 1 January 1962, but constitutional autonomy and commitment to embodying significant elements of culture and tradition in building the new nation would not shield Sāmoa from even more powerful external forces for change. While the new government was united in its desire for independence, its members were by no means as united in their vision for the new state or how it was to be achieved (Meleisea 1987b: 208–10).

As Western Sāmoa's leaders focused on building a nation, winds of change that could not be deflected were gathering force beyond the horizon. During the Second World War, New Zealand governments had become aware of the country's vulnerability and had resolved to restructure the post-war New Zealand economy to ensure greater economic security and industrial self-sufficiency, primarily through the expansion of the manufacturing industries. However, the country had suffered heavy losses in World War II and, even after rural Maori were persuaded to move to work in the cities where growth was gaining momentum, domestic labour supplies were soon exhausted. The New Zealand government turned first to western Europe and then to its former Pacific 'territories' for labour to drive the expansion of manufacturing.

Sāmoans were among those from the Pacific who 'answered the call' for labour from 1945. Their numbers in New Zealand grew rapidly, as the table below shows.

TABLE 1 SĀMOAN POPULATION IN NEW ZEALAND

YEAR	SĀMOAN POPULATION
1945	716
1951	NA
1956	3740
1961	6481
1966	8663
1971	22,198
1976	27,876
1981	42,453
1986	66,254
1991	85,743
1996	101,754
2001	115,000
2006	131,100

Note: The proportion of New Zealand's resident Sāmoan population born and raised outside Sāmoa has risen steadily throughout this period.

Much attention has focused on the consequences of this migration in the receiving society, but the departure of significant numbers of mainly young Sāmoans for New Zealand and, later, other destinations would have a profound and growing effect on Sāmoa's demography, polity, society and economy.

The new nation's population growth rate declined as significant proportions of the economically active population were relocated. Many of those who migrated would eventually establish their families abroad, a factor that explains, in part, the rapid growth of the expatriate Sāmoan population. Population growth rates, which had increased steadily as public health and sanitation measures were implemented during New Zealand's administration, fell dramatically and quickly and reduced pressure on both the economy and environment. While migrants no longer contributed directly to the Sāmoan domestic economy, they were not lost to it.

Early migrants were often chosen by their families on the basis of evidence of their willingness to serve, *tautua*, their families.

Their strong, ongoing commitments to their non-migrant kin ensured a steadily increasing flow of remittances in cash and kind from New Zealand (Macpherson 1974; Pitt and Macpherson 1974: 28–49). These remittances expanded the Sāmoan economy and might have had a limited effect but for the fact that remittances flowed in different ways and redistributed power within families and villages (Shankman 1976: 51–84). Remittance income was no longer invariably controlled by *matai* in the ways that income derived from family land had traditionally been controlled. But remittances did not increase productivity: as Shankman showed in a classic study (Shankman 1976), as remittance volumes grew, so both agricultural activity and productivity in Sāmoa declined. Remittances also created a steadily increasing degree of reliance on the economies and labour markets in which the migrants worked. Contractions in those economies and reforms in those labour markets, over which Sāmoa has had no influence, have had profound effects on the Sāmoan economy and society.[12]

The remittance-driven expansion of family and village economies removed the constraints that were formerly imposed by their local factor endowments, and made new social and technological options available (Macpherson 1988). Families with migrants abroad could engage in activities for which they would not formerly have had the financial resources. This possibility appealed particularly to families that were less influential in the 'traditional' village hierarchy. They could use remittances to engage in business, build larger homes, educate their children, purchase freehold land, challenge traditional authority, enter politics and generally stake their claims to greater recognition within the village. These new tides of money increased the dynamism of Sāmoan society as competition between traditional 'elites' and newly wealthy villagers intensified. Meleisea outlines such a case in his own village (Meleisea 2000) and in Matāutu (Meleisea 1987b). Similar cases have been recorded in many other villages (Tuimaleai'ifano 2000; Macpherson 2004) and surface regularly in evidence in cases heard before village councils and courts.

Migrant remittances have had a profound impact on Sāmoan society, but in the period since independence another force, overseas development aid, has also had a comparable impact. During the cold war, Pacific states were routinely courted by metropolitan states seeking their support. Western Sāmoa was no exception, and significant amounts of aid flowed into the new state from New Zealand, Australia, the US, Europe and various international financial agencies. These new resource flows allowed successive Sāmoan governments to embark on ambitious new development programmes from 1966 on.[13] While the Department of Economic Development formulated the programmes, parliament made decisions about allocation of these resources, and parliamentarians who could secure projects and resources for their constituents gained sociopolitical prestige and ensured their political longevity. Considerable amounts of energy and money were expended to get into parliament, and this transformed traditional institutions that the Sāmoan constitution was designed to protect in significant ways (So'o 1998: 289–304).

Matai suffrage, provided for in the constitution to maintain continuity of *matai* authority, meant that only chiefs could vote for members of parliament. As long as the numbers of *matai* were fixed, lesser chiefs could not hope to enter parliament. At some point in the 1970s, the flexibility of the *matai* system was exploited to create new *matai* by 'splitting' a title formerly held by one person and conferring the title on several, thereby increasing the number of eligible voters and opening the parliamentary race to competition. It is likely, as Meleisea notes (1992), that those who engineered these changes could not have anticipated, or were unconcerned by, the unforeseen consequences of their actions. The consequences were mitigated by a referendum in 1990 that provided for universal adult suffrage, but by that point much had changed and, some 50 years on, the consequential impacts in the chiefly system, *le fa'amatai*, have been very significant and have recently been outlined in an important collection of essays on the subject (So'o 2007).

As emigrants became wealthier and returned to Sāmoa, sometimes temporarily and sometimes permanently, they too began to transform the country. While many remained fiercely loyal to the land of their birth, some were also critical of elements of Sāmoan custom and practice, *fa'asāmoa*, and areas of the chiefly system of governance, *fa'amatai*. Some began to challenge these principles and practices in court. In this they were able to invoke the constitution that, while recognising and enshrining elements of traditional governance, also recognised and entrenched a series of individual freedoms. Thus, traditional agreements about the importance of collectivities such as the village, which were embodied in both the constitution and other legislation, were contested by people who invoked individual rights to freedom of speech, worship and association embodied in other parts of the constitution. These recent political changes and responses have been canvassed by Meleisea 1987b; So'o 2000; Va'a 2000; and Macpherson and Macpherson 2006b.

Conclusion

Sāmoa has, despite superficial appearances, been confronted by a series of external forces and agencies almost since its settlement. These agencies have transformed Sāmoan society in different ways and to varying degrees. There are two views of Sāmoan engagement with global forces.

One contends that Sāmoa has been reasonably successful in confronting and managing these forces. Today, some 81 per cent of Sāmoan land remains customary land under traditional tenure; a further 15 per cent is held in trust by the Sāmoan government on behalf of the Sāmoan people; only 4 per cent has been transferred to freehold title (Australian Agency for International Development 2008b, volume 1: 4). Sāmoan society, this view contends, has engaged with and embraced the Christian religion[14] while retaining a distinctive Sāmoan worldview and culture. Sāmoans exerted early influence on the ways in which the gospel was interpreted and the church was organised, which is reflected in the organisation of mainstream Sāmoan churches. Sāmoa has engaged with and 'seen off' numbers of people who believed Sāmoan society was dying: today, some 92.6 per cent of the population claims Sāmoan descent; 7 per cent are of Euronesian descent; and less than 1.0 per cent is European. Those people sought to transform the Sāmoan polity and yet, after some 150 years of engagement with colonial powers, Sāmoa emerged with a constitution that embodies elements of the *fa'asāmoa*, the *fa'amatai* and the Westminster constitution. The Sāmoan language is widely spoken and remains the language of government and of daily life. Sāmoans, in this view, are justified in claiming that they have selectively engaged with the church, commerce and colonial powers, and have successfully taken from them the elements that they value and have incorporated them into Sāmoan custom. This view of history lies behind the confidence with which Sāmoan people assert that in Sāmoa practices may change but its institutional foundations remain intact: *e fesuia'i faiga ae tūmau fa'avae*.

Another view contends that Sāmoan society has undergone deeper and more fundamental change than the first suggests. It holds that closer scrutiny of Sāmoan history reveals not only variations in practice, but also fundamental transformations in core Sāmoan religious, economic and political institutions: its *fa'avae*. Sāmoan society has consigned an indigenous religion and various associated social institutions to that part of history referred to as the *aso o le pouliuli*, or days of darkness, and adopted a new religion with its attendant worldview and lifestyle in an act that signalled the beginning of the *aso o le malamalama*, or period of enlightenment. Sāmoan society has embraced markets in land and labour, and the Sāmoan economy is increasingly engaged with and conditioned by the requirements of global capitalism. Sāmoan society has seen its traditional polity reorganised with the replacement of the *pāpā* and *tafa'ifā* by the *tama a āiga* as the most powerful figures in the 'traditional' Sāmoan polity (Tuimaleai'ifano 2006b). In the process it has embraced new forms of governance: a nation state, courts, a bureaucracy and a constitution that have curtailed the rights of traditional leaders and the traditional polity (Davidson 1967). There have also been fundamental transformations in both kinship (Macpherson 1999: 71–95) and the *fa'amatai* (So'o 2007). This analysis leads to a somewhat different view of Sāmoan society's engagement with global forces. Transformations in the organisation of each of these areas of Sāmoan culture and social organisation reflect a continuous, dynamic and creative process of engagement with global forces. In this view, Sāmoan society is so flexible that, although it has undergone significant and real changes, it has emerged without a sense of historical disjunction and is still able to assert that its cultural foundations remain intact.

But irrespective of which view one takes of Sāmoa's historical engagement with global forces, Sāmoa is now confronted with new and rapidly intensifying incursions and impacts. The increased level and experience of migration have the potential to transform Sāmoan society more quickly than any factors in earlier periods of movement. New ideologies promoted by influential external agencies using novel forms of leverage and new media have the potential to impose new norms and values on Sāmoan society. New technologies have the potential to redistribute productivity, and to undermine traditional social, economic and political relations and organisation. Can a society of some 185,000 people hope to resist, or even control, these global forces? The following chapters will draw on Sāmoa's experience with earlier globalising influences to provide a context for discussions of the impact of these contemporary influences.

3.

Migration and social transformation

Migration has, over the last 200 years, both scattered and transformed the families that comprise the village. It has extended the global reach of families and villages and, in the process, has changed each of them in fundamental ways: both entities would be very different had this flow of people not occurred. In this chapter we examine the history of migration and the ways in which it has shaped the village and its families at various times. We contend that as the volume of migration has increased, its impact on the organisation of the village and its families has intensified and is likely to continue to intensify.

Movement is such a common topic of daily conversation that one is always vaguely conscious of the global reach of the village. People who see smoke from an earth oven in the air in the middle of the week routinely assume that a family must be preparing an *umu* to cook delicacies for a departing relative to take to overseas *āiga*. People wearing new clothes, or carrying new tools, are often asked whether a relative from abroad has been visiting. These conversations usually focus on individuals, and on the circumstances of their arrivals and departures, so it is easy to lose sight of the larger picture, which is that people have been coming and going from the village for several hundred years at least. Only occasionally do larger formal events, which bring people from around the world together, lead one to consider the significance of the steadily expanding global footprints of villages and families.

A recent wedding led us to think about the increasing global reach of the village and the ways in which it is shaping and reshaping both family and village. During the wedding we began to reflect on some of the differences between that event and others we had attended in the village some 40 years earlier. At the earlier weddings, telegrams and letters came from the few relatives who were living in temporary exile in American Sāmoa, Auckland and Wellington. Each of the expatriates was well-known to all present and was, indeed, something of a local celebrity: a person who had left the safety of the village to live in a distant, cold place from whence they sent formerly unimaginable amounts of money and presents to their relatives. The messages in those earlier telegrams, which were almost always written in Sāmoan, were formulaic: injunctions to hold tight to one's faith, references to passages from scripture on the meaning of love and the sanctity of marriage, and assurances of love and support.

At the recent wedding, the best man read a list of telegrams, email messages and text messages from absent relatives and friends from as far away as Dunedin, Dubai and Dundee. Whispered discussions occurred around the tables as people tried to establish the identity of senders whose names were not recognised. This confusion was not surprising: some had been gone for many years and, in several cases, decades; some had married non-Sāmoans and now had surnames that were not recognised; others had anglicised the names by which most of the village knew them; and some had been born abroad and had never been seen in the village. On this occasion, many of the messages were in English, which did not bother the best man who read them in a heavy American accent acquired during a period working in a tuna cannery in nearby American Sāmoa. On this occasion, too, the content of the messages was rather more varied, less formal and decidedly more 'secular'. Some of the advice to the new couple would have been unthinkable 40 years earlier, and the best man had to pause briefly to censor some of the messages before translating them into Sāmoan for older guests who might have been surprised by what people now felt able to say in public.

We were with a group of people in their sixties and conversation soon turned to the impact of migration on the village over the last 50 years. Some present recalled a time when only one person from the village had been abroad, to Europe as a soldier in the Second World War, and how he had recounted his experiences of Europe to spellbound young audiences. Others remembered a time when only one person in the village had travelled on an aeroplane: from Apia to Auckland and back on a TEAL[1] Solent flying boat. She would recount her experience, complete with sound effects and a description of the aircraft bathroom, to anyone who would listen. She had stayed overnight in a hotel in Fiji and could provide a commentary on Fijian society and culture and on the wonders of life in hotels. Another recalled a man from the village who travelled to New Zealand by ship and was told to disembark at the first port of call. After the ship was diverted from its original destination because of a storm, he got off at the wrong port and was only eventually re-united with his family by the New Zealand police.

Nor were the triumphal returns of those early emigrants forgotten. Some recalled the woman who returned to the village in the 1950s with money stuffed into her clothing to circumvent New Zealand currency export regulations, and bought her family the first refrigerator in the village. That led to recollection of the woman who brought the first television set to the village and of the crowd of people who gathered at the family's home in the evenings to watch American television programmes[2] even though few spoke much English at the time. Others remembered expatriates returning from New Zealand for village weddings laden with dresses, shoes, diamantes and cosmetics for entire bridal parties, and huge wedding cakes. The repatriations of the first people to die abroad, the expensive coffins in which they returned, and the large numbers of expatriate relatives and amounts of cash that accompanied them, were also recalled with more than a little nostalgia.

On that occasion, stories focused on the steadily increasing frequency of movement that has occurred since 1948 when several young men from the village first went overseas to work. The recollections focused on changes that had occurred during the lifetimes of those present and spoke of the increasing ease and frequency of movement over that time. Indeed, as one person noted, arrivals and departures are so common that travellers' names and prayers for their protection are no longer offered in church services as they once were. We soon realised we were talking as if the globalisation of the village, and of its families, had commenced after World War II. In reality, the post-war period is only the latest phase in a very much longer history that has seen people come and go through the village, changing it in the process. The village and its families have been exposed to the global community and economy for at least 150 years, and evidence of this earlier globalisation is all around. In fact, ironically, it is so readily apparent, so embedded in areas from culture to technology, that it is almost 'invisible'.

The 'invisible' past

The culture

The most conspicuous evidence of the village's exposure to global forces is the large, white church that occupies the physical, spiritual and social centre of the village. It has stood in the village since the first Europeans established it in middle of the nineteenth century and represents, as we will argue in the next chapter, a watershed in village history, culture and social organisation. But while this is so 'obvious' in some ways, it is 'invisible' in others. The church is not thought of as evidence of the village's exposure to global forces. The identity of the village is now so completely intertwined with the church that it is almost inconceivable to think of the village without the church, or the church without the village. It is as though the church has always been the foundation of the village, its history and its social organisation.

The village flora

Evidence of this earlier globalisation also abounds across the range of village flora, in the presence and various uses of familiar plants. Several examples are highly visible in food plants that grow everywhere and are eaten regularly. The lady finger banana, *fa'i misiluki*, that the village is fond to claim as its own was, in fact, brought to Sāmoa from either Java or Brazil and is now so widely established that it has displaced some native varieties. It has been identified as *Musa balbisiana*. Another is the popular dwarf banana cultivar, *fa'i fua maulalo*, that was brought to Sāmoa by the Reverend John Williams from the Duke of Devonshire's estate at Chatsworth in the mid-nineteenth century. It has been identified as *Musa nana* and is also known as the Cavendish or Chinese banana, and has become a staple food in the village diet. They are two of a group of four introduced cultivars, known collectively as *Eumusa*, that Sāmoans call *fa'i papālagi* and are now preferred in the Sāmoan diet to the native plantains (Parham 1972: 24–28).

While we were studying Sāmoan medicine (Macpherson and Macpherson 1990), we discovered plants in use that were not recorded in any of the early Sāmoan plant collections and were clearly not natives.[3] In the first instance, inquiries soon revealed that the plants were brought back to the village by a Sāmoan pastor who served as a missionary in the Solomon Islands in the late nineteenth century. There, he had studied Solomon Islanders' uses of plants and had later collected and repatriated the most useful of them. In Sāmoa, his mother, a Sāmoan healer, had incorporated them into her medicine and had, effectively, rendered their origins invisible: they were now a part of Sāmoan 'traditional medicine'.

Soon after, we came across another cluster of exotic medicinal plants that, it turned out, had been brought back to the village by a pastor who had served in Papua New Guinea in the early twentieth century. He too had brought these back for his wife's mother, a well-known village healer, who incorporated them in her medicine. The process had continued throughout the twentieth century. Another plant widely used in 'traditional medicine' was, in fact, brought to the village from Papua New Guinea in the late 1970s by a young man who had worked there as a rigger and had discovered its therapeutic properties while hunting with locals who used the plant to relieve muscle cramps. Another medicinal plant was brought to the village more recently by a returning Mormon missionary who had seen the plant used by first nations communities in Colorado and had offered it to a Sāmoan healer who integrated it into her 'traditional practice'.

Similarly, it was revealed that some exotic decorative plants were brought to the village by an Australian woman who married a local man after the Second World War, settled in the village and created a much admired flower garden. Another prominent decorative plant was imported from Hawai'i, propagated at the government plant research station and distributed to villages for use in village beautification programmes from the 1990s.

The village fauna

Evidence of this earlier movement is also found in the village fauna. Coconut palms are still attacked by rhinoceros beetles, *Oryctes rhinoceros*, that were accidentally introduced in 1909.[4] The dogs that dominate the village dog packs look very much like Australian blue heelers and, it turns out, were indeed introduced by an Australian who had come to manage an Australian trading company in the 1950s and lived in the village for some 20 years. Two bird species, the common mynah (*Acridotheres tristis*) and the jungle mynah (*Acridotheres fuscus*), which increasingly dominate the bird life in the village, were introduced to control cattle ticks, in 1965 and 1988 respectively. Village gardens are now periodically ravaged in wet weather by voracious snails known as the Giant African snail (*Achatina fulica*) or *sisi afelika*, a species introduced into Sāmoa in late 1994, probably from American Sāmoa.

The technology

Evidence of this earlier globalisation is also found in a range of technologies used in the village. The large simple church was built with a lime cement made from coral harvested at the reef with steel crow-bars, brought ashore in canoes by men, and passed by long lines of women and children to large fire pits. The lime produced was then mixed to form the building's foundation slab and walls. On top of the lime cement walls sit huge, beautifully machined beams and bolted trusses that support the dark-stained, sarked, tongue-and-groove ceilings. Set in the walls are stained-glass windows with wonderful nineteenth-century renderings of religious images. It was the first lime cement building in the village and replaced the simple traditional structure that had served the smaller village congregation earlier. Yet, despite the fact that most people in the village spend at least some time each week in the church, and contemplate its ceilings and windows during services, few see it as an example of introduced technology.

Two palms whose fronds are preferred to thatch roofs, and to weave blinds for those houses that still have them, are known in Sāmoan as *niu māsoā* or arrowroot palm, and *niu olotuma* or the Rotuman palm, identified as *Metroxylon salomonense* and *Areca catechu* respectively by Parham (1972:

89–90). The first, known also as the Solomon Islands sago palm, is said to have been brought by Solomon Islanders who worked on German plantations at the turn of the twentieth century, and the second is evidence of the earlier presence of a Rotuman family who are said to have had their relatives bring the plant from Rotuma when they realised it was more durable than the local palm that was in use in the village.[5]

A variety of the Derris plant,[6] known in Sāmoan as *'ava niukini*, can be used to manufacture a neurotoxin that, when spread in pools on the falling tide, temporarily stupefies fish and makes catching them easier and more efficient. Enquiries revealed that the plants, and their use, were thought to have been introduced to the village by Solomon Islanders who had been part of the indentured labour force taken to Sāmoa to work on plantations in the early twentieth century. These men had remained in Sāmoa and had married into the village in the early 1900s.

The ever-present bush-knife, or *sapelu*, without which no self-respecting farmer would go to the plantation, was one of the very earliest items sought in trade after its utility became obvious to those who saw them used on British and German plantations. It was soon joined in service by the invaluable steel file, or *'ili*, and the steel crowbar, or *kolopā*, that are essential pieces of equipment in plantation work on the stony, recent volcanic soils of the village.

Village diet

The village diet also reflects a long and diverse contact history. On any 'traditional' occasion where a family or village is required to show hospitality, the menu invariably includes a range of savoury dishes including *alaisa*, rice, *siaumegi*, chow mein, *sapasui*, chop sui, *pisupo*, corned beef, *pua'a*, pork, *manu pālagi*, beef, *povi masima*, salt beef, *salati pateta*, potato salad, *sosisi* or sausages, and *sua eleni* or herring stew; and a range of desserts including *keke*, cake, *puligi*, steamed puddings, *salati fuala'au*, fruit salad, and, increasingly, *aisi kulimi* or ice cream. Of these, rice, probably because of its versatility, has become so pervasive that the price of a sack of rice has become a popularly used index of the cost of living in the village. At the same time, some traditional foods have been progressively displaced from the diet and parents complain that their children prefer rice and canned food and will no longer eat such dietary staples as breadfruit, talo and green bananas.

Village land tenure

This earlier globalisation is also evident in land tenure patterns throughout Sāmoa. Some 4 per cent of all land in Sāmoa is currently freehold land. Much of the 15 per cent of the land presently owned by the Sāmoan state was freehold land that was seized from German interests during World War I and returned to the Sāmoan government after independence.

A survey map of village land reveals tracts of freehold land, *fanua tau pālagi*, in the midst of customary land, *fanua tau Sāmoa*. The creation of freehold land, where there was once only customary land, reflects the fact that in the mid-nineteenth century an English surveyor married a local woman. Her family gave the new couple some land that the husband promptly surveyed and registered as freehold land, thus creating a fundamental division within the village between two very different forms of tenure. Other Europeans followed, married into the village families and, over time, secured by purchase or marriage significant parts of what was formerly customary land. Their descendants have retained that land and live on it today. In the 150 years since, various other parts of the village estate have become *fanua tau pālagi*; and yet, despite the very different rights that attach to each type of land, this is not obvious in either daily life or conversation.

The faces of the people

But evidence of this earlier globalisation is most obvious in the faces of the people. While the majority are visibly Sāmoan, there are others who reflect the waves of immigrants who, for various reasons, have settled in Sāmoa. Some 7 per cent of the Sāmoan population is described as 'Euronesian', that is, of mixed Polynesian and European descent, but this population tends to be concentrated in some areas around Apia and is probably more obvious in those places. Smaller percentages are descendants of marriages between Sāmoan and immigrant labourers. Chinese-Sāmoans, sometimes known as *'afa Saina*, and Sāmoans with Solomon Island ancestry, known as *'afa Solomona*, were generally integrated into the village, while this was not always the case with those of mixed Sāmoan and European ancestry (Stace 1956: 39).

A significant number of people in the village bear the names and features of English and German settlers who established small businesses and plantations around the village in the late part of the nineteenth and the early twentieth centuries.[7] They set up homes and had families, and over time were fully absorbed into the village. In most cases their children married into the village and became part of its genealogy and history. In some cases these settlers' families have become so completely embedded in the village social organisation and their names have been so Sāmoanised that their origins are only faintly obvious. So the Pomasa family turn out to be the descendants of one Augustus Burmeister, formerly of Berlin, and the Pilitati family turn out to be the descendants of an English couple, the Pritchards, who settled in the village and were well-known as missionaries, and later as traders, in Sāmoa and throughout the Pacific.

The woman who runs the barbecue stall near the main road and sells food to bus passengers turns out to be a descendant of one of several Chinese men, brought to Sāmoa as plantation labour, who remained after his compatriots were sent back to China in the early twentieth century. He married a Sāmoan woman and started a small business in the village. His children have since had their own children, all of whom bear his name and features, and are now respected members of the village elite. Interestingly, some 100 years later, a more recent Chinese immigrant has married a village woman and established a new store and bakery at the other end of the village.

The bus-operator is a grandson of one of several thousand Solomon Islanders who worked at a nearby DHPG copra plantation in the early twentieth century before leaving the plantation and settling in the village. He married a village woman and formed close bonds with her family. His children and grandchildren are now respected members of the village polity and its social elite. Ironically, the bus-operator recently bought and settled on some freehold land that was formerly owned by DHPG and on which his grandfather had once worked.

The woman with stunning blue eyes in the village shop turns out to be one of the descendants of a marine who was stationed briefly in Sāmoa during the Second World War. After the war he returned to the village and married a local woman whom he had met. They started a shop on her family's land and had eleven children, all of whom are said to have had the same blue eyes.

This overwhelming evidence of the village's long history of exposure to global population movements becomes apparent only when one asks about it. The individual pieces are not subjects of daily conversation: indeed, they rarely warrant any comment. This is not to suggest that there is a conspiracy of silence about this earlier period or some collective denial of its impact. On the contrary, some of the evidence of earlier globalisation is clearly marked linguistically and readily apparent to all who stop to think about it. It is simply irrelevant in most matters that are considered of any significance, and is evidence of a situation in which incomers and change have become part of the life of the village.

Linguistic markers

The weed that overtakes plantations and makes farmers' lives so hard is known as *vao maligi* or *vao elefane*, also called marines' plant (*Pseudelephantopus spicatus*). It turns out that it was brought to Sāmoa during the Second World War on the earthmoving equipment that US marines, who had a large base in Sāmoa, used to build airstrips to support the advance of US forces in the Pacific (Whistler 2000: 209). The bananas mentioned above are routinely referred to as *faʻi papālagi* or European bananas, and the palms used in thatching are known as *niu olotuma* or Rotuman palm. In each case, these markers are used only when necessary to distinguish between cultivars.

Certain illnesses, thought to have been introduced at different times during this earlier period of globalisation, are also clearly marked linguistically (Macpherson and Macpherson 1990: 68–72, 88–89, 117). There is a group of illnesses designated *maʻi papālagi*, or European diseases; and there are individual diseases whose names identify their supposed origins, such as the *lafa toʻelau* or ringworm from Tokelau, scientifically known as *Tinea imbricatea* (Milner 1966: 93). But in each case, these pointers are used only to help people distinguish between the illnesses and to identify appropriate healers, rather than to draw attention to some profound, culturally significant, difference. Land tenure is similarly marked. Land held in Sāmoan customary title is known as *fanua tau Sāmoa* to distinguish it from freehold land that is referred to as *fanua tau pālagi*. In this case, the latter is used only occasionally to signify the different legal rights that attach to it.

Occasionally, people's ethnic origins are also marked linguistically. While for the most part people in the village are referred to simply by their given names and without any qualifier, various families are occasionally described as *le 'au 'afakasi*, the mixed descent people; *le fanau a le saina*, the descendants of the Chinese; *le fanau a le olotuma*, the descendants of the Rotuman; or *le fanau a le maligi*, the descendants of the marine. But where such distinctions become necessary, it seems only to be a way of differentiating between genealogies rather than as a marker that carries some profound genetic or cultural significance. This is hardly surprising: descent has little apparent influence on the ways these people live their day-to-day lives within the village.

Even when the exotic origins of the various introductions are marked linguistically, they are not spoken of in a way that suggests a deeply immutable difference. They do not seem to draw attention to a cultural divide between what is 'indigenous' or 'authentic' and what is not. They are certainly not considered evidence of a series of disruptive intrusions into village life. Why is it that the quite significant impacts of this earlier period of globalisation are routinely ignored in daily life even when they are 'marked'? Why is it then that, when the evidence of this earlier exposure to the world beyond Sāmoa is so pervasive, it is routinely overlooked?

Explaining the 'invisibility'

It is probably because the impacts of these earlier introductions seem to have been so completely incorporated into the life and organisation of the village that they are now practically invisible. Those who left the village and lived abroad during this early period of globalisation apparently returned, settled and resumed life in the village. Neither their experiences abroad, nor their return, seem to have been associated with major social dislocation in the village. In the case of some who went abroad as missionaries, their experiences of life 'among the heathen' confirmed their view that life in the Sāmoan village was infinitely superior in every way to life in other places, such as Papua New Guinea, and was certainly not in need of radical social transformation.[8] So too with those who went abroad as sailors on trading and whaling ships. There are tales in village families of sailors who were badly treated and suffered poor health on ships and who were grateful to return to the social and physical security of the village. The stories of life abroad, among both 'godless' savages and sailors, apparently gave few people any reason to advocate wholesale social transformation in the village, which was a secure, ordered and god-fearing haven.

It is, of course, too simple to presume that all who returned simply merged back into the security of village life. It is entirely possible that some who came back were uncomfortable with life in the village and that they did not stay, either because they could not live with what they found, or because the village could not accommodate them. Village polities had, and still have, the right to exile individuals and families whose conduct threatens the order of the village or challenges the authority of its chiefs. It is possible that such people went, either voluntarily or involuntarily, to live in Apia where different standards of social conduct prevailed and where one could escape the restrictions of highly structured village life (Davidson 1967: 5, 280, 288, 407; Gilson 1970: 162–87). Irrespective of why these people did not settle in the village when they returned, the effect was the same: the village averted potential challenges from external forces to its social structure and organisation.

So too with people who came from beyond Sāmoa to live in the village. They arrived in relatively small numbers and seem to have been quietly incorporated into the village over time. In most cases, settlers appear to have lived in the village at its pleasure. There are no tales of confrontation between the settlers and the villagers. This is not surprising: they were for the most part individuals or couples who were heavily out-numbered by villagers and were not in a position to assert much influence on either the organisation or governance of the village. Where they gained any influence, they did so through their Sāmoan spouses' connections, by employing villagers or by involving themselves in, rather than asserting themselves over, village politics.[9] Eventually, they were incorporated on the village's terms into the genealogy, polity and, eventually, the history of the village.

The same applies to the plants and technologies that have found their way into Sāmoan medicine and agriculture. They have become part of everyday life and reality in the village, so much so that they are no longer thought of as evidence of the outside world's impact on the village or of the human movement that produced it. Highly invasive introduced plants came to dominate niches in the local flora displacing indigenous varieties in the process. In the cases of *vao maligi* and *vao elefane*, three generations of farmers have now grown up and worked in plantations in which these are prolific, and it is hardly surprising that they are now regarded as a local plant: there is probably no one alive who can remember a plantation in which they were not present.

The 'new' globalisation of the village

One might argue, on the evidence above, that the village and its families had 'managed' this earlier phase of globalisation, in effect incorporating people who fitted in and innovations that seemed socially or technically valuable without major disruption to its way of life. People acknowledge some change during this earlier period but point out that this was cosmetic and that the foundations of the village's Sāmoan culture, its *fa'asāmoa*, have not changed.[10] One might then reasonably ask why a village that had 'managed' its exposure to global forces and had incorporated elements of these into its social fabric over a long period with apparently minimal disruption would be unable to 'manage' the consequences of more recent movements. There are, we believe, reasons why the movements of people in the most recent phase of globalisation, that which has occurred in the last 50 years and continues today, will have more significant impacts on the village than those earlier ones.

The extended reach of globalisation
The first reason is that recent movement involves more people and has significantly extended the global reach of the village and its families, exposing them to more global influences than any of the earlier movements could have done. This is readily evident throughout the year during such events as the presentation of various special offerings to the church. Every Christmas, for instance, those who trace their roots to the village, and who wish to mark that connection, make donations to their village church. During the service a church official reads a roll of donors, their locations and the amounts of their contributions, providing calculations from originating currencies into Sāmoan currency, to the admiring congregation. Fifty years ago that donor roll included the names of about ten people who were working in factories in Auckland, Wellington and Pagopago. Now, the roll includes the names of soldiers and security contractors in Iraq, teachers in Denmark, postgraduate students in London, nurses in Edinburgh, professional rugby players in Wales, a professional gridiron player in California, customs officers in Melbourne, restaurateurs in Sydney, factory workers in Auckland, taxi drivers in Wellington, fruit-pickers in Hastings, and fishermen and gold miners in Fiji.

The impact of this larger range of contacts on the village and its families is more significant than that generated by the earlier, more restricted range. Previously, small numbers of people went abroad as missionaries, sailors, traders and spouses. The cost of international travel and communication limited visits and contact between those who were abroad and those who remained in the village. Contact between migrants and their families was confined to occasional visits and to letters that inevitably restricted the influence of those abroad on those at home and, to some extent, buffered the village and its families from external impacts. Most people in the village knew only indirectly of other peoples and places.

The village now has a larger expatriate 'footprint'. More people go further, remain away for longer, work in a wider range of occupations and earn higher incomes. The 'footprint' grows as migrants and their overseas-born children move ever further afield, meeting and marrying non-Sāmoans as they go. Many village families now routinely include non-Sāmoans in their genealogies. The range of sources of information, experiences and influences to which people in the village are commonly exposed through these expanding social networks is larger than ever before and continues to expand.

Once, the influence of this extended network might have remained at a distance from the village but, as costs of travel have fallen and the frequency of services has increased, more expatriates visit the village each year. The patterns are shaped by expatriates' assessments of the utility of maintaining connections with the village that, in turn, are influenced by their longer-term plans (Macpherson 1994) that change as individuals' circumstances change. While some have severed all contact with the village, others return periodically to visit parents and grandparents or for family vacations. Later, some return for longer periods to care for older relatives who are reluctant to leave the village. Still other expatriates remain more actively involved in village life and politics, maintaining homes in the village and returning periodically to attend weddings, funerals, baptisms, and cases in the Land and Titles Court; and to take *matai* titles in ceremonies known as *saofa'i* and to look after other family affairs.[11] Other migrants have returned later in life, and after long periods abroad, to settle in the village.[12]

All of these expatriates' visits and stays influence the social organisation of the village and its families in various ways. Some of those who have returned to live in the village in retirement have been remarkably influential and have been able to bring about significant changes in a number of areas of village organisation. Others who have not left the village, but who have acted on advice from their expatriate children, have also been able to bring about changes in the organisation of village activity and protocol. Some *matai* routinely discuss village proposals and seek advice from their expatriate children by telephone, whose input finds its way into the final courses of action. Family matters almost inevitably draw on expatriate resources and must therefore accommodate the views and aspirations of their expatriate members in people's daily lives in the village.[13]

But the impact of movement is not generated only by expatriates, returning or otherwise, and their advice. Many families now have significant numbers of children living overseas, and a generation of family members is being born and growing up abroad. Bonds between onshore and offshore kin remain strong and, in any given year, a significant number of older people from the village will be absent for varying periods of time visiting their expatriate children and grandchildren to maintain these bonds. A recent conversation reminded us just how many parents routinely spend time with their children and grandchildren living abroad.

We had just arrived in Sāmoa and were asking one relative about the whereabouts of various others whom we had not seen around.

'So where is the old man, U?'
'He's in America having an operation on his eyes.'
'Is he staying with his son A in Los Angeles?'
'No, he's in Missouri with one of his other sons.'
'So where are our other neighbours then?'
'The old lady is in London with the daughter and her husband.'
'Is her husband, E, here?'
'No, he's in Alaska with his other daughter and her family.'
'Which daughter, R?'
'No, the younger one: the one who used to live in Washington.'
'When will they be back then?'
'I don't know. They may not come back this year. They're going to New Zealand later this year for a church opening.... But M is here. She has just arrived from New Zealand, but I don't know how long she'll be here. Oh yes, and some of P's family are here from Brisbane for their case in the Land and Titles Court. They'll be here for a couple of weeks.'
'What about the family living near the seaside? Are they there?'
'The husband, the *pālagi*, is there but the wife N is still working in Sydney. Oh, and you know the other family living near the sea –?'
'You mean T's family?
No, I mean the Tuvaluan family. Well, they've gone to their grandson's graduation in Wellington, but they'll be back soon.'

One such regular traveller pointed out that it would be far more convenient for everybody if her children and grandchildren were in the village. Then, she noted,

> I could just walk over and see them, or they could walk over and see me. The children could stay with me and help out around the house and I could explain things they need to know to them. The way things are now, it's much more inconvenient, and much more expensive, for everyone. Now, I have to go to Auckland, and then Wellington and then to Brisbane to see all of my children and grandchildren. My children like me to go, but they don't want me to go when it's cold over there: they don't want me to get sick. So I have to go each year when it is warm over there because my children will worry that I will get sick if I go when it is cold.

It is tempting to see this increasing frequency of movement as no more than an expansion of the earlier process, but it is important to ask whether it is somehow qualitatively different. We believe that this movement is indeed different and that it will have a greater impact on the village and its families than the earlier ripples of people away from and back towards Sāmoa.

Changing perceptions of the 'self' and 'other'
The second reason why the movement of people in the most recent phase of globalisation has a greater impact than earlier movements is that routine absences of people from the village and visits of those living overseas have a direct and personal bearing on those involved. Increased mobility and reach inform the way the people of the village see and think about themselves in relation to the world; and more and more of them now journey out of the village as travel becomes easier and more affordable. This, in turn, has the potential to increase the knowledge that is available within the village, to undermine social stereotypes and to redefine expectations of relations in the social world. Increased direct, and indirect, exposure means that people now have a larger social mirror in which to reflect on social conduct. The impacts of these, often highly significant, personal experiences are evident in many conversations about travel. An older woman who had recently

returned from her first visit to New Zealand told us about her stay with her daughter, who had married a Pākehā New Zealander:[14]

> I was a bit nervous at first. You know, I thought that *pālagi* might chase me out of the house, so I didn't say very much at first. I would wait in my room until my daughter's husband went to work and then I would come out and my daughter and I would talk. Sometimes, my other daughters would come around to the house and we would have a meal and I told them about the family in the village. But, do you know, her husband didn't mind at all.
>
> Over time, the *pālagi* was very polite and he was really friendly to me. My daughter told him I liked to eat chicken and so he would often bring me chicken and *pisupo*, even though he didn't eat it himself. He always asked me to say grace and he didn't mind if I said it in Sāmoan. His parents and friends came over to the house and they were also very polite and very respectful to me and my daughters. On my birthday, he took us all out to dinner at a restaurant. It was very nice. I must say I was a little surprised . . .

Some elements of the expatriate lifestyle and worldview lead those who go abroad to reflect on their own lives and beliefs. An older man, who spent a month abroad every year, told us:

> Some of the things that my children's children in Australia do make me sad. Those grandchildren never do anything around the house to help their parents. They just seem to read books, watch television and play those computer games, while their parents and aunties seem to do everything. You know, that's a thing that you see often among our people abroad and in my view that's not good. In my opinion, children should accept their roles and show respect by doing things to help out in their family. But on the other hand, they are very polite and respectful to me and to their parents. And they are doing very well in school and their parents did go to Australia to get them a better education than they had. Perhaps it may be a better way, I'm not so sure any more . . .

But one does not have to leave the village to meet people whose conduct defies the social stereotypes. More expatriate families are arranging reunions in Sāmoa to introduce overseas-born children to the 'village' and the 'family'. These family reunions bring the village-based family face to face with its increasingly cosmopolitan overseas 'branch' in situations that have the potential to transform the view each has of the other. An older friend told us about her grandson's *pālagi* girlfriend who had stayed with them during a recent family reunion in the village:

> She was a small girl, you know, thin and pretty pale. When I first saw her, I thought she might be too weak to stay in the village but she was really strong and very active. She went out with the girls and helped collect the food and then with the work in the kitchen. She didn't talk too much and she was very polite. She also dressed very well, very modestly, not like those young *pālagi* girls you see on the television. She spent most of her time here in the village. She didn't want to go to Apia much. She would go for a swim in the afternoon. My grandson must have told her that young people looked after older people in Sāmoa because she would make a cup of tea and bring it to me with a biscuit. She must have come from a good family. She was not at all what I expected, and was much more like a Sāmoan . . .

Not all of the reflections in the larger mirror are positive. Some expatriates return and compare the village lifestyle with their own and feel that their relatives might benefit from their experience. It is not uncommon for people to criticise their resident relatives. A mature woman, who returned periodically with her husband and family from Europe, made the following comments:

> My relations are pretty happy when we go back to Europe. They get tired of me always growling about things I'm not happy with. But someone has to tell them. I look at my brothers and they just go to the plantation to get some food and then sit around the house. That's because I send money and they don't have to work. I get angry when I think that I have to go to

work every day on the train and the bus, and in snow in the winter, to earn money and they just lounge around and eat.

I told them I have been working ever since I left the village 18 years ago but I don't see any evidence of their work: the family's plantation is no bigger than it was when I left and all I see is more children. I told them if they spend more time in the plantation and less time in bed, there would be fewer children and more food. I suppose in one way it's my fault. I tell them I'm not going to send them money so that they will have to work, but they know that even if I only send the money to my parents, they'll buy food for everyone.

Another was disappointed at the changes she saw in the village on her visits and she made her disappointment clear:

You know, when I first came home to Sāmoa, some 30 years ago, our extended family would have a thanksgiving service and a meal. Over the next few days, friends and relatives would come and welcome me back. It was good to catch up and we would talk into the night about what had happened in New Zealand and in Sāmoa. They would bring small presents of food and my parents would give them small gifts out of respect. But now people, including some I don't know, just come wanting money like so many beggars. It also seems everyone now has a title and thinks that entitles them to respect and gifts. Well, when I went back last time, I gave some money to my mother and told her that when that was finished to tell the scroungers they were too late . . .

The increased scale and frequency of movement between the village and its sub-village enclaves produces a new range of personal experiences, and has a more significant impact on the way people think about and act in the village than the smaller numbers of earlier movements could have had. Set alongside the increased range of 'virtual movement' produced by television and film representations of life beyond the village, these diverse personal experiences have significant real and potential impact on the social organisation of the village. But the impact of movement is not confined to personal experience.

The socio-demographic consequences of recent migration

The third reason to believe that the impact of recent, larger scale movement on the village and its families will be greater than that of earlier waves of mobility has to do with its demographic consequences. Previous movements involved the temporary absence of relatively small numbers of people, most of whom returned to the village. Post-war movement has involved steadily increasing numbers of people who have remained away longer and in many cases have not returned permanently, producing more significant demographic impacts.

Throughout the New Zealand administration, a combination of public health programmes, improvements in sanitation, and the establishment of new health care facilities that were enthusiastically promoted and supported by women's committees resulted in increasing, and ultimately unsustainable, national population growth rates.[15] By the mid-1950s, the national population and many village populations, especially those on the northeast coast of Upolu, were increasing at unsustainable rates of around 3.5 per cent per annum and were forecast to continue to grow into the future. These rates were bound, in the absence of augmented agricultural productivity and increasing import prices, to produce a declining standard of living throughout the country (Stace 1956: 3, 7, 11, 63).

These trends were felt in the villages as well, especially those in the most heavily populated areas of the country. In the village, public health programmes had, with the untiring activity of the village women's committee, *komiti tumamā*, resulted in improvements in health and increasing population density. Without more village land available to accommodate its increasing population, this pressure on available agricultural land and competition for new house sites in the village's residential area had several effects: the spring-fed fresh water pool from which the village drew water and in which people bathed was being used to capacity; there was a shortage of local building materials and of the stones used to build house foundations; and at the same time, land needed for domestic food gardens and for pigs and cattle to forage close to the village was declining in quantity and quality. Growing pressure on the reef and lagoon saw fishing yields falling and people forced to buy formerly subsistence elements of the village diet.

These various pressures were combining and producing mounting tension within and between families in the village. As population grew, people removed the top courses of rocks from the stone walls of pig pens to build foundations for new houses. Where space was constrained and building materials were in short supply, new houses were smaller and more crowded and closer to one another. People spoke with some nostalgia about the time when the village was less crowded:

> In those days the village was very beautiful. Most families had a large house, some smaller houses and there was space around the houses and a lot more trees. Many families had small gardens and some fruit trees. But when the families started to grow there were a lot more houses built and they were closer together. There were more people in those smaller houses and only some families had enough land to keep their large houses. It was not good then because there were toilets everywhere, especially before the Peace Corps toilets were installed.[16]

But pressure continued to grow and, as pig pen walls became lower and thinner, pigs escaped and ruined neighbours' gardens. Families became embroiled in conflicts with their neighbours over reparations for pig damage. Some frustrated garden owners eventually killed other people's valuable pigs and the conflicts escalated. People began to complain that their chickens, which had previously roamed free in the village until they were needed for food, were increasingly going missing, and where these complaints led to accusations of theft, further tension developed. As population densities increased, long-standing rights-of-way over families' lands were withdrawn and replaced, out of necessity, with domestic food gardens. Further tensions between families arose over the resulting inconvenience.

Soon after the government water supply arrived in the village, its capacity was exceeded by the demand from the growing population, and those living at the end of the pipe line often received only a trickle of water at certain times of the day. This water supply problem led to tension between neighbours near the main line who were running domestic taps all day and those at the end of the line who were getting very little water.

Even the deceased were not exempt from the consequences of this growth. As population density increased, families faced pressure from newly-married members for house sites, and the mortal remains of people whose graves were occupying scarce land had to be exhumed and re-buried in tombs in a series of ceremonials known as *liutofaga*.[17] Discussions about these moves contained their own potential for tension between and within families. These tensions were exacerbated in urban and peri-urban villages where people from rural areas moved in order to be closer to Apia for employment and education.

Emigration started to relieve population and environmental pressure from the 1950s and gained momentum in the 1960s and 1970s as more significant numbers of mainly young people left the village, married and had their families abroad. The loss of this cohort, and of its reproductive potential, checked village population growth rates quite suddenly and for some time,[18] and had a significant effect on the later shape of the village population. In the late 1970s, at the height of out-migration, the village population seemed to be comprised largely of older people, some teenagers and children: it was as if many of the younger adults had gone missing.

The congregation that once filled the church was much smaller, and the singing that had once overwhelmed the piano was almost drowned out by the new electronic organ, a gift from migrants abroad. Where earlier, the congregation had to sing five verses of a hymn to allow sidesmen to collect the offering, by the late 1970s, it was only necessary to sing two verses to collect the much depleted congregation's gifts. People began to complain of labour shortages to do such simple things as weeding plantations, and tasks that had been carried out by younger people were neglected.

This departure of numbers of young adults had another demographic consequence: it produced higher dependency ratios within the village as declining numbers of 'economically active' people who remained were called on to support the stable 'economically inactive' population. The dependency ratios themselves were probably not as significant as the circumstances in which they occurred. Some of those who remained in the village began to compare their own situations, and life chances, with those of their expatriate peers who were thought to enjoy a higher standard of living and to live less constrained lives abroad. Those who stayed in the village began to consider themselves relatively deprived. Where this loss of young adults resulted in increased workloads for those who remained, it was associated with some social pathologies such as increasing alcohol consumption and abuse, and fighting. Ironically, as parents sought to discourage this 'bad behaviour' by imposing harsher discipline and restricting the freedom of those who remained, they may have inadvertently confirmed their children's belief that their life was worse and their prospects poorer than those of their expatriate peers. This perception lay behind a number of cases we studied in an analysis of the increasing incidence of youth suicide in the 1970s and 1980s (Macpherson and Macpherson 1987).

However, depopulation also relieved pressure on village resources and defused some of the social and political tensions that were developing in those villages in which rapid, and ultimately unsustainable growth, was occurring. The relocation of some of the village's most 'fertile' people meant that growth, which might have further increased pressure in the village, occurred elsewhere where it did not produce the same social tensions and environmental impacts. The redistribution of the village population effectively expanded its boundaries and, in the process, relieved some pressure on its scarce resources, thus arresting some of the environmental degradation that had been occurring.

The reconfiguration of families and villages

Migration did more than relieve some emerging pressures: it fundamentally reconfigured the village and its families. This is the fourth reason why recent global impacts have had such an effect on Sāmoan society. Because the village is defined by the nature of interaction of its members rather than by a set of defined spatial boundaries, reduction in the size of the 'local' population did not signal the 'loss' of the 'village' population but rather its 'relocation'. The same was true of families that are also defined by the nature of interaction among their members: the physical 'absence' of members did not signal decline in family size or strength because many who were physically absent remained socially and economically engaged. But new ways of thinking and talking about village and family, which reflected the new spatial realities, emerged.

The chain migration process that shaped migration patterns of both villages and families tended to concentrate expatriate populations in locations in which the early emigrants had settled (Macpherson 1974 and 1978; Pitt and Macpherson 1974). The aggregations of the village population that were forming in Auckland, Wellington, Sydney, Honolulu and Los Angeles were increasingly regarded as and referred to as *pitonuʻu*, or sub-villages,[19] in the same way as similar entities within Sāmoa. They were, in other words, extensions of the village with limited autonomy. Only occasionally, usually in discussions of village affairs, will someone make a distinction between our people 'here' and our people 'outside', *o tatou tagāta nuʻu la ei fafo*. This continuity is reflected in various ways. When a storm damaged the village school, its leaders set out to raise funds to rebuild it. The idea was to use the labour of local villagers and funds from expatriate villagers to complete the project. The plan, as one leader explained, involved, 'sending a delegation to each of the village's large *pitonuʻu* to talk to its leaders and to outline the rebuilding plan and timetable. But, at the end of the day it was for each of the *pitonuʻu* to decide how it would raise funds. We were confident they would not let us down because it is still their village and all have family here.'

Only occasionally do events draw attention to the significance of having such a large part of the village population living abroad. We were reminded of this by a very public argument and confrontation over a family house site in the village that was claimed by a family member returning from New Zealand to retire. During an increasingly heated exchange, various parties revisited aspects of the family history that were better left alone, accused the family *matai* of being unable to solve the issue, and threatened to take the matter to the Land and Titles Court for judgment. This was significant because it challenged the chief's right and competence to resolve a matter and, ultimately, the family's autonomy and leadership. After the tension had subsided, an observer asked quite seriously, 'If that is what happens when one family returns, imagine what would happen if all of those who had left were to return!'

Emigration also redistributed family members and altered their demographic profiles, but families, like villages, are defined by the character of interaction between their members rather than by their spatial location, and they also cohere despite their dispersal. Occasionally, in discussions about family affairs, someone will make a distinction between our people 'here' and our people 'outside', *o tatou āiga la ei fafo*, or our people in Auckland. In planning a funeral, for instance, a set of tasks was assigned to those in Sāmoa and another to those in New Zealand: a funeral in New Zealand and the dispatch of the deceased would be organised by the New Zealand part of the family and a second funeral and burial in the village would be handled by the Sāmoan branch of the family.

But, despite the spatial reality, in much daily conversation in Sāmoa speakers often see no need to refer specifically to the fact that someone is not actually resident within the village's spatial boundaries: they simply assume that most people know where expatriate family members are. In an account of a funeral, a woman outlined in great detail the contributions made by various parts of the family and the roles various family members had played during the event. She saw no need to explain that many of those whom she mentioned were normally resident abroad. Only when she was asked why certain people were not mentioned did she say that they were probably unaware of the death because they were 'outside' at the time and could not be contacted.

For these reasons, one is only occasionally conscious of the large population that is now living beyond the village's physical boundaries. Every so often, events that focus on locating and harnessing the combined resources of the family remind people of the significance of having such a large part of the family living abroad. One such event was a discussion of the whereabouts of family members who might be persuaded to contribute to the rebuilding of a family's guest house, *fale tele*, in the village. The exercise resulted in a family roll being drawn up[20] that showed that over one half of the family now lived beyond the spatial boundaries of the village. But the evidence is all around: there are now unoccupied family homes in the village and there is a new term to reflect this new reality – 'the family's house is locked up', *ua loka le fale o le āiga*.

These events raise the very real question of what would have happened in both the village and in families without emigration that, by redistributing population, has restricted growth and relieved pressure on the available physical resources within its boundaries.

The economic impact of migration

The fifth reason to believe that the most recent phase of migration will have a larger impact on the social organisation of the village is its greater economic significance. The evidence is everywhere: many of the homes in the village have been rebuilt in permanent materials since the 1960s, and new, modern houses spring up periodically. Every month containers of various sizes, filled with building materials, home appliances, household goods and tools from expatriate relatives, are unpacked in the village. The scale of these transfers has had a profound effect in several areas of the village economy.

The expansion of the village economy

The most recent phase of globalisation has effectively expanded the village economy, raised the average wage of the village and made new resources available to those who have remained there in a way in which earlier globalisation never did.[21] It has extended the range of sources of capital, credit, ideas and technologies in a way that has freed the village from the constraints of its traditional factor endowments. Villages whose economies and sociopolitical influence were once constrained by their limited natural resources are now no longer so constrained. Small villages with committed expatriate populations can, and do, undertake significant capital development projects that can rival those of better-endowed larger ones.

Similarly, families whose wealth was once constrained by their access to local resources now have opportunities to increase their wealth and extend their influence within the village. The dispersal of family members has provided access to new sources of income for families that are now able to accumulate physical capital in the form of houses and purchases of freehold land. The same dispersal has provided new capital and opportunities for village entrepreneurs who are investing in small stores, fishing boats and taxis. But there are now also larger businesses such as a successful hardware store in a nearby village. The owners' expatriate children, nephews and nieces reside in Singapore, New Zealand, Australia and the US and act as procurement agents for the business. They source and price stock in various locations, pass the information to the managers who determine where stock will be sourced, and then buy and ship the stock home. Access to global personal networks and resources has extended opportunities in ways that village entrepreneurs can operate.

The expansion of the village, and family, economies has increased the amount of wealth available to families and has intensified competition in the village. Families compete with one another to demonstrate their new wealth in various forms of conspicuous consumption in a range of activities. One might argue that these transfers of wealth within the new 'global village' have also even had an indirect influence on national politics. People who now have access to the resources of a global village no longer look only to the state to provide resources and to fund local development. At the same time, those who have access to new wealth may choose to invest this in campaigns for seats in parliament, a practice that has led to the intensifying competition evident in national elections (So'o 1998: 289–90).

The transnationalisation of the village economy
The most recent phase of globalisation has also effectively diversified the village economy. The modern village economy is now, in effect, a transnational one with a series of nodes at which different types of economic activity occur, and between which resources can be transferred as need arises. In any given year, textiles, *siapo*, fine mats, *'ie toga* and traditional food are produced in one part of the village economy and sent to others for use in rites of passage: baptisms, weddings, title bestowals and funerals.[22] In turn, cash, equipment and commodities are produced or acquired in another part of the village economy and flow back.

The transnationalisation of economic activity has redistributed risk in fundamental ways and has made the village economy more robust. The village is no longer as vulnerable as it once was to natural disasters, simply because its economy is no longer located in one place. The village can no longer be devastated by a single hurricane or by a crop blight that could, over night, reduce village food supplies and incomes by 90 per cent for sustained periods while crops were replanted. Similarly, rising levels of unemployment or declining incomes in some nodes can be countered by movement to others.

The growing efficiency of the village economy
The globalisation process has made the village economy more efficient. New tools sent home by migrants have allowed individuals to do more work using less labour in less time. Where once breadfruit trees fell after more than an hour of rhythmic chopping by razor-sharp bush-knives wielded by groups of men, they now fall in a matter of moments to the scream of a chainsaw wielded by a single man. Where once Saturdays were marked by the regular swoosh of bush-knives cutting the grass around houses, they are now disturbed by the racket of two-stroke grass trimmers and motor mowers. Where once the women sat and sang as they weeded the plantation over a couple of hours, a silent man with a backpack sprayer now applies a herbicide to the same area in 30 minutes.

Furthermore, since these new technologies are available to more people, there are opportunities for those who formerly had restricted access to these labour-saving technologies to compete on more even terms with those who have traditionally controlled the village.[23] This, in turn, has created a more competitive village economy and in the process disrupted some connections between rank, wealth and influence and produced challenges to traditional village elites who face competition from upwardly mobile villagers supported by migrant kin (Meleisea 2000: 189–200). Not all of the benefits of access to new technologies undermine tradition: some are used by individuals to enhance their status within 'traditional' family and village politics (Macpherson 1988: 1–24). The new village economy is potentially even more efficient.

The expansion and diversification of the village labour market
The globalisation process has also effectively expanded and diversified the village labour market in two ways. The new village economy no longer

consists of the local population and a small number of expatriate labourers in a limited range of industries. Social mobility, and entrepreneurial activity in migrant enclaves abroad, has extended the range of occupations in which expatriate villagers are now involved that has, in turn, created opportunities for others. In the recent past, people have moved to California to work for an uncle who has set up an aluminium window installation business; to Sydney to work for the aunty who needs a nanny whom she can trust with her children; to Auckland to drive a van for a cousin who is trying to expand a courier franchise; and so on.

Globalisation has diversified the village labour market in another way. New domestic economic activities are beginning to lessen dependence on the local agricultural economy and to redefine the meaning of work. The establishment of the Yazaki plant in Sāmoa, which assembles automobile wiring harnesses, has generated employment for between 2000 and 4000 people including a number of young people from the village.[24] That operation was established in Sāmoa in 1991 because the hourly wage rate there was approximately 5 per cent of the wage rate in the Melbourne plant in which the harnesses were formerly manufactured. The factory has generated employment opportunities within the village that have lessened dependence on the local agricultural economy and have transformed local definitions of 'work'.

The growth of alternative income sources has also influenced social relationships. Some people who no longer derive their livelihoods from the use of village and family lands are starting to ask fundamental questions about the control of their income. Why, they ask, should they contribute their income to their families at the same levels as they did when they owed their livelihood to village and family? This concern is not yet widespread, but disputes carried in the evening air suggest that it may become more common as time goes on.

Some neo-liberal economists contend that this 'dependent development', which relies on 'external' resource flows that may or may not be available in future, discourages real autonomous development within 'nations'. This may well be true, but for the village and the family, which pay little attention to neo-liberal economists, there do seem to be some real social and economic advantages from harnessing the resources of the new global village and family. Some of the resources that have found their way to Sāmoa have stimulated significant growth in the village and family. Even now, fledgling businesses in the village are started with capital from family and supporters abroad, because the banks show less faith in the new entrepreneurs than their families do.

The new village

The final reason to believe that this expression of globalisation will have a more profound impact is the transformation of the character of the village. Strictly speaking, much of the village population is, effectively, permanently absent from the village's physical and political 'centre'. Aside from gifts that many migrants send to their family and village church at Christmas, Easter and White Sunday,[25] and occasional visits, they will have little direct impact on either the demography or politics of the village's 'centre'. They will not be called on to provide labour for the new entrance of the church, to clear the rubbish from around the village, to form its access road or to plant shrubs around the village for the annual beautification contest. They will not debate emerging moral and social issues that confront the village in its *fono*, or formulate new regulations to protect it from threats to its authority.

But, in practical terms, many emigrants remain very much part of the village. They are, in a lot of cases, active members of expatriate branches of the village. They may meet in places as far apart as San Diego, Melbourne, Auckland and Invercargill to socialise and to raise money for the village; host its rugby teams and entertainment troupes; and buy raffle tickets to support village projects. In the wake of Cyclones Ofa and Valelia, it was these expatriate 'branches' that hired containers, filled them with food and building materials, and dispatched them to the village. Many of these same people then took leave, followed the containers, and helped to rebuild their family homes and the village school and the church.

Clearly, the village retains a very important place in the hearts of those who went abroad. How important is apparent from the numbers of people who bring their children, and in some cases their grandchildren, back to visit the village and their families, and to see their land and their forebears' resting places. Some of the same people choose to return there to live out their lives and, eventually, to be buried alongside their families in cemeteries in the village. A number of our neighbours in Sāmoa are people who have returned, after their working lives in New Zealand, to live in houses built on land on which they grew up.

But the demographic reality is that while the village may be the affective centre for many people, it is no longer the demographic centre. In some villages, more people now live abroad than live in the centre. After a recent death, the burial was postponed for some nine days to allow members of the family and friends to return from as far away as London, San Diego, Christchurch, Invercargill and Kansas City. In Sāmoa, they joined others who had travelled earlier from Auckland and Sydney to be with the woman as her health had deteriorated. In that remarkable cosmopolitan gathering, there were almost as many people from beyond the village as there were from within the village. But as quickly as they had come, they left for the four corners of the new global village.

Rethinking the global village
This raises the question of whether 'village' and 'family' need to be re-conceptualised to acknowledge and reflect their transnational character. While each still has a physical centre, its boundaries have expanded as a consequence of globalisation. The eminent demographer, Richard Bedford, in an article on contemporary Pacific populations, talks of the 'effective population' of Pacific nations, referring to the population that at any given time acts as a nation: this captures nicely the increasingly globalised reality that is the Pacific 'nation' (Bedford 2007: 71). The same metaphor can be usefully applied to the Sāmoan village. A village's 'effective population', as opposed to its resident population, comprises all who remain actively engaged in the organisation and economy of the village. It can be extended still further to the Sāmoan family, the effective membership of which comprises all who remain engaged in the activities of the family.

But it is useful to go beyond the transnational character of nation, village and family to capture the character of interaction between the various nodes of these entities. In their work on MIRAB states,[26] Bertram and Watters (1985 and 1986) likened Pacific kin-groups to transnational companies that act globally, deploying and employing resources and capital designed to maximise advantage to the company at any given time. This idea, captured in the term 'transnational kin corporation', can be usefully applied to the modern transnational Sāmoan kin group that in various circumstances acts as a transnational corporation moving its resources between its nodes in ways designed to maximise its advantage. The metaphor can be usefully extended to the modern transnational Sāmoan village that routinely, and quite deliberately, seeks to identify and harness the strengths and resources of various nodes of the village to its advantage. Many of the churches and school buildings that are being built are only possible because village leaders are acting globally, which is, in turn, only possible because of the size and wealth of the village's nodes, or sub-villages, created by migration.

If we are unable to conceptualise these modern transnational villages and families, it may be the consequence of our lack of imagination. The sociologist, Professor Epeli Hau'ofa, explained this as a problem of cultural metaphors that are shaped by the way different peoples think about the sea. As early as 1993, Hau'ofa suggested that we need to regard the Pacific Ocean as something that connects islands rather than something that separates them (Hau'ofa 1993 and 2000). Extending the metaphor can help us to think of the sea as something that connects, rather than separates, the parts of the modern village and family. These transnational entities, connected by the ocean, look much more like the villages and families as they are conceptualised by those currently living within them. For Sāmoans, the family comprises all those who claim ties to the family land and its leaders without reference to where they might reside at any given time. The family comprises those who act as family. The same idea can be extended to the village whose population comprises all those who claim ties to it and to its leaders, and who acknowledge and act on these ties.

Can it last? A reality check

This model, while interesting, raises the very real question of whether modern transnational villages and families are sustainable realities, or brief windows of opportunity that may close as quickly as they opened. These transnational entities will only exist as long as people in various parts of the village and family continue to identify with and support them. While many emigrants have continued to support their villages, their overseas-born children are, in some cases, lost to the villages. At least one, and as many as three, generations have now been born and grown up beyond the original village. In many cases, those born abroad have had somewhat limited contact with the village. The ties of the original migrants' descendants with the village are attenuated over time for a number of reasons.

In some cases, they lack the sense of history and loyalty that their parents feel for the village that is born of shared experiences of life in the village. They have not experienced the excitement of being part of the village rugby team that won a prestigious district competition; part of the village dance troupe that performed with distinction at the national Teuila celebrations; or part of the committee that beautified the village and won the national competition. The lack of these real experiential links may limit their commitment to the village. But it is not simply the result of a lack of actual participation that changes these people: real differences between the experiences and worldviews of people born in different parts of the transnational village are emerging that may prevent them from understanding and empathising with one another. The New Zealand-based Sāmoan/Scottish playwright Victor Rodger's 1995 play, *Sons*, about brothers brought up in different parts of the village, captures some of these real differences and their consequences.

In some cases, declining fluency in the Sāmoan language, which is increasingly evident in the overseas-born villagers, constrains their ability to 'experience' the village, to understand all that is happening around them, and to take a full and active role in the life of the village. Their lack of fluency in the Sāmoan language marks them as different from those for whom the language is a fundamental element of Sāmoan social identity.

Some New Zealand-born villagers spoke of the frustration of not being able to take part in conversations and of their embarrassment when their attempts to use Sāmoan led to blank stares or, even worse, amusement. Some interpreted these reactions as public attempts to exclude them and spoke of their reluctance to try again afterwards.

The lack of other social and physical skills may also mark these people from abroad as incompetent, expose them to unwelcome attention and cause them some embarrassment. Sāmoans from overseas spoke of the fear of being asked to perform traditional dances and their apprehension about being likened to tourists who are routinely asked to do this to the amusement of Sāmoans. Others mentioned having been embarrassed by their inability to perform such basic daily tasks as husking and desiccating coconuts, throwing fishing nets and using bush-knives.

But the emerging differences are not simply the consequences of various skill 'deficits'. Some people born abroad talked of their annoyance with aspects of village life and their frustration at feeling unable to express an opinion about those things because of local sensitivities. Some were frustrated by the treatment of women, children, young people and others by the dominant elderly, male elite; and others by the unquestioned adherence to religious dogma and the apparent reluctance to consider other ways of thinking about the world. Those who raised their concerns about such matters found themselves labelled *palāgi*, or European, and, worse still, *fiapālagi*, a disparaging term that is used to describe someone who aspires to be a European, which carries the negative implications that they reject their 'Samoanness' and consider themselves above or beyond the village. The New Zealand-born anthropologist, Melani Anae, has written very poignantly about this experience (Anae 1997 and 1998).

But globalisation also transforms those who left the village and spent time abroad, and their view of the village.[27] In some cases, the reluctance of people who have been born or live abroad to accept certain key premises of life in the village leads them to conduct their business in Sāmoa from the safety and privacy of a hotel. This, they say, protects them from the constant visits and requests for money and provides them with the privacy to which they have become accustomed. But it also marks them as people who cannot or will not live in the village and to the criticism that they see themselves as 'above' the village. There are some cruel jokes told about visiting expatriate villagers who alight like royalty from a taxi, deliver a royal message to their subjects and then depart for the comfort of their hotel, 'leaving nothing for the village but words'.

But just as the family and village inevitably lose the commitment of some who are no longer able or willing to submit to the expectations and demands of life in Sāmoa, there are always new people, those who are born in the village and leave, and those who are born overseas and return, and all the flux and flow in between these extremes that ensure that the global village remains a real entity.

A look into the future

The paradox of emigration is that it generated significant new resources for families and villages that they then invested in various forms of competition as they sought to enhance their respective positions in 'traditional' hierarchies. Thus, emigration and remittances fuelled and intensified a competition that had formerly been constrained by families' and villages' factor endowments. This competition pitted branches of families, and families and villages, against one another in public events in which significant amounts of capital were consumed in what has been described by the Prime Minister of Sāmoa as a 'financially draining game of one-upmanship' that was 'spiralling out of control' as families competed to out-do one another in events such as weddings and funerals.

The irony of this situation is that the very things that fuelled the competition – emigration and remittances – are the things to which people are now forced to turn to continue to participate in the competition. Even more ironically, continuing emigration has become necessary for many families who have become dependent on remittances to maintain their participation in, and growing commitments to, the increasingly expensive 'traditional' *fa'asāmoa* that, before migration, worked well without either cash or large quantities of imported commodities.

The Prime Minister has become so concerned with this form of inflation that he has spoken openly, over some years, about the increasing costs of ceremonial and has made a number of moves to reduce the costs of participation in *fa'asāmoa*.[28] Despite some initial resistance to his 'interference' in the affairs of families and villages, there seems to be a greater degree of acceptance of the benefits of the measures. But this has not defused the competition. The debates are now being aired in the mass media and are occurring more widely in families and villages. Even where families are acutely aware of the high financial costs of participation, they are equally cognisant of the potentially high social costs of being the first to withdraw from a competition.

Defusing the competition may require bold initiative by village councils that force entire villages to act together to reduce both the financial costs of participation and the social costs of withdrawing from it. There are early signs that this may be happening. Recently, the villages of Sala'ilua and Sili in Savai'i became increasingly concerned about the growing expenses of participation in *fa'asāmoa* after village families were left financially ruined. Those villages have now banned the use of imported canned fish, various red meats and chicken pieces in ceremonial exchanges. The Ministry of Women, Community and Social Development's Internal Affairs Division has recently established a national committee of leading *matai* known as the Fale'ula o Sāmoa to look at a range of practices that are leading to what have been described as distortions of the 'true' *fa'asāmoa*.[29] The committee's programme, *Fa'afaletui ole Aganu'u,* or Questioning Our Customary Practices, has set out explicitly to consider whether ceremonial inflation practices are in fact shifting the foundations of Sāmoan custom and leading to poverty, and to find ways of correcting this trend.

But aside from escalating costs of *fa'asāmoa*, which may in time be managed by concerted, collective action by government and village councils, there are other forces that will fuel interest in emigration. One of these is the rising rate of youth unemployment that means that even those who would willingly work in Sāmoa may not be able to find paid work. Larger cohorts of better educated young people are now leaving secondary and tertiary educational institutions and entering the workforce, but Sāmoa's current economic growth rate cannot produce enough paid jobs to absorb all of those seeking work. The government of Sāmoa, with assistance from the ILO, is looking to training that will help young people develop skills that will allow them to earn a living from new skills and from development of under-utilised land.[30]

As a consequence of the factors above, the number of people who are either moving or contemplating moving is growing. Interest in emigration in families and villages remains high, and many people spend a lot of time considering how to ensure that some at least of their children can go abroad. Visitors are routinely asked for information and advice about access to labour markets beyond the village. The most recent discussions we have had with family and friends have focused on opportunities for their children to emigrate. People routinely canvass such issues as the costs and possible benefits of succeeding in an annual ballot that picks a maximum of 1100 pre-qualified people to migrate to New Zealand with secure permanent residence; the possibility that New Zealand companies and government departments might again offer longer-term employment where they are unable to recruit sufficient staff in New Zealand;[31] the likelihood of gaining access to short-term horticultural and viticultural labour contracts such as those offered under the New Zealand Recognised Seasonal Employment scheme (RSE) that carry with them the opportunity for productive employees to work regularly in New Zealand; the hope that the Australian government will offer a similar programme to secure short-term labour for its horticultural and viticultural industries from 2009; various similar, unofficial church-based short-term labour programmes; the chances of going to Pagopago in nearby American Sāmoa to work in one of the tuna canneries; and the prospects of scholarships to study overseas.

An unanticipated, and unfortunate, outcome of emigration may be that, over time, it has created the impression that life abroad is somehow more challenging, more fulfilling and more materially rewarding, and that talented people will invariably go abroad, which by implication suggests that Sāmoa is somehow less desirable. A second unfortunate, and unanticipated, consequence of this is that families now look to invest in children's education to ensure that they have better opportunities to go abroad. A relative whose son had recently qualified as a plumber in Sāmoa asked us if we could find out whether additional qualifications from the local branch of the Australian government's regional trades training programme would improve his opportunities of getting in to Australia. It was, as he noted, increasingly difficult to live with only three adult salaries and only two children abroad. Thus, ironically, remittances intended originally to augment villages' and families' resources, and to make life at home more comfortable, may have gained such significance that emigration, which was once a means to an end, may have become an end in itself.

Traditional houses, fale o'o, *which could be built with locally available materials and dismantled and moved, are being replaced by larger, more substantial houses which cannot.*

World Bank–financed infrastructure project: The increasing dependence on external development agencies for funding effectively increases their ability to bring about change.

4.

Ideas and social transformation

Introduced ideologies have been transforming the Sāmoan worldview and lifestyle for almost 200 years. The evidence is seen in shifts in the organisation of both families and villages. This chapter explores the influence of introduced ideologies on the organisation of the village and its families. It contends that Sāmoan society was changed early, and fundamentally, by such ideologies as Christianity, capitalism and colonialism, but that these were appropriated and managed by leaders in Sāmoan society in ways that limited their impact on the organisation of society. Newer global ideologies and ideas, generated beyond the Pacific and inextricably connected with migration, trade and aid, may not be as easily resisted or controlled

A discussion about the cost of repairing a house in Sāmoa led us to consider the powerful role of ideologies, and the ideas that comprise them, in the transformation of the village and its families. A neighbour was complaining to a group of friends, many of whom had returned from abroad, about the difficulties and costs she had faced in getting some repairs done to her house. She pointed out that in the 'old days' one could ask relations to come and do the work. As long, she noted, as you fed them and thanked them appropriately, the work was done and everyone was happy. When those who had helped you needed assistance, you went and helped them in turn. That was the essence of *fa'asāmoa*, the Sāmoan way. Now, she noted, even kin wanted to be paid for their work and fed and thanked. The neighbour concluded that, in the 45 years she had been away from Sāmoa, people had come to see the world differently. People thought more and more about money and less and less about their obligations as kin. Money, she speculated, was now becoming more important than kinship in Sāmoa.

Each new 'theme' brought forth more anecdotes and, before long, those present were outlining other changes that had occurred in the village, mostly for the worse, in that time, and lamenting the passing of the old Sāmoa or what is referred to as *o aso nā*, 'those days'. One person after another presented evidence of shifts in thinking from different spheres of social life. A change in people's attitudes to nature was identified. People recalled a time when nature's rhythms structured life: when, one man noted, the locusts chirped in the evening people stopped work to return to their homes. Now, he complained, people have their stereos playing so loudly that you often cannot hear the locusts' chorus. People mentioned shifts in attitudes to kinship. A woman recalled a time when local fishermen shared their catch with family and friends. Now, she noted, they took surplus fish to sell to neighbours or in the fish market. Shifts in attitudes to religion were also referred to. People remembered when they awoke to the sound of morning devotions in nearby homes. Now people did not seem to feel that morning prayers were necessary and the noise of some families' radios prevented others from saying their prayers in peace. Others recalled a time when families gathered in their houses for evening prayers when the village church bell rang in the evening: now some families do not even turn their television down when the bell tolls, much less gather in prayer. Changes in attitudes to the village were outlined. One woman recollected a time when families kept areas around their houses very tidy to avoid the embarrassment of being fined by the women's committee inspectors for failing to meet the village standard and, by implication, letting down both family and village. Now, she noted, some people are no longer ashamed and do not seem to care. With so much rubbish around, she said, it was not surprising that the mosquito problem was getting worse. The general consensus, that people think differently now, was expressed in the following way by several speakers: '*ua 'ese a le mafaufau o tagata Sāmoa i lenei vaitaimi*'.

Our neighbour argued, and most present agreed, that significant changes in the ways people in the village thought about the world had occurred over the past 50 years, and that this seemed to have begun when 'people started to go abroad', '*Ae pei uma lava ua amata mai ile taimi na o ai tagata i fafo*'. She was correct in saying that life in the village has altered significantly in the last half-century, but probably incorrect in suggesting that the most significant changes have occurred in that time. In focusing on differences they have noticed in their lifetimes, those present were, understandably, drawing attention to trends they had experienced and for which they could offer evidence. The focus on those shifts obscured others that predated them that may actually have had a greater influence on the village.

In fact, some of the most significant ideas and ideologies that transformed the culture of the village had arrived in Sāmoa very much earlier. From the early nineteenth century, three introduced ideologies transformed the ways Sāmoans thought about and acted in the world: Christianity, capitalism and colonialism. Sāmoa was, as we have already noted in chapter 1, exposed to each of these over 150 years, and while to some extent each overlaid the other and some drew on a common stock of ideas, several key factors in this earlier transformation can be identified. Each signals a significant departure in the ways certain fundamental elements of Sāmoan culture, its worldview and lifestyle were altered.

The new religious ideology rested on acceptance of a new theocracy. The embracing of central tenets of the Christian gospel signalled the beginning of an enormous transformation in Sāmoans' understanding of the spiritual realm and of relationships between humans and their gods. The ideology of Christianity required acceptance that a single, omnipotent, omniscient and omnipresent god replaced a number of district and family gods that had previously controlled human life and determined the outcomes of everything from illness to warfare.[1] The newly arrived religion required belief in a new creation narrative that had its origins in another part of the world. The narrative was embodied in a previously unknown history peopled by unfamiliar mythic heroes and marked by extraordinary feats.[2] The new ideology prescribed a new set of relationships between Sāmoans and the new god, and determined that interpersonal conduct was to be shaped, not by power, but by a set of clearly articulated proscriptions. It prescribed new relationships between humans, and proscribed certain elements of former relationships such as war and polygamy. Furthermore, all of these ideas were prescribed and, initially at least, mediated by a set of agents who had no formal status or position in 'traditional' Sāmoan society.[3]

The new religious ideology clearly required the most wide-ranging shifts in both the Sāmoan worldview and lifestyle of the day, but it was not the only incursion into the Sāmoan way of life.

The second ideology to impact on Sāmoa was capitalism, the foundation of which is the sanctity of private property. Individual ownership and exclusive access to land, and the owner's right to retain profits from its exploitation, are central to successful capitalism. These ideas were, quite literally, foreign to Sāmoans for whom land was vested in families that were defined, as noted in the previous chapter, as those who were bound to the lands and the chief in whom control of the land was vested. Land was used by individuals during their lifetime, and re-assigned by *matai* after death to other members of the *āiga*. Parts of the proceeds of the exploitation of land, including both produce and cash from the sale of produce in the market, were retained by the individual to meet subsistence needs, and part was placed at the disposal of the *matai* who used it on behalf of the *āiga*. This 'rent' was used as sociopolitical capital to establish, maintain and enhance the standing of the *āiga* within the *nu'u*.

The arrival in Sāmoa of unrelated individuals seeking to 'buy', 'own', occupy and use land to which they had no rights through kinship was a new phenomenon. So too was the proposition that they would retain 'profits' from 'production' for their exclusive use. The would-be 'buyers' wanted to institute a new form of land transaction that differed from the Sāmoan practice by which powerful *matai* occasionally transferred lands and chiefly titles to families who had served them. In these transactions, the subject land was defined only by reference to landmarks and was registered only in families' oral histories. The would-be buyers wanted to use new technologies to measure and define land boundaries, and written records of transactions were formally registered in an office controlled by a third party. The acceptance of the idea that land was a 'commodity' that could be permanently 'alienated' for a 'value' set in a 'market' and transacted in a new currency signalled the beginning of the transformation of Sāmoans' perceptions of, and relations with, the land on which they lived. If capitalism produced significant changes in the ways Sāmoans thought about and related to land, it also produced other shifts.

A further premise of capitalism is that labour power is a private 'commodity' that its 'owner' can assign for a 'price' that is established in a 'market'. This idea was also quite literally foreign to Sāmoans for whom an individual's labour power was controlled by the *matai* and *āiga* on whose land he, or she, resided and from which they derived their livelihood and identity. The labour power of individuals was, in effect, a collective good that was employed by the *matai* on behalf of the *āiga* to establish, maintain and, where possible, to enhance its sociopolitical status within the village polity for the benefit of all of its members. Part of an individual's labour power could also be assigned by the *matai* for use by the village *fono* on projects chosen by the village polity. The arrival in Sāmoa of people who sought to 'buy' and 'use' labour power for a 'price' that was set in a labour 'market', and to retain all 'profits' from its use without concern for the social dimensions of the relationship between 'buyer' and 'seller', required significant shifts in Sāmoan thinking about the nature and value of labour. Acceptance of the idea that labour power was a commodity that could be 'bought' and 'sold' signalled the transformation of relations between humans, as did the idea that labour bought in this way was placed at the exclusive disposal of an unrelated person and that the price paid for that labour bore no relation to the value of its output.

Colonialism was the third ideology that produced changes in Sāmoan society from the nineteenth century on. Colonial authority rested on the acceptance of an ideology of governance that had only recently been formulated and was still being refined in emerging western 'nation states'. This model embodied new ideas including the concept of a 'nation' in which power, authority and administration were centralised primarily for the convenience of colonial powers. In this 'nation', administrative precepts and procedures, applied consistently by 'impartial officials' and official bodies and without regard to the relationships between, or relative status of, those involved were capable of delivering 'superior' outcomes for the 'citizens' of a 'nation'. Sāmoans who had governed themselves on an entirely different basis for many centuries[4] were understandably reluctant to embrace this ideology that challenged their established autonomy and the forms of power and authority on which it rested.

Sāmoan leaders resisted the idea of the superiority of colonial governance and many of the claims of colonial agency, and exploited divisions between various consuls, effectively dissipating and limiting their influence on Sāmoan society. They also resisted the suggestion that governance should be transferred to *papālagi* consuls and officials who claimed to understand the system and to accept positions on the periphery of Sāmoan society and politics. Where colonial claims of authority were rejected, colonial agents were shown to be somewhat impotent. They could only resort to the exercise of force to secure Sāmoan compliance in the case of serious breaches.[5] Despite the limited early impact of this ideology, its arguments did provide Sāmoans with the opportunities to consider alternative models of governance and led eventually to limited participation in some structures promoted by these powers.

Over a period of 150 years, the ideology and forms of Sāmoan governance have been transformed. The polity has now embraced a number of institutions that were once vigorously resisted and that have over time curtailed the power and authority of those who traditionally controlled Sāmoan society. Sāmoa has embraced the 'nation state'; a 'constitution' that defines the individual citizen without reference to kinship or land; a set of individual rights that transcend those of the collectivities to which they belong; and a new means of electing those who will exercise power over the Sāmoan 'nation'. At the same time, there have been significant changes in the organisation and exercise of the power of the traditional polity.

The three major ideologies described above were the most significant sources of new ideas but did not exhaust the range of new models to which Sāmoans were exposed during that tumultuous time. For example, the scientific model of health, primitive though its early form was, had at its heart an aetiology of illness that effectively excluded supernatural agency, and was based on new models of biology, physiology and anatomy. It promoted the idea that natural agencies such as bacteria and viruses could be responsible for illness in a body that could be understood primarily as a physiological machine. This signalled the beginning of the transformation of ideas about the human body and condition and the explanation of the nature and causes of illness.

The 'invisible' past

This transition is not unique: many societies have undergone similar transformations over the same period. What is of interest in the Sāmoan case is the way in which the impact of this transition is minimised in Sāmoan accounts of Sāmoa's history. Each of the 'new' ideologies represented major departures from Sāmoan models of society, and yet each seems to have been incorporated into the worldview and lifestyle of the village so completely that they are no longer thought of as having origins beyond the village. This raises the question of how profound changes have become so embodied in the worldview and lifestyle that they are effectively 'invisible' in daily discourse. In what follows, we suggest that while each of these new sets of ideas transformed life, each did so by adding to rather than displacing existing knowledge. New knowledge was grafted onto and eventually incorporated into existing paradigms and effectively extended the range of ways in which things could be understood. Thus, while very significant paradigm shifts occurred, these did so gradually so there was apparently never a point at which profound, cognitive dislocations between paradigms occurred.[6] Since *papālagi* were not in a position to control Sāmoan society, it is hardly surprising that Sāmoans dominated the discourse in both social and political spheres.

Christianity

The first, and arguably the most significant, of these ideologies was the belief in a single omniscient and omnipotent god who controlled all of the affairs of humanity. This new god was all-powerful but eschewed war and instead preached forgiveness and love of one's enemies. He defined all other gods as idols and demanded the complete and exclusive allegiance of those who wished to worship him, offering the possibility of salvation and eternal life to those who set aside other gods and served him. This new ideology redefined supernatural authority and marginalised district gods, family gods and various animal totems that formerly controlled the earthly lives and fates of humans (Stair 1983: 210–41, 259–70; Turner 1983: 16–77; Krämer 1994: 24–26).

Christianity was so completely embraced in Sāmoa that it is now seen to be a central institution, and indeed a pillar, of village life, and few if any people routinely think of it as an imported ideology. Indeed, all that existed and was believed in before this was apparently consigned to a space known as *aso ole pouliuli* or the days of darkness.[7] All that followed the acceptance of the gospel became known as *aso ole malamalama* or enlightenment (Meleisea 1987a: 144ff) or *aso ole tala lelei*, the days of the good news. This division is routinely used and acknowledges and defines a fundamental paradigmatic shift. Indeed, as the national coat of arms proclaims, the new nation of Sāmoa is founded on this God: *Fa'avae ile Atua Sāmoa*.

Yet while the Sāmoans claim to have embraced Christianity in its entirety and to have dispensed with 'heathen' beliefs of the former time of 'spiritual darkness', the same people who assert that heathen beliefs have been dispensed with are the very same people who continue to acknowledge these same spirits and beliefs in their daily life: the new god, while omnipotent and omniscient, did not displace all of the other spiritual agencies that once dominated the life of the Sāmoans. Spiritual agencies, *aitu*, continue to influence the daily life of humans in the village in many unexplained matters, especially as they impact on human health and wellbeing. For example, family graves and graveyards are cleaned regularly out of respect for the spirits that reside that in the area; boiling salt water may be poured into graves whose occupants are thought to be responsible for problems that are disrupting social life; women do not use certain forms of bodily adornment because they believe that particular female spirits such as Saumae'afe and Telesā will become jealous of those who compete with them in this way and may seek vengeance on them; whistling ceases after the locusts call in the evening; mirrors are covered at night; pregnant women do move alone at night or wear floral garlands; babies are not carried facing backward at night; what the village dogs are 'seeing' when they bark at night, and where the *ve'a*[8] stops calling during the evening are matters of considerable interest.

This may seem incongruous when the same people assert that Sāmoa is founded on the God of the Holy Scriptures; when the life of the village and family revolves around, and is premised on, the teachings of this god;

and when the morning begins with prayers to this god to guide, guard and protect the supplicant and ends with thanks. When people are asked to explain the simultaneous belief in *aitu* and the omnipotent God of the scripture, the former are explained as 'demons' that, in scripture, were cast out by Christ but continue to roam the world of mortals creating mischief among them and testing their faith in God. What the scriptures did was simply to clarify the nature and purpose of this malicious agency, once these teachings became available and ushered in the age of enlightenment or *aso o le malamamala*.

The new ideology also challenged and transformed chiefly authority in fundamental ways (Meleisea 1992: 21–23). Missionaries were elevated to the status of *aliʻi paʻia* that set them alongside the highest ranks of Sāmoan chiefs. But elevation of missionaries to the status of 'sacred chiefs' did not displace the existing chiefs (Meleisea 1992: 21). Indeed, the latter became the sponsors and protectors of the former, and retain that status to this day (Macpherson 1997). The pastors were installed in a relationship with the village and its polity known in Sāmoan as *feagaiga*, or covenant, that is marked by mutual respect and carefully balanced power. The best known *feagaiga* relationship is that which exists between a brother *tuagane* and sister *tuafafine* in which the brother holds executive power and the sister holds consultative rights.[9] The pastor, who is addressed ceremonially as the *faʻafeagaiga* to capture the character of the relationship, is thus related to the village in the same way as a brother is related to his sister. In this relationship, the village is the 'brother' who holds executive power and the pastor the 'sister' who holds rights to consultation (Tuimaleaiʻifano 2000: 172–3).

This symbolic, if slightly asymmetrical, balance is matched in political practice. Despite their religious authority, and the secular influence and respect accorded them, pastors serve at the pleasure of the village polity and cannot survive without the political patronage of the chiefs of a village.[10] Thus, while a powerful new elite was installed by the new religion, its members remained under the effective control of the Sāmoan elite in a relationship, called the *feagaiga*, named to enshrine its asymmetrical character. It is therefore not surprising that the church is not seen as having inserted itself in and dominating Sāmoan custom. It is seen rather as something that Sāmoans inserted into the Sāmoan hierarchy in ways that ensured they maintained control of both the institution and the hierarchy.

Capitalism
Capitalism and land

Capitalism is the second transformative ideology that has impacted on Sāmoa. Capitalism holds that land is a commodity that can become the inalienable property of an individual and be bought, sold and exchanged by unrelated individuals. This model of the nature of land, which underpins the idea of a land market, differs markedly from the pre-existing Sāmoan model in which land was vested in a kin group and was part of an indivisible corporate estate in which use rights were allocated to group members for use during their lifetimes. The idea that land could also be a commodity was embraced and village land was alienated by gift or sale while that was possible.[11] So why is this effectively invisible in daily life? Why is it that when people are aware of the existence of freehold land within the village, and while it is a fact of village life, few if any people think about this as the by-product of an imported ideology and a major departure from Sāmoan custom?

Firstly, it is probably because the new form of land tenure did not replace the earlier form: some 80 per cent of the land area of the country remains in customary tenure, and a further 10 per cent is held by the government as crown estate[12] (Australian Agency for International Development 2008b, volume 1: 4). Only some 10 per cent of Sāmoan land, which was alienated in the nineteenth and early twentieth centuries, is freehold and it is closely held by a relatively small number of individuals.[13] While Sāmoans distinguish between *fanua tau Sāmoa* and *fanua tau pālagi* and acknowledge that different forms of rights attach to each (O'Meara 1987 and 1995), for most, life is lived out on customary land; and land matters that consume most time and energy relate not to freehold land but to the land held in customary tenure in which both rights and control are more frequently and publicly contested.

Secondly, in the village, there are often no clearly defined social boundaries between those who occupy freehold and customary land: in many cases they are kin of long standing. When family or village *fa'alavelave* arise, all members are called on, as *āiga*, to participate and to support the family in its hour of need. No distinction is made in the expectations of those who live on freehold land and are therefore, technically at least, less dependent on the family. Within village and family affairs, freehold land owners are treated in the same way as other family members: as *āiga*. When, as they invariably do, they respond as kin, their action demonstrates that kinship is more significant than land tenure. As long as those who occupy the freehold land continue to acknowledge their kinship, recognise and discharge their obligations to the *āiga*, and participate in kin ventures, they are regarded primarily as kin and the nature of their land rights will be largely irrelevant and effectively invisible.

Those who occupy freehold land do, however, have different rights that they could exercise if they chose to. They could, hypothetically, argue that their obligations differ because they do not derive their livelihood from the family land and should therefore be exempted from the 'rental' component of the levy on them as kin. However, in the village,[14] land owners may be reluctant to exercise or to draw attention to their rights, because they are well aware of their dependence on their *āiga* for various forms of support, and conscious of the social tensions that can arise and complicate life if they were live in the village but choose to separate themselves from it. So, families living on freehold land in the village, who could appropriate and sell all of the produce on their land, choose to give a certain amount to kin who ask for it in order to maintain good relations and to build social and political capital. They explain their action as an investment in good social relations, and as a form of insurance for the future. Thus, a woman who routinely gave produce, firewood and medicinal plants to any kin who asked explained:

> This way makes more sense in the village. As long as people ask, and show that they respect our rights, I don't mind giving them things that they need. After all there is more here than we can use, and if we refused to

help them, we will give us a very bad name and people will steal things that they need. This way we give them things they need when they ask and they respect us and will help us when we need something. That's quite important because our children are no longer here to help us and so if I can go out and ask the boys to come and help me, it's more sensible. If I have a bigger job, I can get them to do the job and give them food for their family. That way everybody feels happy.

While their actions serve all of these purposes, it also explains why the nature of the tenure remains effectively invisible. It is, as they note, somewhat philosophically, a necessary part of *fa'asāmoa*.

Capitalism and labour
Capitalism also held that labour power was a commodity. It was the 'property' of an 'individual' who controlled it, and could be bought, sold and exchanged between unrelated individuals. This idea, which underpins the concept of a labour market, differed markedly from the belief that labour was, in effect, the property of the kin group to which one belonged. In exchange for the rights to use its land and to enjoy its protection, members were expected to place part of their labour power at the disposal of the leaders of that kin group. The amount of labour that one was expected to place at the disposal of the kin group was shaped by genealogical status, gender and age. The outputs of that group's labour were employed to generate sociopolitical capital for the kin group. The same principles applied to the labour that was assigned by family *matai* to the village polity for its use.

Wage and salary employment has been so completely embraced that in 2002 some 20.7 per cent of the adult population worked full time and a further 0.6 per cent worked part time for wages and salaries[15] (Sāmoa Statistical Division 2002: table 1.2). This figure was highest in Apia where 35 per cent of the adult population worked full time and a further 0.8 per cent worked part time for wages or salaries and declined with distance from town. In the next most populous area, Northwest Upolu, the comparable figures were 22.9 per cent and 0.6 per cent respectively (Sāmoa Statistical

Division 2002: table 1.2). These official figures understate the real extent of wage and salaried employment because they are based on formal sector only and recent censuses suggest that informal sector employment is significant.[16] It also understates the level of dependence on wage labour because it does not incorporate the multiplier effect of a single wage. Now, approximately one quarter of adults in the village work for wages and salaries, in government departments and businesses in town, at a nearby factory or as self-employed contractors. All retain at least some of their earnings from the sale of their labour for their exclusive use. Those without access to land or paid work may even sell their labour power to kin in the village on a casual basis and there is a new set of terms being used to refer to this hybrid employment relationship.[17] And yet this departure from 'traditional' ideas about the nature of labour is not seen as imported ideology. Why is it that the sale of labour power escapes much comment and seems to be simply a fact of village life?

The first reason is that wage labour has become a necessity, particularly in villages with limited land that is under more pressure. The numbers of people now living in villages with restricted access to agricultural land continues to grow, especially in Apia and in the more densely populated villages of the Northwest Upolu area. These people seek employment in either the formal or informal sector to meet their economic needs that, in turn, limit their ability to maintain productive subsistence gardens. They join a significant number of Sāmoan migrants who work for salaries and wages abroad and whose inclusion in the 'rate' would make this form of employment the norm. Indeed, a relation who was explaining where each of her adult children was living made no distinction between the 'oldest son, U, who stays in the village and looks after their cattle; the next two sons, P and E, who work in government departments in Apia; the two daughters A and E who work in New Zealand; and the youngest daughter F who works in the US'. In Sāmoan terms, their kinship is more important than the way in which their labour power is used. But kinship and labour relationships are connected.

The second reason is that access to reliable cash incomes from salary and wages is more and more important to the increasingly cash-hungry *fa'alavelave* at the centre of the *fa'asāmoa*. Family, village and church make regular demands on their members for contributions in cash and kind for various *fa'alavelave*. These include marriages, funerals, title confirmations, some birthdays, baptisms that are sponsored either by one's family or village, and periodic church demands, *taulaga*, at particular times of the year. Since the timing of these events cannot always be anticipated, individuals and families may find themselves facing pressure to participate in more than one event at the same time, which places significant pressure on those involved. Competitive pressures on participants to demonstrate 'generosity' in conspicuous ways lead to an increasing value on the wages that can be used to secure the cattle, pigs, tinned meat and even fine mats that are redistributed on these occasions.[18] In essence, income from the sale of labour power has ironically become the mainstay of the events that are at the centre of the *fa'asāmoa*.

Beside these *fa'alavelave*, people's help is routinely sought by kin to help pay church donations, school fees, medical expenses, court costs and fines, vehicle repair costs and other expenses that people cannot meet at a given time from their own resources. Both of these sets of events place a premium on savings and cash. In all of these situations, employed people are important because they are not only a source of cash but also of access to credit. They are able to leverage their earning power, to borrow against their National Provident Fund contributions and to use evidence of employment to secure loans from the private finance companies that are springing up around Apia to service the growing demand for cash. On any evening on television, there will be a series of advertisements from companies offering almost instant loans to meet the demands of *fa'alavelave* to those who can bring in a payslip or other evidence of employment. Given the significance and importance of the sale of labour, one might expect that those who can make the difference on these occasions might have been able to leverage this to gain some independence from, or at least recognition of their importance to, the family.

While those who live and derive their incomes from employment beyond the village, and not from the use of family land, might seem to be free to absent themselves from these demands, this is rarely the reality.[19]

They could argue that they derive their livelihood without using the family or village's resources and therefore should be exempted from the 'rental' component of such levies. But even people who are now apparently independent and employ their own human capital to earn wages are not seen in this way in Sāmoa. One of the villagers told us:

> Even if those people are big shots and make big money in town, they know they have eaten their family's sweat to get to where they are. That is why they will still feel they have to come. It's the same with the village, even the very important people know that they became who they are when they lived in the village. They have eaten the village's sweat too to get to where they are. Some pretend that they owe nothing to the family or the village and refuse to support *fa'alavelave*, but people have no respect for them because they forget the truth.

This reasoning may explain why even those who sell labour continue to place some part of their income from wage work at the disposal of leaders of the kin group who then employ it to generate sociopolitical status for the *āiga*.[20] Those who work for salary and wages are looked to for help to meet family expenses and routinely commiserate with one another about the costs of the *fa'asāmoa*. They may even seek to avoid or to minimise their contributions by pleading that all of their wages have been used up in *fa'alavelave*, but confronted with a demand, few refuse.

Given this dependence on wages and salaries, one might suppose that the importance of wage and salary employment would be very apparent. In fact, it is not. When people outline and detail the resources contributed to family and village *fa'alavelave* and to church offerings and special collections, scrupulous attention is paid to the donors and amounts, but no mention is made of the source of the money. This creates something of a paradox. As long as those who are employed continue to contribute resources to the projects of their families and villages, and to make these projects possible, the availability of income will be more significant than its source, thus making the real importance of wage labour invisible.

Governance and law

The third transformative ideology derives from colonialism and is the idea that governance is best centralised and law can be formulated and administered by people who are neither in, nor of, the village. Governance instead derives from a set of criteria from beyond the village, for the benefit of an entity that did not previously exist: the nation state. The idea that a national system of governance and law, which regulated significant parts of the conduct of those in the village but was administered impartially by people from beyond its boundaries and without regard for the relationships of the parties, differed fundamentally from the idea that those in the village and its families had the right to define acceptable standards of conduct, to regulate the conduct of those within its boundaries, and to determine and impose punishments for those who transgressed them (Meleisea 1992: 13). Furthermore, it differed significantly on the importance of relationships. In Sāmoan society, social relationships were all-important in government and law.

Yet now, parallel systems of law and justice are so deeply embedded in the life of individuals that the imported law is not seen as an imported ideology. People distinguish between the village's law *tulāfono a le nu'u* promulgated and administered by the village council or *fono*, and the nation's law *tulāfono a le mālō* promulgated by its parliament and administered by courts and government agencies. This raises the question of why the idea of a body of 'national' law, formulated and administered by the 'nation state', is not seen as an imposed system that challenges the 'traditional' bodies and their practice.

This may be because, in practice, they complement rather than compete with one another. The two sets of agencies and the two bodies of law relate to and regulate different spheres of social life. The state depends on village *fono* to maintain law and order in the villages[21] and has, in the Village Fono Act of 1990, delegated some of its authority and power to village councils to formulate local by-laws, to hear and adjudicate on violations of these, and to impose a range of penalties from fines to banishment from the village. In some matters that could be heard in state courts, those involved may try to have them heard in the *fono* and resolved in the village because there is a widely held belief that those involved will know more about the parties and will be able to deliver a judgment that better reflects their expectations and aspirations. Disputes over land and titles, and some criminal matters that cannot be resolved in the village where they originate, are resolved in the courts of the state. Thus, while a national system of law exists, it comes to many people's attention only when matters that cannot be dealt with in the village legal system are passed to it for resolution. The introduced origins and significance of national law may escape attention because for most village people, for most of the time, the village legal system has the most immediate impact on their daily life and conduct.

Furthermore, the systems do not seem to be as clearly separated to Sāmoans as one might assume. Most of those who work in the various branches of the nation's administration and legal system are Sāmoan, so it is popularly assumed that these entities are extensions of the 'Sāmoan system' and that the Sāmoan values that underpin village law and administration also underpin national law and administration. This impression is confirmed for many people because they are able to use kinship and friendship links to access various sections of the bureaucracy and the legal system[22] and, in some cases, to influence outcomes so that neither may seem as distant and impenetrable as one might expect (Macpherson and Macpherson 2000). In fact, the extent of this access was a matter of some concern to the Auditor-General, Su'a Rimoni Ah Chong, who drew attention to it after reviewing the affairs of a large number of government ministries and trading operations (Controller and Auditor-General 1994). This gave rise to an extensive governance reform programme, widely supported by Sāmoa's development partners, and intended to limit private influence in the operation of the national bureaucracy.

The human condition
The final transformative ideology redefined the human condition. It derived from a 'scientific' model of human biology, and embodied the idea that health and illness might be regulated by a set of microscopic biological agencies that could be transmitted in hitherto unforeseen ways (Macpherson and Macpherson 1990). This model differed quite fundamentally from the idea

that health and illness were influenced primarily by supernatural agencies, which observed the conduct of their living descendants and intervened, in the form of illness, to signal their displeasure with elements of that conduct. The nature and course of an illness were studied by healers to identify the conduct that had provoked the supernatural displeasure and to determine appropriate remedies.

But new knowledge of human biology was grafted on to earlier beliefs to extend the range of explanations of the human condition. It did not displace them. Now, parallel and complementary models of health and illness exist alongside each other. A series of illnesses assumed to have been introduced by outsiders, and known by the generic term *ma'i papālagi*, are thought to be most appropriately understood and managed by those who have been trained to understand and manage them. Equally, a series of illnesses that have been in Sāmoa from time immemorial, known by the generic term *ma'i Sāmoa*, are regarded as most appropriately managed by those healers who best understand them.

The finer distinctions between the two models, and the fact that they have somewhat different aetiologies and diagnostic models, are not often canvassed. While one of the first tasks in diagnosis is to determine whether an illness is a *ma'i Sāmoa* or a *ma'i papālagi*, this information is necessary primarily to make sure that the appropriate healer is located as early as possible and to secure prompt relief for the patient.

The invisibility and pervasiveness of ideological change

New ideas, and the ideologies from which they were derived, altered fundamental tenets of Sāmoan society: the foundations of its theocracy, the essence of the human condition, the aetiology and causes of health and illness, the nature of land and labour, and the character and origins of governance and law. This begs the question of why they are apparently 'invisible' in much contemporary Sāmoan thinking. Our contention that this was possible because they could be grafted on to existing bodies of Sāmoan belief raises the question of how earlier elites might have managed these introductions so as to minimise their impact on the Sāmoan worldview and lifestyle and on their personal standing. Elites had no interest in the promotion of ideas that would have undermined their personal standing, and maintained a balance between a traditional conservatism that protected their status and the adoption of certain ideas that they embodied in the *fa'asāmoa* in ways that obscured their origins and, over time, made them seem part of it.

We argue that this was possible because the power to define and redefine the meanings, and place, of these new ideologies in Sāmoan life was concentrated in the hands of a united and powerful elite. This elite, whose authority and word were in effect final, comprised respected chiefs and, later, missionaries and pastors, who were able to redefine reality for the village without fear of public contradiction. The collaborative relationship between the chiefs and the missions was mutually beneficial and guaranteed each a significant influence over Sāmoan society (Macpherson 1997: 19–24). There were, as Meleisea and Schoeffel note, authorities who effectively defined which knowledge was incorporated into existing paradigms (Meleisea and Schoeffel 1987: 1–20) and the form in which it entered local practice. When the elite accepted and promoted an idea, it was incorporated; and when they disapproved of one, it simply languished and, in some cases, was actively stamped out. A few examples will suffice to explain how this process of incremental augmentation and inclusion may have occurred.

When these elites identified and promoted ideas, they did it in ways that ensured that the new ideas did not directly challenge existing ones. In fact, in many cases, the new ideas that were promoted consolidated and extended the authority to those who controlled the process. A book entitled *O le Tala i Tino o Tagata ma Mea Ola 'Ese'ese e iai fo'i o tala i manu ua ta'ua i le Tusi Pa'ia* was written and translated into Sāmoan by the missionary Powell (1886), to help Sāmoan pastors interpret and explain for their converts animals, concepts and processes mentioned in the Bible with which they were unfamiliar. The text contains a number of assertions about physiology that contradicted existing beliefs, but the book contains no explicit suggestion that existing Sāmoan knowledge was incorrect. The net effect of the publication was to extend, rather than displace, Sāmoan knowledge of flora, fauna, and plant and human physiology.

This process of adding new, fundamentally different ideas to existing bodies of belief continues daily. During our research on traditional medicine, we came across ideas about medicine that were of particular interest because they seemed to be unique (Macpherson and Macpherson 1990). An elderly healer, who specialised in the diagnosis and treatment of *ma'i aitu*, prescribed and dispensed her medicines in ways that linked the strength of the dose to the body mass of the patient. When we enquired about the basis of the belief, the healer thought only briefly before explaining that she had been involved as a public health nurse in a filariasis campaign in 1965. Everyone was weighed before the dosage of the filariasis medicine was calculated and the results were so impressive that she had adopted the idea and incorporated it in her 'traditional' practice.

In some cases, such as religion, this expansion can be explained by examples of omissions rather than inclusions. For example, the Reverend John Williams' party was escorted to Sāmoa by a Sāmoan *matai* named Faueā. On the way to Sāmoa, Faueā warned Williams that to succeed in Sāmoa, he should avoid wholesale criticism of, and attempts to ban, Sāmoan practices. Williams, who later thanked God for Fauea's advice and insight, decided to avoid early criticism of large areas of Sāmoan life in favour of discouraging a few particularly problematic ones. When Williams was asked what changes the church would seek in Sāmoan society, he initially named only a few relatively minor areas of practice and planned to transform others as the mission gained influence. The unintended consequence of this decision may well have been the formation of the impression that the paradigms were not as distinctly different as they were and of an implicit acceptance by the missionaries of significant areas of Sāmoan religious belief and practice.

The same elite was able to stop other arguably less contentious ideas from gaining currency. When the linguist George Milner[23] edited a superb *Dictionary of the Samoan Language* in 1966, a disagreement about the translation and interpretation of certain ideas in that work led to a ban on the import, sale and circulation of the dictionary in what was then

Western Sāmoa even though the work's copyright was jointly held by the governments of Western Sāmoa and American Sāmoa.

Should the elite have worried that ideas in a dictionary could disrupt Sāmoan society? Probably not. As late at 1948, the Secretary of Sāmoan Affairs at the time, F. J. H. Gratton, in *An Introduction To Samoan Custom*, warned people who might seek to force change upon Sāmoan society that –

> . . . cultural change is not something that can safely be contrived by European opinion and applied overnight. Democracy, or any other form of cultural development, is a sensitive growth that does not transplant well: the seed is most likely to flourish and come to fruition where it sprouts *in situ*. . . .
>
> There are influences at work in Samoan society at the present day which it will be impossible to obstruct effectively as it would be imprudent to endeavour to force it in some other direction . . . (Gratton 1948: 157)

But, as Gratton noted prophetically, 'It is true that there seems to be a present resilience about Samoan custom, something that one observer has called its bamboo-like quality, its ability to give without breaking and to spring back into place to all appearances undamaged; but this, of course, cannot go on indefinitely' (Gratton 1948: 157).

The invisibility of some of these earlier introductions may be a consequence of the fact that they were quietly incorporated into existing models over time and on terms the Sāmoan elites were able to control. So is there reason to believe that Sāmoan social, political and religious elites could not simply combine their influence to select and incorporate new and powerful ideas that are now circulating on their own terms, as they have done with others in the past?

We believe there are three reasons why Sāmoa may no longer be in a position to manage the introduction of new ideas as effectively as it was able to manage earlier ones. Firstly, Sāmoa is increasingly exposed to new ideologies, and elites may no longer be able to control either the content, speed or the ways in which these enter and are incorporated into Sāmoan culture and society. Many new ideas are available in media, such as the internet, over which the elites can exercise little or no control. Secondly, Sāmoan elites are becoming more diverse than was once the case and may not be able, or willing, to form a single view on new ideas or to agree to a consensual course of action as was once the case. An essay in a book published in 2000 on Sāmoan attitudes to governance documented the diverse range of responses in Sāmoa and argued that these were evidence of growing plurality in Sāmoan society (Huffer and Schuster 2000: 45–58). The interviews for that study were conducted in 1998 and, in the ten years since, the ideas expressed have probably gained wider currency and been more formally articulated. Finally, those agencies promoting these contemporary ideologies may have greater leverage than those that promoted some of the earlier ones and may not be as willing to allow Sāmoan elites to control the process.

Another chapter in the same book argues that new 'good governance' ideologies that were being promoted by international development and financial agencies required nations that used their services and funds to identify and address existing social inequalities and to create more equitable social structures (Macpherson and Macpherson 2000: 17–20). These agencies deliberately target social ideologies, such as patriarchy and gerontocracy, that generate the arrangements that produce identifiable, ongoing disadvantage among groups such as women, youth and people on low incomes. These forms are typically institutionalised and reflect core cultural values. While governments may be given some latitude in the ways and the order in which they confront these ideologies, they are required to define targets and programmes for their mitigation and to report regularly on progress toward their elimination. We believe that these three factors will present challenges to the authority of the traditional elite and will reduce its ability to filter and to manage new ideas.

Some challenges to the authority of traditional elites might be described as 'internal' insofar as they emerge from changes in Sāmoan society itself. Others may be described as 'external' insofar as they emerge from ideologies promoted by agencies beyond Sāmoa. In addition, the traditional elite comprises both a secular and a religious entity that each faces somewhat different challenges to its authority. In what follows, the internal and external challenges, as well as the secular and religious entities, are dealt with separately.

Emerging challenges to traditional authority

Internal challenges to the secular elite: the family and the village
In a recent volume on changes in the organisation of the secular elite entitled, *Changes in the Matai System: O Suiga i le Fa'amatai*, Asofou So'o noted that, 'There is a general feeling among Sāmoans that the *fa'amatai* is gradually eroding under the pressure and magnitude of changes that have accompanied modernization and, more recently, globalization. Although a relatively tiny place in the Pacific, Sāmoa has not been left untouched by these two major influences of our time' (So'o 2007: 7).

In a series of case studies in that volume, the various authors, notably Chan Mow, Fuata'i, So'o and Toleafoa, describe their personal experiences of this transformation. This volume focuses on case studies and, as So'o notes, it proved difficult to identify discrete themes within each chapter, as it can be argued that a set of interwoven processes has contributed to the declining unity and increasing frequency of challenges to the authority of the *fa'amatai*.

The authority of secular leaders, who once controlled families, villages and the state, is increasingly subjected to challenges from within Sāmoan society that may, in turn, constrain the capacity of the leaders to assert their power as effectively as they once did.[24] Sāmoa's current secular leadership is nowhere near as united in its views on many different issues as it was 50 or even ten years ago. Meleisea and Schoeffel have argued that even during discussions about independence, the elite was divided on the appropriate development agenda for the new state (Meleisea and Schoeffel 1987: 158–60). Such difference is, in part, a consequence of the changing character and organisation of secular leadership, known as the *fa'amatai*.

To appreciate the extent of change, it is useful to understand the process by which *matai* were selected and appointed some 50 years ago. An *āiga* title then was held by a single person,[25] often chosen by the previous holder and revealed on his or her deathbed in a *mavaega*, or by senior members of the family who met in convocation, as the *āiga potopoto*, to consider candidates from whom they selected the most promising. In choosing leaders, families sought candidates who had provided unstinting service, or *tautua*, to the *matai* and family; who knew and understood the family's history and genealogy or *gafa*; who were articulate orators and advocates for the family; and who were well-educated in both Sāmoan and non-Sāmoan cultures.

Families would go to very considerable lengths to identify one candidate from among their number in whom its *mana* would be embodied, whole and undiluted. This candidate was installed in a ceremony, *saofa'i*, in which the family's choice was made public, and in several other ceremonies in which the new titleholder and the family 'fed' the village and, in some cases, the district, before the title was officially registered at the Land and Titles Court in Mulinu'u. The family, having elected the new titleholder, was then bound to serve its *matai* for as long as he or she maintained unity within the *āiga*, represented them effectively and with dignity, and maintained or enhanced their sociopolitical status and influence within the village and, in some cases, the district.[26]

The candidates considered, and the *matai* finally chosen, in this process were almost always people who had lived in the village, who had served the family and its *matai*, and who, in the process, had gained a firm grounding in the history and politics of both the family and the village. Once selected, they would join other *matai*, chosen for similar qualities by their families, in the village *fono*. There they served a form of apprenticeship in which they honed their skills by emulating the senior members of those bodies and mastering the esoteric knowledge of Sāmoan society, politics and oratory. These *matai* represented their families in village affairs; their villages in district affairs; and Sāmoans in the various Sāmoan bodies established by consuls, colonial powers and in the early post-independence government of Western Sāmoa.

The involvement of the extended family, *āiga potopoto*, in the selection process produced a certain *matai* 'profile' that is widely acknowledged, with some nostalgia, by those who think about it. In discussion of his current *matai*'s conduct, one elderly man summarised this sense in the following way:

> Do you know when I think back to the *matai* that looked after the family and village in the time when I was young, I can see very clearly the difference between those people and our current leaders. It's true that the old *matai* may not have had that much formal education. Some did not speak any English but they were very knowledgeable and very wise in the Sāmoan language and custom. It was probably because they only became *matai* when they were older and when they understood the *fa'asāmoa*. They were very dignified and their mastery of formal speech reflected their knowledge of history and custom. They only spoke when they had something to say and when they spoke all the people listened because they had chosen them to lead the family and really respected them. We never had the sorts of problems which bedevil the family now.

Another woman said of those earlier *matai*:

> [They] were respected in the family because once the family chose them to lead, they gave the rest of their life to leading the family. Their whole focus was on how they could use their knowledge and skills to keep the family strong and united. They were good at this because they lived in the village and knew what their people were thinking and what they expected and they knew how to persuade people to achieve this. They knew because they had served the family all of their life. That is the origin of the saying, the 'path to power is service'.[27] Those *matai* might not have been to university, but they knew some more important things and they used a lot of proverbs to illustrate these things very clearly to their people. That's why families were more united in those times: they were united in respect for the *matai*, and a *matai* kept them united and committed to the family. P used to say a disunited family is like a broken comb: it is useless.[28]

Origins of Internal Challenges to Secular Authority

Why then has the authority of Sāmoan secular leadership been subject to more challenges than it was in the past? It is, in part, the consequence of a rapid increase in the numbers of people holding *matai* titles. The historian Malama Meleisea notes that in 1960, shortly before Sāmoa's independence, some 4595 or 4.1 per cent of the population held registered *matai* titles in Sāmoa.[29] By 1975, the number of registered holders of titles had expanded to 11,000 or 7.3 per cent of the population, as families elected multiple holders to titles that were once held by a single person.

Sāmoan scholars such as Meleisea and Schoeffel contend that this trend was, initially at least, a consequence of the 1963 Electoral Act that restricted the franchise to titleholders, and led families to increase the numbers of titleholders and to create new titles to increase their electoral influence (Meleisea and Schoeffel 1983: 100). There is little doubt that the creation of new titles, *matai palota*, that had no history, land or untitled people to serve them, and were created solely to gain families electoral influence, had a negative effect on the authority of titles. Concern with this devaluation of titles led to the passage of legislation to prevent the practice and to rescind those titles. The pressure to split existing titles to gain electoral influence was eliminated in 1990 when universal suffrage replaced *matai* suffrage and effectively reduced the influence of *matai* in the electoral process.

Despite this, the practice of electing multiple holders of titles continues. While the families that control prestigious national titles strive to limit the number of people who hold these titles (Toleafoa 2007: 211–12), within other families the number of titleholders continues to proliferate as the award of titles is used to provide leaders for rapidly growing families, to relieve tensions between rival claimants and their supporters (Tcherkezoff 2000: 118–20), and to raise funds for a variety of purposes (Tuimaleaiʻifano 2006a). In the past, families struggled to find male successors and to fund the *saofaʻi*, but now within rapidly growing families there are large numbers of claimants with the financial resources to pursue titles. Families routinely bestow titles on between 20 and 30 members of the family who have paid between $SAT2,000 and $SAT10,000 for the privilege.[30] Some titles are bestowed outside the village in which they exist, without evidence of service to the family, or knowledge of its history, or the oratory that is so central to maintaining family standing. Many of these people have only a tenuous connection with the village.

Toleafoa describes this process in his own family in the following way:

> Today there are seven titleholders including two females, a first in the family. Two are males married into the family, again another first. Only one titleholder is permanently resident in Fasito'otai. One has a house there and takes part in village affairs, but lives mostly in Apia. Three live in Apia where they were born and raised, and the rest live overseas where they migrated.
>
> Most of these *matai* have had what can only be described as a passing acquaintance with Fasito'otai village, or with the seat of the title, a paramount requirement in earlier days for becoming a *matai*. Within the time span of three generations only, the selection process had moved from one suitable male heir only to choose from, to scores including females and *faiāvā* [in-marrying males], who pressed claims, on the basis that they are heirs or are married to heirs. This is a common pattern in almost every Sāmoan family today. (Toleafoa 2007: 211)

If the commodification and relaxation of criteria for the endowment of titles has had an impact on their status, so too have the protracted absences of *matai* from the village in which their families and lands are found. Absentee titleholders are often unaware of the issues that involve the title and the family at a given time and are unable to contribute to the most pressing day-to-day business of their *āiga*. This means that the burden of leadership often falls on those *matai* who live in the village, that can result in resentment within families. As one resident *matai* complained:

> Those *matai* living outside the village just carry the title but don't carry any of the responsibility for the day-to-day duties of the *matai*. Some of our *matai* living abroad send money for some *fa'alavelave* here in the village. That is fine, and beside they represent and serve the family at our *fa'alavelave* overseas and that can be a heavy load. But some of them are

just living and working in Apia and yet we never see them in the village, even when they know about the *fa'alavelave*. They just call themselves *matai*, but don't act as *matai*. Sometimes those of us who serve the family in the village get very annoyed with those absentee *matai* who come to family meetings and give advice but are never seen at *fa'alavelave*. They just play at being *matai*.

The accession ceremonies, *saofa'i*, were important events in which families and their new *matai* publicly and formally committed themselves to serving each other. Further formal ceremonies followed in which the new *matai*'s family fed the village, and in some cases the district, before finally taking a seat in the village council *fono* and sharing 'ava with new peers. The solemn ceremonial was a rite of passage for the new *matai* and conferred considerable social import on the accession process. Some of the ceremonies that were once considered an essential part of the formal process have now been dispensed with, a factor that in many people's eyes has lessened the standing of the titles and those who receive them in these truncated *saofa'i* (Tuimaleai'ifano 2006a).

This is especially true where those receiving the titles fly in to Sāmoa briefly to receive them and, as one young man told us, 'often do not have time for all of the Sāmoan ceremonial formalities':

> Of nine of us who received the family title on that occasion, three were from New Zealand, two were from Australia, two were from the US and one was from American Sāmoa. Only one was resident in Sāmoa. We were given a choice between having the *saofa'i* in the village from which the title comes or having it in a village near Apia. Everyone was pretty keen on doing it in Apia because it would have been much more expensive and would have taken a lot longer if we had gone out to the village and done all of the *fa'asāmoa*.
>
> Because we did it in Apia, we only had to put on a cup of tea for the *matai*, but if we had done the *saofa'i* in the village we would have had to feed the whole family and the village. They reckoned it would cost us about another $SATI,500–2,000 each to feed everyone. We had already paid our

fares to Sāmoa and had given them the money and so that would have added a lot to the cost. But it was also the time involved and we would have had to make a whole lot of speeches and a number of us didn't really speak Sāmoan and certainly not well enough to do what would have been expected of us in the village.

This speaker makes another important point: numbers of people, many who are now awarded *matai* titles, have a less than adequate grasp of either the language or culture and, in many cases, of the family's history. Migrants brought up outside Sāmoa frequently have very little facility with the formal language and practices of *fa'amatai*, and in-marrying titleholders often have a limited understanding of the family history because of the reluctance of families to disclose significant parts of their genealogy, or *gafa*, and history to non-members. One man spoke of the effect of this on the dignity, *mamalu*, of the titles:

> In those days, titles were held by people who knew a lot about Sāmoan custom, could speak well, and acted with concern for the standing and dignity of the title. They thought a lot before they spoke or before they acted because they knew their conduct could influence the status of the title. Now you see men who don't seem to care about the effects of their behaviour on the title's dignity. They speak badly and can't even use the chiefly language properly. They make their ignorance even more apparent by trying to use figures of speech and proverbs which they don't understand. One man started to say something and couldn't even finish it: people who see that must think 'what sort of family appoints a clown like that to preserve their reputation?'

The proliferation of titles also creates new tensions within families that once spoke with a single voice, but are now beset with tensions that reflect competition between titleholders for power within families, and for the right, *pule*, to administer family land. Furthermore, the tensions can be time-consuming, expensive and have the potential to further divide families and to expose them to unwelcome scrutiny from others. People in the village routinely discuss these problems.

A young man who had returned to the village for a land case that involved litigation between several branches of his family complained that:

> These things go on and on because people's pride keeps them from conceding in these family matters. I can't understand this, and sometimes despair, because after all, all of those who are involved are part of the same family. This is the third time I have been to Sāmoa in two years for this case. It's not just this family either: my wife's family has a similar case and most families have these sorts of cases going on and on today. In the old days, the *matai* just listened to people who knew the family's genealogy and history and then made the decision. But now you have too many people, with too little knowledge, all wanting to be big shots. Time, and resources, are wasted with people who don't know much arguing with one another about things they don't understand.

A senior *matai* complained that he had agreed to the creation of new titleholders within his *āiga* to broaden the base and share power, but that:

> I now find myself wondering why I did that. As the senior titleholder I was entitled to do that and I had thought the new titleholders would represent the various parts of the family. They would bring their families' views to me as the *sa'o*[31] and I would make the decision after I had considered these. But those people and their supporters are forever arguing with one another and the tension is dividing the family.
>
> Now, some are even challenging my authority, even though I created them. I once thought we would be able to resolve everything in the family by discussion, but now we find ourselves in the Land and Titles Court because many of those new titleholders don't think of the whole family: they just think about themselves. If they thought about the whole family, they would realise that all of this argument makes the family look very weak and divided to other people. A divided family is, as a proverb says, like a broken fish trap: it is useless.

Another older observer, who had lived abroad for some years, noted that many of the families in the village were using a lot of time, energy and resources on internal conflicts that were further dividing and weakening the family. He noted that this internal conflict dissipated families' resources and prevented them from doing the sorts of things that might strengthen them. As he said:

> If they [the family] spent half of the time and money which they spend on discussions and court cases, on developing the family's lands they would be very powerful and everybody could be well off. If they developed their access road and bought a tractor and truck, they could make use of all of that very productive land that they have inland. But instead, they spend much of their time and resources on discussions before court cases, court cases, and post-mortems after court cases. In the mean time, the land just grows weeds.
>
> When I look at these things, I can see it is just the pride of some individuals which keeps these things alive. It all looks futile to me, but I don't think other people see it that way because most of the families are involved in similar sorts of things at some time or other. It's become 'normal' because there are too many *matai* with the money to push these things in the families.

Some of these tensions within secular leadership are exacerbated by increasing divergence of views among titleholders on a range of issues. Many new titleholders have higher formal educational qualifications and a wider range of social and technical experience than their predecessors had. This fact, on the surface at least, would seem to have extended the range of skills to which families now have access. But this is not always the case, and sometimes attempts to introduce new thinking are unwelcome. People in the village complained that titleholders from 'outside' (*matai mai fafo*) brought ideas from outside and tried to tell people in the village how to run their affairs.

Thus, one described how:

People from outside come and think that, because they have been living outside, that they know how to run the family better than we do. I get angry when I hear these new *matai* from outside telling us, that in New Zealand they do this and that, or in the US they do this and that. Then when they've given us the benefit of their 'wisdom', they just get on a plane and go home. When I hear them going on and on, I want to tell them, this is Sāmoa and we'll do it in this way because that is the Sāmoan way. Some of the things that they say reflect their lack of understanding of Sāmoan custom or protocol. That just annoys us because we can see that they don't understand what they're talking about. So although they may know a lot, they just seem to be ignorant as far as Sāmoan things are concerned, and to be giving gratuitous advice, *fia poto*.

Similar divisions have emerged within the secular leadership in districts, *itūmālō*, as people who have become accustomed to challenging tradition within family and village contexts have begun to challenge traditions in these wider contexts. The evidence of these divisions has been outlined and discussed in a recent book (So'o 2008). In the past, it was held that *matai* within a constituency should meet and determine which of the available candidates would best serve and represent the interests of the district in parliament. The district could then agree to nominate a single candidate, which obviated the need for an election. The process also ensured that the candidate was obligated to the entire district and was bound to use that office to serve their interests. But these unanimous decisions are becoming increasingly difficult to reach as more and more candidates assert their right to stand against those favoured by existing power blocs and have, indeed, been willing to go to court to challenge their powers.

There are also challenges to *matai* authority from people within the family who claim they have the right to act as individuals rather than as part of the collective (Macpherson and Macpherson 2005). For example, in a case where the *matai* of a family accepted a ceremonial apology, *ifoga*, on behalf of a member of the *āiga* who was the victim of a sexual assault, the acknowledgement of guilt and the making of a public apology by the offending family, and its acceptance and the extension of forgiveness by the offended family, closed the matter within the village. However, the victim of the assault, a well-educated young woman, challenged the right of male *matai* to determine that an apology was sufficient and made it clear that she wanted the matter prosecuted in the courts. The *matai* asserted that as leaders they were charged with making a decision in the interests of the family, and that they had done so. In reply, the woman pointed out that the assault was on her, not her family, and she insisted that the case went to the courts. The offender was subsequently tried, convicted and imprisoned.

The families involved were divided over the issue: some agreed that the *matai* were within their rights and that the victim should have acknowledged their duty to act as they did since they were concerned with resolving the matters between the families. It was pointed out that the family that tendered the apology had been humiliated publicly for what had been done and that the woman should have accepted that this was sufficient – that this was the way these things are handled in the *fa'asāmoa* where the interests of the collective had to take precedence over those of individual members. Others thought that while the *ifoga* resolved the matter between the families and was an appropriate outcome, the woman was entitled to have her personal grievance addressed and that she should be free to take the case to court without criticism.[32] This incident illustrates perhaps the increasing difficulties that emerge over the extent and character of the rights of the secular elite even within their own families.

Internal challenges to secular authority: the Constitution

Other internal forces are also reducing the capacity of secular elites to agree on courses of action and undermining their solidarity and authority. The first of these is the growing willingness of individuals and groups to challenge the authority of traditional secular leadership (Macpherson 1997: 45–48; Meleisea 2000: 193–9; So'o 2000: 133–50). These contests have invoked individual rights, enshrined in the Sāmoan Constitution in 1962, that were for many years largely untested and remained somewhat academic, and used these to question the power of village elites (Macpherson and Macpherson 2006b: 145–9) in a growing number of challenges to the authority of village councils.

People, for instance, once accepted that the village council was entitled to determine what would happen in the village. The state seemed to confirm this power when it formalised these village powers in the Village Fono Act of 1990. Where, for instance, the village council determined that there had only been one denomination and one church in the village and that there would be only one, most people accepted its right to do so. Those who did not want to worship in their village church simply travelled to another village and worshipped in the denomination of their choice. This accommodation allowed the village to retain its autonomy and villagers to acknowledge the village council's authority in this area while exercising their freedom to worship in a denomination of their choosing. When people challenged this 'arrangement', they frequently found themselves banished from the village, and where this occurred, most of the people who remained in the village supported the council.

More recently, growing numbers of individuals have been willing to question the authority of village polities that, they contend, have effectively denied them rights guaranteed them by the constitution (So'o 2000: 133–50). Some people, dissatisfied with these arrangements, have sought to establish a second or third denomination in villages in which there had previously been only one or two churches. They soon found themselves in conflict with the village councils that strenuously resisted challenges to their authority and sought to stifle these by various means. But some people persisted, asserting that their constitutionally guaranteed rights to freedom of assembly and freedom of religion allowed them to introduce new denominations into the villages. Before very long, there were confrontations between the village councils representing the rights and authority of the collective and the new religionists representing the rights of individuals and the authority of the constitution.

In yet another set of confrontations between individuals and their secular leaders, people have challenged the right of the collective to make decisions about the conduct of life and business within the village. These people, who have often lived outside of the village, have also found themselves in confrontations with the village councils that have traditionally enjoyed the right to regulate acceptable conduct within the village boundaries.

In these cases, the councils contended that those who reside within the village are bound by the laws of the village. Others claim that as long as they do not violate any law, they are free to exercise their constitutional rights. Such disagreements have resulted in other confrontations between representatives of two ideologies: those who advocate collectivism and those who support individualism.

In still another set of confrontations, the power and authority of the village council has been challenged publicly by the state. As the guardian of the constitution, the state is bound to uphold individuals' constitutional rights and has done so by over-ruling some decisions taken by village councils (Va'a 2000: 151–69). These confrontations pose a problem for the state. It is bound to uphold the constitution but, in practical terms, may lack the resources to enforce decisions that go against villages. It therefore had to avoid courses of action that resulted in large populous villages challenging the state when it tried to enforce a decision without the necessary police resources.[33] The state depends on villages for local government and administration and has been reluctant to alienate village elites by direct confrontations over enforcement.

In the past, the problems of conflict between individuals and village polities have been solved by asking those people who have won judgements against villages to accept the practical difficulty of enforcement. This has been resolved in freedom of religion contests by asking promoters of new faiths to accept the difficulty of enforcing the decision in the face of a united council and to move to villages where they would not face opposition to their religion. In other cases, those whose appeals against banishment were upheld were asked to stay away from the village for a while to allow passions to wane and for negotiations to take place over the terms of return. This worked for some time, but now people have started to challenge this solution and have gone to court to have their rights confirmed and enforced. A number of court challenges by individuals and families against decisions of village *fono* have been upheld by the nation's courts, which have over-turned villages' decisions and directed councils to accept the return of people whom they had banned from the village.

These decisions have been particularly significant when they have been made in the Land and Titles Court, in which Sāmoan values and practices are well understood by its judiciary, and have pointed to the limitations of the power of the *fono*. Where village elites have conceded and accepted the courts' directions, their authority has been challenged and diminished. Challenges to the power of the *fono* are not without risk. While the direction of the courts establishes the superiority of national law and the relative power of the state, where the latter lacks the resources to uphold these decisions it, in turn, may look weak and ineffective. This type of action can also alienate village leadership and this, in turn, further fragments a formerly cooperative and united relationship between the state, districts and the villages.

Internal challenges to religious authority

For many years, three major denominations, the Congregational Christian Church of Sāmoa, the Methodist Church and the Roman Catholic Church, known in Sāmoan as the *Lotu Ta'iti, Lotu Toga* and *Lotu Pope* respectively, enjoyed the allegiance and commitment of the vast majority of the Sāmoan population. At one time, these churches commanded the support of over 97 per cent of the people, and some 75 per cent of Sāmoans currently belong to one of these denominations. Adherents are in most cases regular worshippers, active contributors and participants in a range of church activities. The early and managed entry of the churches into villages ensured formation of close balanced relationships between village leaders and village pastors, and parallel relationships developed between national secular and religious polities. Senior figures from both village and national polities held lay leadership positions within the churches and ensured, where necessary, that the churches' needs were well understood in secular bodies. Leaders in the three areas were in some cases related to one another. The appearance of a united religious authority was reinforced by the creation of the national Council of Churches that from time to time considered and clarified a church position on a number of policy issues. The theological authority of the leaders in the dominant churches was almost unchallenged and the population looked to them for guidance in both religious and secular matters. This guidance was interpreted in the villages by pastors who were considered God's representatives on earth and shown the deference and respect appropriate to such a status.

This is no longer the case.[34] The emergence of a public critique of mainstream churches seems to have been gaining momentum and focuses not so much on the theology or organisation of the churches as on the conduct of some ministers, their families and certain officials. This conduct is now subject to more intensive scrutiny and criticism in both private and public spheres. There is a clear connection between the growth of mass media and the emergence of a more critical discourse, but whether the critique is fed by increasing media coverage of ministers' activities or whether increasing public discussion has tempted the media to be more critical is impossible to tell. The private, and more recently public, criticism of the conduct of God's servants was unthinkable 50 years ago, and open discussion of ministers' behaviour reflects an increasing willingness to challenge their authority.

Thus, for instance, when the editor of the *Samoa Observer*, Savea Sano Malifa, reported a plan to hold a convention on religious freedom in Sāmoa at the National University of Sāmoa in early December 2008, there was significant support for the idea. What surprised some Sāmoans was the explicit and open critique of the churches that this implied. One expatriate Sāmoan wrote in a letter to the editor of the *Samoa Observer* that:

> According to Savea, the convention's rationale is: 'Religious freedom is a fundamental human right.' Savea went on to ask what I consider to be a very relevant and very powerful question: 'So why is it that not one of the hundreds of pastors who have religiously stood up there on the pulpit around the country twice every Sunday over the years, has told us about this little secret?'
>
> Well, it's [because of] this very question that I believe such a convention is warranted. And if the convention is to uncover this little secret, I wonder as to whether the hundreds of pastors who have been champions in masking this little secret have been invited? I wonder as to whether the village councils who have been fooled and unjustly misguided by this little secret for so long have been invited to hear that religious freedom is

a fundamental human right? That is, neither churches nor village council has the right to interfere when an individual or a family exercises that fundamental human right.

It [freedom of religion] has been the subject of countless litigation. People have been left homeless, persecuted, banished and even killed because of absolute lack of respect for religious freedom in Sāmoa despite the fact the Constitution stipulates it clearly as you correctly pointed out.

And it's for that reason as well as to why I do support such a convention. However, it must be aimed at the right people. And the right people should not be Lawyers and Academics. It should be aimed at the perpetrators. In the case of Samoa, the normal perpetrators are the village councils, often inspired by their religious leaders – the hundreds of pastors that Savea referred to. (Letter to the Editor, *Samoa Observer*, 3 December 2008)[35]

Our point is not that this view is typical of Sāmoan attitudes to the church: it is not. Our point is that the public expression and publication of such a critical view signals a growing willingness to confront the power of the elite in the mass media, and that this critique may arise from those who reside abroad and live beyond the reach of the institutions that are criticised. However, these conversations are also occurring in the village though they may be more muted. Discussion, prompted often by media coverage of a particular incident or case, periodically turns to consideration of the general conduct of ministers. A number of themes seem to dominate these conversations.

Some of the criticism arises from comparisons of the current generation of pastors who enjoy large 'stipends', live in relative luxury and are supported by their congregations, with the pastors of old who were much poorer and were often compelled to cultivate their own food albeit with some help from village children. One woman noted that:

My grandfather was called as a pastor to a small village in the district of F. When he went there, all he took with him was a glory box and his Bible. That was all he had. The village had built a small Sāmoan house for him.

There, beside all of his preaching and pastoral work, he caught his own fish and looked after his own plantation. The village gave him land a long way from the village and he had to walk over a number of hills to get to his plantation before he could start work. There weren't many people in the village because it was a poor village so he didn't get very much help from the congregation which would normally have supplied some labour. His wife made all their mats and also went fishing. Even then he shared his food with members of the congregation. He was a thin man and always sun-burned but very strong because he was always working.

She went on to compare the pastor in the past with the present incumbent, pointing out the growing gaps between the standards of living of the pastors and their flocks:

> . . . when I see the village pastor today I see there is a big difference. Our fellow is a big, lazy man. The village buys all his food, pays for his house, pays for his petrol, pays for his power and water, and gives him around $SAT4,000 a month. When the village called him, he came with his wife and asked the village to do this and that to the house, to buy a new fridge, stove and television before he came. Then, when he arrived, he asked the village for a four-wheel drive vehicle.
>
> He doesn't run a pastor's school, and he doesn't visit the members of the parish on Saturday. I don't know what he does with his time. He doesn't spend it on preparation because sometimes his sermons are the same. Well, I do know where he spends some of his time: playing billiards on the big billiard table which the village bought him. And do you know that even though he gets a very generous fortnightly offering, *alofa*, and many other gifts for officiating at weddings, funerals and other *faʻalavelave*, he doesn't share it with the poorest people in the congregation? He just sticks everything in the big freezer and gives it to his own family.

Some criticism of mainstream churches revolves around the theological paradox that the 'shepherd' is now exploiting the 'sheep' he was chosen to protect. A woman who had seen her neighbours asking for food after they had given money to the church offering pointed to the paradox:

> If you think about the modern pastor's conduct: it is wrong. He is supposed to be like a 'shepherd' whose job is to protect the 'sheep'. The shepherd is supposed to lead them to food and protect them while they grazed. Now the 'sheep' are busy finding the 'shepherd' food and supporting him while he grazes. Meanwhile, the sheep and the lambs are going hungry. But shepherds who do that must know that this can only end badly for them.

Similar observations were made by a man whose neighbours had requested a basket of breadfruit for a meal. When he asked why they did not use the breadfruit from the tree near their house, the neighbour told him that the fruit from that tree was used to feed the pastor's pigs. He went on to comment:

> That is unfortunate. Even though the pastor is well-supported by the village – after all, no one else in the village earns as much money as he is given every fortnight – he takes the food from the table of that family. He lives next door to the family and so you would think that he might see that they do not have much land on which to grow their own food. But that is the problem: he is not looking at the situation of the people around him. That is not the behaviour of a Christian.

The conduct of pastors in the Congregational Christian and Methodist churches was sometimes compared with that of pastors in some evangelical fellowships in which ministers held full-time jobs to support themselves, and with the Latter Day Saints whose bishops supported themselves and whose 'missionaries and their families raised their own funds to allow them to dedicate time to the Lord's service'. Other inter-faith comparisons surface in these conversations, one of which focuses on the biblical injunction to give tithes to the church. The Mormon Church and several other smaller denominations, which ask parishioners to give one-tenth of their income to the church, were cited as examples of correct, biblically sanctioned form, and their practices were described as earthly expressions of divine intention. Conversely, attempts of other denominations to exhort parishes to give more than that wilfully ignored the biblical injunctions on giving and were therefore 'against the word of God'.

This issue of the personal wealth of pastors is a recurrent theme of conversations. The growing involvement of some pastors in the administration of their parishes' finances has led to some well-publicised cases of theft and fraudulent use of parish funds by pastors. Public concern with this matter was highlighted when Prime Minister Lupesoliai Malielegaoi Tuilepa Sailele alluded to these difficulties and advised ministers gathered at an annual church meeting that pastors might be well-advised to follow scripture[36] and to focus on theological and pastoral concerns, leaving the financial and secular issues to the laity. Those with whom we watched the speech when it was broadcast on national television immediately commended the PM for venturing into the area and went on to discuss widely known cases, citing them as evidence of some pastors' growing concern with their personal prosperity and a declining interest in the spiritual wellbeing of their congregations.

Challenges to the traditional churches' authority are being mounted as people become dissatisfied with the standard and direction of leadership. Some of the concern arises from comparison with denominations whose leaders have different, and often more egalitarian, relationships with their congregations. People explained that after the 1991 cyclone a number of families in the village changed denominations because –

> After the cyclone the Mormons were going around the village giving other families from the Congregational Church food and other supplies from their welfare cupboards. I think this made a big impression on families in the Congregational Church because they were desperately trying to get food and get their *alofa* for their pastor while the Mormon Bishop was going around giving families whose plantations were destroyed interest-free cash loans to help them buy food. Then the Mormon school system gave new books and a photocopier to the government school so that it could re-open after the storm.

Less obvious are challenges involving the transfer of membership from mainstream churches to those newer denominations that are organised in different ways, and that make fewer financial demands on their members. While the established denominations still enjoy the support of some 75 per cent of the population, this figure is down from earlier levels of 98 per cent and the change seems to be gaining momentum. Support for mainline churches may decline as senior figures in families and villages, who have effectively guaranteed support for mainline churches, die and people feel free to exercise choices. A taxi driver remarked casually when he was driving us home that:

> All of T's family has changed churches since the old man died. They now attend the Mormon Church in P. That means that all of the people on that western side of the road now go to the LDS Church. When you think about the village now, there are big differences: the other family goes to the Seventh Day Adventist Church and most of the family on the inland side of the road now attends the Assembly of God. Do you recall the drama which used to accompany changes of faith? People used to stone houses and banish families. Now, if you want to change, you just change to a faith which seems to be more your style.

Not all criticism of the mainline churches is directed at their ministers. Some Sāmoans argue that, since the village controls the church, responsibility for some of the problems in the church must be placed at the foot of village elites. The same people noted that, in the case of the Methodist and Congregational churches, villages had some knowledge of their pastors' views when they called them, and that they selected candidates whose beliefs were similar to their own or whom they believed they could control. The same people contended that if mainline churches operate in certain ways, it is probably because this suited a local elite's interests, and it is wrong to assume that what was done in their name necessarily reflected the personal desires of the pastor.

One example cited by advocates of this view was that the church provided a legitimate and public site for families to compete with one another within the village.[37] They argued that if the various regular offerings within a parish are considered excessive, it is within people's rights to reduce their offerings. If they choose not to, it may be because of public pressure and family pride rather than because of pressure exerted by its pastor. One person offered the following view:

> In our village, it is the important families which compete with one another that drive up the value of the *alofa*. They compete with one another all the time. They always have competed. If they chose to, they could arrange to cap, or even reduce, the *alofa*. They did once before to discipline the pastor when he tried to limit participation in the White Sunday service. But neither family wants to because they are reluctant to take the first step in case people think they can't afford to keep up their contributions.
>
> The village doesn't want to pull back either because they judge themselves against the other villages in the district and always want to be number one in the district. You could say in this case that it is history and not the pastor who is causing the problem. But it suits people to blame it on the church rather than accept responsibility for it.

Notwithstanding that view, the conduct of pastors is now more closely scrutinised and more openly criticised in print media, in the work of Sāmoan authors and poets, in popular music, and in *faleaitu* or comedies where it is satirised, sometimes in public performances. DVDs of the New Zealand cartoon series *BroTown* in which the Sāmoan minister is characterised as a philandering hypocrite circulate and are widely enjoyed in Sāmoa.

Villages ensure that leaders who violate the trust embodied in the *feagaiga* are dismissed and removed from the village. Pastors' families have been forced to perform public ceremonial apologies, *ifoga*, to the village when their pastor member has violated the norms of the *feagaiga* relationship (Macpherson and Macpherson 2005: 117–23). Matters involving clergymen, which might once have been overlooked or resolved within the village, now become the subject of criminal complaints. Police investigate and prosecute, and courts try to convict pastors for a variety of offences. These matters, and evidence from court cases, are covered in the media and quickly become the subject of public discussion. While these events relate to only a small number of individual pastors, each of the incidents chips away at the formerly unquestioned authority of the ministry.

The authority of both secular and religious elites is being progressively eroded. Both face an increasingly critical people, many of whom have lived abroad and have become accustomed to expressing dissent more openly. These people are less willing to accept 'tradition' as a justification for forms of social and political conduct that they find offensive. It is unsurprising that the current Prime Minister is on record as saying that these people and their political ideologies are a potentially destabilising force, and ruling out their widespread participation in national politics.[38]

But nevertheless, both secular and religious elites face an increasingly active civil society that has proven increasingly willing to challenge the notion that any one group of titled people should have the right to determine what is in the best interests of the nation. The emergence of both better funded and organised non-governmental organisations[39] and an increasingly assertive press has challenged both the churches and the government's judgements on a number of such issues. All of these things speak to growing divergence of opinion over whether there can, or should, be agreement on what is in 'Samoa's' interests, and over who is entitled to define these interests and by what right.

Our point is that for all of the above reasons the coalition of religious and secular elites, which once effectively managed the ways in which new ideologies were incorporated into Sāmoan culture, no longer enjoys the unqualified support or trust of the people. Their capacity and willingness to manage the ways in which ideas enter and are incorporated into Sāmoan society are compromised by the changes above. But these do not exhaust the challenges to the capacity of the elites to manage the content of contemporary Sāmoan culture.

External challenges to the elite

If the elites that once managed Sāmoan society face internal challenges to their authority, they also face external forces. New, powerful discourses that emanate from external sources, promoted by powerful agencies, are also swirling around Sāmoan society and may prove difficult to control or to resist. In Sāmoa, power was once concentrated in the hands of older titled males, and much government policy reflected and consolidated their influence in development policy. This was possible for as long as 'development' was measured in purely economic terms using blunt indices such as GDP growth. As development philosophy and policy shifts occurred in the late 1990s, more attention was paid to social equity as a philosophy and goal. International organisations created new indices aimed at producing more inclusive development.

Sāmoa has, through its membership in various international organisations, bound itself to support a number of conventions that promote values and ideas that are at variance with some 'traditional' beliefs. The most obvious of these is the discourse about the nature of fundamental human rights that is contained in the 1948 UN Universal Declaration of Human Rights to which Sāmoa is bound as a member of the United Nations. This declaration holds that humans are born with universal and inalienable rights that are a consequence of our humanity and are unconnected with age, gender or kinship. This ideology contradicts the Sāmoan ideology that rights of individuals are fundamentally defined and conditioned by age, gender and kinship. The acceptance of the principles of the charter is a condition of development assistance and access to the UN's technical and financial resources, and often calls for the adoption of policies and programmes that redistribute power that is traditionally controlled by elites. Similar pressures come from international financial institutions such as the World Bank and the Asian Development Bank that lend to Sāmoa, and from individual development partners, such as New Zealand and Australia, that have also embraced 'inclusive development' policies.

Active support, promotion and implementation of these rights are required by the organisations as conditions of the financial and technical assistance that the Sāmoan government requires to advance its economic and political agenda. These agencies routinely insist that proposals for general funding explain how programmes proposed by states will redistribute privilege and support activities that result in the creation of new opportunities for groups, such as women and youth, that have traditionally been disadvantaged. Agencies may also directly target programme assistance into these groups to achieve their redistributive objectives.

Increasingly, organisations and aid donors that provide loans and aid funds to Sāmoa are requiring hard evidence of a redistribution of opportunity to younger people and to women as a condition of continued funding of programmes. The UNDP Human Development Index provides a range of ways of identifying social goals and indices for measuring outcomes for UN agencies' activities. The World Bank's Millennium Development Goals has a similarly broad social agenda and clearly defined set of outcome measures for the bank's programmes that all now focus on producing a more equitable distribution of opportunity. These goals have also been increasingly adopted and incorporated into bilateral development assistance programmes. These organisations typically insert clear high-level goals, performance indices that must be measured regularly and benchmarks that must be met to ensure continued funding streams.

The dependence on government for funds from these sources effectively commits the government to undermine the source of the power traditionally held by older men. Thus, the government must acknowledge and promote a set of values and embody these in public policies to secure the funding to meet the rising aspirations of its citizens. Sāmoan governments have embraced these in successive Statements of Economic Strategy since the late 1990s and continue to move in this direction.[40] The extent of this shift can be seen in such documents as the *Joint Sāmoa Program Strategy 2006–2010* agreed on by the governments of Sāmoa, New Zealand and Australia, designating youth, women, rural dwellers, the disabled and the elderly as the most vulnerable groups in Sāmoan society and the targets of social development programmes.

In a more recent document, *Strategy for the Development of Samoa: 2008–2012. Ensuring Sustainable Economic and Social Progress,* the government goes further to define poverty in ways that target equality of opportunity and social inclusion:

> There is no official figure for the incidence of poverty in Samoa. However, participatory poverty assessments confirm that a significant number of

households experience hardship arising from 'poverty of opportunity' that is manifested in three ways: (i) a lack of access to basic services; (ii) a lack of adequate resources to meet basic household needs and customary obligations to the family, village community and church (these obligations absorbed 10% of household income in 2002); and (iii) a lack of opportunities to participate fully in the socioeconomic life of the community. (Ministry of Finance 2008: 4)

The document goes on to broaden the definition of those who fall into this category:

The groups identified as most vulnerable to hardship include landless individuals and families, the unemployed (especially unskilled youth who are found mainly in new settlements nearby to Apia such as Vaitele-fou), single income households, isolated rural households – although they may have more land to farm for subsistence – and families with many children. Elderly persons without family support and the disabled are also vulnerable. (Ministry of Finance 2008: 4)

In acknowledging that such issues exist and are produced by current social arrangements, and by committing itself to bring about change, the government in this document implicitly challenges the authority of groups on which it has traditionally depended for its support.

This process is further aided by the activities of non-governmental organisations and civil society organisations that secure funds, often from international agencies, and provide human and financial resources directly to those groups that have traditionally had difficulty in securing them. Thus, for instance, the YMCA and Women in Business have found ways of generating income for youth and women respectively and have, in the process, given these groups a greater degree of independence than they previously enjoyed. Women in Business with support from New Zealand aid has created a fine mat-weaving programme that provides training in skills that allow rural women to earn reliable regular incomes from weaving high quality fine mats or *'ie toga*. This project had greatly increased the income and independence of rural women who would otherwise be dependent on others for cash. NGOs also support local groups that are forming to articulate and claim rights for sections of the population such as the disabled, and to provide programmes to extend opportunities available to them.

As the global development philosophy has shifted, aid donors seeking to empower 'disadvantaged' groups within society have become increasingly interested in supporting cooperation between NGOs that is designed to make them more efficient, and to allow them to make better use of resources and increase the reach of supporting donors. In Sāmoa this has resulted in the formation of an umbrella group, SUNGO,[41] that, with funding from NZ Aid's NGO Capacity Building Fund, is able to provide training and support to SUNGO itself and its member organisations. Support from NZ Aid's NGO Fund also provides direct funding for NGOs working in key social development areas.

The flow of remittances is another, and highly significant, element in the equation. Remittances continue to make a solid contribution to the Sāmoan economy. In 2007–2008, remittances valued at $SAT292m represented 22.7 per cent of Sāmoa's GDP; of these, 69.7 per cent were sent to individuals (Central Bank of Sāmoa 2008: 14). As Shankman noted as early as 1974, migrants are free to send money to anyone they choose and have shown themselves increasingly willing to divert money from traditional channels and to place it in the hands of people who might not otherwise have access to resources (Shankman 1976: 83). The same points were made in major studies of remittances to Sāmoa and Tonga in the 1990s by Ahlburg 1991 and 1995; and Connell and Brown 1995. Some of those were undoubtedly directed to people who are free and willing to use them in novel ways that may indirectly and inadvertently undermine the power of traditional elites. Finally, the increasing availability of microcredit from a growing range of organisations[42] has provided funds for individuals and groups that lack acceptable collateral and cannot secure capital from commercial agencies. This has enabled them to start small enterprises in their own right that have the potential to exempt them from control of the traditional elites.

A brief look into the future

Under these circumstances, Sāmoan society is gradually becoming reshaped on the basis of redefined sets of interests and rights. A number of rights-based discourses formulated beyond Sāmoa are now being actively promoted within the country. The growth of the Sāmoan NGO sector and the range of rights and interests that NGOs are now defining and promoting are evidence of this broadening debate about rights.[43] The interests draw on new ideologies that, in some cases, stand opposed to those that support the traditional distribution of power. The growing influence of civil society groups, which stand ready to protect those rights against attempts by government to curtail them, and the presence of an active mass media, also ensure protection for advocacy of new ideologies. The Sāmoan government's willingness to enact and expand legislation, to publicise new goals and standards, and to set in place the means of investigating and prosecuting violations of these rights is also helping to redistribute, albeit gradually, the rights and power on which they rest.

A person may remain a member first of a family, and then of a village and then of a district, but they can increasingly see themselves as women, or young, or disabled or gay, and may see their interests as somewhat more conflicted than was the case previously. As people redefine their humanity and their interests, it is increasingly unlikely that any one view of what is 'good' and 'desirable' will be shared by all. New ideologies will be received in different ways by various sectors of the Sāmoan population, but it is doubtful whether any one elite will again be able to manage the reception and incorporation of these ideologies in the ways in which traditional elites have done. It is probable that the contours of debates about what is 'good for Sāmoa' will be far more vigorously contested, simply because more sources of information will be available to more people, and fewer people will be in a position to make uncontested assertions about what is 'good' and 'desirable' and how indeed what is 'good' and 'desirable' is to be determined.

Imported mats are now widely used in place of woven Sāmoan mats because they are reversible, patterned, more colourful, more durable and cheaper. This may lead to a loss of weaving skills.

Laminated beams make new designs possible but are shifted and lifted in the traditional way. As cranes become available the relationships that are developed during labour-intensive building projects may be undermined.

5.

Technology and social transformation

Sāmoan society has been shaped by technology since the Sāmoans' ancestors arrived in the archipelago 3000 years ago and began to explore novel uses for the flora and fauna they found there. The ancestors of contemporary Sāmoans developed new architectural and building technologies to construct larger, more elaborate and sophisticated houses to meet the requirements of an increasingly complex society (Hiroa 1930). They also refined the naval architecture and navigation techniques that made possible the later stages of the exploration and settlement of the eastern Pacific (Irwin 2006: 64). New technologies that were brought to Sāmoa by the growing numbers of European visitors increased the pace and social impact of transformation from the late eighteenth century.

This chapter explores the role of technology in the transformation of contemporary Sāmoa. It argues that Sāmoan society has embraced and incorporated significant new technology over the last 150 years, with apparently limited impacts on social relations within both family and village. The most recently introduced technologies, however, have the potential to transform society more quickly and completely than any technological innovations in the history of Sāmoa. Since our consideration of this question began after two mundane events involving some mats and a bucket, these will serve to introduce the issues.

Becoming aware of the issues of technology

The mat problem
The issue arose when we decided to replace floor mats in our house. We had

always used Samoan mats or *pāpā* (Hiroa 1930: 209–27). These mats were made from pandanus[1] that was grown and prepared locally for weaving by village women who then wove the mats at women's committee meetings. They are durable, light and can be rolled up into bundles that can be carried outside to air and quickly retrieved if a sudden shower should arrive. When they begin to fray, they can be used to dry cocoa or copra and for other tasks where appearance is unimportant. They are biodegradable and at the end of their useful life leave no environmental residue. Buying the mats locally returned money to the village women who made them, and provided cash for people with limited opportunities to earn income. The purchase also gave buyer and seller a chance to talk and reaffirmed social relationships.

So, when we needed new mats, we asked around to find out who was making the mats in the village. No one, it turned out, was still weaving them. Since the women who had made them were still in the village, and since pandanus was still growing around the village, we thought it was simply a matter of bringing the two together. But when we visited a weaver's house to order a set of mats, we discovered that the floors in her house were carpeted with vinyl floor coverings. The weaver no longer wove mats: not many people wanted them and, with increasing pressure on land in the village, it was getting more and more difficult to grow enough pandanus to maintain supply. We could, she suggested, try the market in Apia.

We tracked down some mats in the Apia market, alongside handicrafts sold mainly to tourists, but not in the quantities we needed. Apologetic sellers pointed out that tourists rarely bought more than one or two at a time, that Sāmoans did not buy them much any more and that those who needed them probably made their own. Some directed us to a larger store that they thought stocked the mats, and we ended up in an air-conditioned shop in the centre of town. The shop did not have them but, the slightly puzzled owner assured us, we could still get them in rural areas 'out the back' if we really wanted them. The clear implication of his ever so slightly patronising suggestion was that the mats are found only where people cannot afford anything else.

A neighbour, to whom we mentioned our difficulty, suggested we call in and look at the new mats he had just bought. In the house was a set of mats that, as the owner noted, were probably from China or maybe even India. His wife listed the advantages of their new mats. They are light, have straight, bound edges and fit together very neatly; they come in large sizes that can be used whole, or cut into two panels of different sizes or three panels of equal sizes; they come in a range of patterns and colour combinations; they are reversible so that you can let one side fade in daily use and keep a good side for visitors; they can be easily matched in larger areas; and are durable and waterproof. They are, the wife noted as an afterthought, lighter, more decorative and interesting than Sāmoan mats, and are approximately one quarter of the cost of the *pāpā*.

And so now the floors of our house are covered with a set of polypropylene mats made in China, sent by freight to New Zealand, purchased in Auckland and then shipped to Sāmoa. They are indeed durable, reversible and more colourful and can be arranged in different ways, but they are also made from byproducts of fossil fuel and have a huge carbon footprint. They are not biodegradable and burning them at the end of their useful life will release a variety of toxins into the atmosphere. They are also cheap, but buying the Chinese mats does nothing for the village economy; nor does it provide incomes for women in the village. Furthermore, buying these mats further limits the range of cooperative activities that once created bonds between village women who formed the weaving circles, *fale lalaga*, that made the Sāmoan mats.

The basket and the bucket

A second event, shortly afterwards, reminded us that this was not an isolated phenomenon. A boy who had helped us in the plantation asked if he could collect some papaya for his family who had limited land. We told him to take as much as he needed, and suggested he wove himself a couple of baskets, *'ato launiu*, from coconut fronds, and cut a carrying pole on which to carry the baskets. What we were suggesting was an age-old solution to his problem: a simple, highly effective basket woven from one half of one frond of a coconut palm (*Cocos nucifera*) that can be used to carry everything from large stones to *talo* to tools to cooked pigs (Hiroa 1930: 189–209). With a leaf 'liner', it can also be used to carry gravel and soil.

The raw material is readily available and the palm can be stripped of fronds without damage to the tree. A single frond will make two baskets that, even with heavy use, will last for at least a month. They can be woven in about 7 to 10 minutes by a skilled weaver in a range of sizes that can be chosen on the spot for a particular use. A basket can carry up to 25 kg, and its carrying capacity can be increased by a few manufacturing modifications including selecting a larger frond, increasing the amount of weaving in the bottom seam, and closing up the warp and weft. Two, four and occasionally six baskets can be carried, counter-balanced, on a single pole over the shoulder. They can be flattened for storage and take little space. When they start to wear, they can be discarded and are biodegradable.

The boy looked somewhat puzzled and explained that he did not know how to weave a basket. He asked if he could borrow the bucket, or better still, the wheelbarrow that he had seen while he was storing tools. What he was talking about was a 10-litre plastic pail that, when filled, had to be carried home for him because it was too heavy. The bucket is created from fossil fuels. It requires ongoing maintenance as UV rays lead to rapid degradation of the plastic and cause splits that have to be repaired, which involves, in this case, plastic sheathed copper wire. When the handle fails, as it invariably does, it too requires more copper wire to repair. The plastic bucket has a limited life and is not biodegradable, so when it is finally burned it releases a number of toxins into the atmosphere. It is imported and is a cost to the local economy and returns nothing to that economy.

When we mentioned to a friend that a village boy claimed not to know how to make a basket and seemed reluctant to use this cornerstone of Sāmoan technology, she was not at all surprised. She pointed out patiently that the bucket has a number of obvious advantages that had apparently escaped us. It could carry liquids, powders and fine gravel; it had a tight-fitting lid; it did not have to be made before it can be used; and several buckets could be slung on a carrying pole in the same way as baskets. A drive through the villages confirmed that while baskets are still 'used in the back', the bucket is gaining ground among farmers and their families just as polypropylene mats are. These incidents raised several questions about the impact of technology in general on family and village life.

'New' technologies

While imported mats and buckets drew our attention to the impact of technology, they are only among the most recent technologies to find their way into Sāmoan village society. Much more significant technologies have been incorporated and are now effectively invisible for reasons outlined in earlier chapters. New building technologies and materials, for instance, have been incorporated into Sāmoan village architecture and have transformed the built environment and appearance of the 'Sāmoan' village. European-style houses, *fale papālagi*, that were originally built in and around Apia by the wealthier part-Sāmoan commercial elite, are now being constructed in increasing numbers by many Sāmoans in their villages. A drive through rural Sāmoa shows how completely these new building styles have transformed the built environment of the village in the past 50 years. But Sāmoans do not think of these real, and obvious, technological transformations of their built environment as making the village somehow less 'Sāmoan'. Morgan Tuimaleali'ifano describes Falelatai as an ultra-conservative and traditional village despite obvious evidence of introduced building technologies and significant transformation of the built environment. But, as Tuimaleali'ifano notes, what makes the village 'traditional' and 'ultra-conservative' is not the built environment but the ways people interact within the built environment (Tuimaleai'ifano 2000: 173–4).[2]

The construction of these new houses has also changed the way of life of the village. The traditional Sāmoan house, *fale o'o*, and its associated cooking house, *umu kuka*, was an open structure that could be secured against the weather by a series of blinds that were dropped to exclude sun and rain. The only internal partitioning was provided by curtains that hung from strings and were used occasionally to provide privacy for visitors. The only storage was on racks in the void under the domed roof, in glory-boxes or food safes. Families' wealth and standing was evident solely in the size of the house and the height of its foundation, the dimensions of the glory-box, and the number and quality of sleeping mats and fine mats stored in the roof at any given time.

The houses could be built cheaply with local materials that were sourced and collected from the bush, the shore-line and around the village. For example, sinnet, or *'afa*, which was used for lashings, was woven from the husk of the coconut; the blinds, or *pola*, and the thatch used for the roof, *laupola*, were made from woven fronds of coconut palms; and the stones, *ma'a*, used for the foundation, were collected from plantations. Once the materials had been gathered, the house owners and their families prepared the materials for use and then worked as a team to construct the house. Throughout the construction process, a number of relationships were identified and activated to secure the materials and labour necessary. By the time the house was built, a series of outstanding social debts had been acknowledged and settled, and a new set of debts had been incurred and remained to be settled at some time in the future. The houses were simple and could be moved within, and even away from, the village as owners' circumstances changed.

By contrast, new permanent houses are built, often on a concrete slab or foundations, in permanent materials with external walls, windows and doors that can be locked so that they can be secured against both weather and intruders. Many contain internal partitioning and permanent rooms that can also be locked, and some now have lockable wardrobes, glory-boxes, food safes and refrigerators to secure the steadily increasing amounts of personal property that families are accumulating. Some also have lockable lean-to structures in which to store the more valuable tools that are being acquired. These homes cannot be built cheaply by owners: the building materials have to be purchased and specialists have to be engaged to build, at least, the basic structure. Nor can these houses be moved easily: many have fixed septic tanks and are almost impossible to shift, which reduces some of the flexibility that existed earlier. *Āiga* can no longer re-position houses within their area of the village as their populations increase and their circumstances change.

The privacy afforded by these 'European' houses makes it possible for people to live and interact in different ways in both their houses and in the village, although, as people note, there are as many eyes and ears around as there always were, and sometimes more because of growing population density in many villages. The new houses are often closer together, and even walls and doors will not contain families' secrets. One secret that people do not seek to conceal is the owner's wealth, which is on display in everything from the size and design of the house, to the amount and style of furniture, and the number and age of the appliances that line the walls of kitchens and living rooms. But this display, in turn, highlights growing material inequalities within the village and leads more families to seek to secure their property against theft and borrowing with lockable doors, security screens and windows. While security screens may be explained as keeping out mosquitoes to avoid the implicit suggestion that there may be thieves in the village, they actually signal the fact that a house contains much valuable property that needs to be kept safe.

Confronted with such apparent contradictions, Sāmoans often say that ways of doing things change but the foundations that underpin them remain intact, *e fesuia'i faiga ae tūmau fa'avae*.[3] This reflects the view of the famed anthropologist of the Pacific, Te Rangi Hiroa, Sir Peter Buck, who in 1930 wrote:

> The pleasure derived from the exercise of native institutions is
> perhaps the most important factor that has led to the persistence of
> Samoan customs and helped them to resist the disintegration that has
> taken place in other parts of Polynesia. The Samoans are thus more
> conservative than other branches of their race and their satisfaction with
> themselves and their own institutions makes them less inclined to accept
> the changes that foreign governments consider would be of benefit to
> them. (Hiroa 1930: 5)

Technological innovation has clearly occurred in the village, with apparently minimal social impact, as the example above illustrates. Our contention is that, even where incremental change is incorporated so that it is effectively 'invisible', it is still change; and the fact that its impact on the social fabric of the village is not routinely discussed does not mean that it is not real. Can technologies and their impacts be incorporated without changing the foundations of the worldview and lifestyle that constitute the culture of the village? And can they be incorporated in the same way as earlier ones: incrementally and invisibly?

These questions raise two related issues. Firstly, does the current climate of technological adoption differ from earlier technological incursions and acceptance and, if so, how? The next section examines a set of factors that influence the current availability and uptake of new technologies. It argues that a combination of social factors and government policies has led to the removal of obstacles to the introduction of new technologies and makes the current climate significantly different from that which existed earlier. Secondly, how and why might the impacts of new innovations differ from those of earlier ones? Later in the chapter, we examine the ways some technologies that are now taken for granted, such as the reticulation of water, have transformed the social fabric of the village. We then consider the observed and potential impacts of some of the latest technologies on family and village life, and argue that these will produce greater impacts on social relations than earlier ones.

Influences on the uptake of new technologies

Image: social status and innovation

We believe the uptake of new technologies is more than a matter of practicality. The woman in the Apia handicraft shop, who told us that the mats were still made and available 'out the back', was talking about rural Sāmoa. But her reply was not simply about the availability of the mats: it was about 'image'. Why, she implied, did we want Sāmoan mats when we could buy imported mats that better reflected our 'status'?[4] Her comment also reflected an urban Sāmoan stereotype of rural Sāmoa and rural Sāmoans.

Thirty years ago many 'new' technologies were available only in Sāmoa's urban area. This was partly because the political and commercial elites resided in Apia; most of the salaried civil service and business community worked in Apia; urban incomes were higher than rural ones; and the country's leading schools,[5] secular tertiary training institutions[6] and 'cultural' organisations were concentrated in Apia. Electricity, piped water, telephone lines, tar-sealed roads and department stores were more readily available and radio reception was better in Apia than in rural districts. The hinterland was actually rendered more remote because roads were poor, public transport services to rural areas were basic and physical infrastructure was limited, although a few powerful politicians from rural areas were able to secure some of these services in their constituencies. The lifestyles of the urban *papālagi* and part-Sāmoan elites differed from those of people in rural villages (Hirsch 1958). Some children from Savai'i, who went on a school trip to Apia in 1965, wrote essays about their visit that reflected, with some awe, on the fact that the families with whom they were billeted had such things as cement floors, beds, indoor kitchens, glass windows, lockable doors, telephones, radios, steel buckets, tape recorders, ice-boxes, refrigerators and even fences around their houses.

This 'uneven development', which is common throughout the Pacific, was a consequence of financial and political decisions taken by aid donors and governments and not lack of interest on the part of rural people. The development model was produced by financial cost-benefit analyses that favoured early provision of services to areas with highest population densities and resulted in the relative deprivation of the rural villages. Since those who made the decisions typically lived in urban areas, this development rationale, known as 'modernisation theory', had an obvious personal appeal. These facts lay behind a perception, which persists today, that the residents of rural areas are somehow less 'sophisticated', and are unable to appreciate or take advantage of these technologies. This is a little ironic since many of those who took, and still take, this position have themselves grown up in villages.

Now the gap between rural and urban lifestyles is shrinking as rural Sāmoans embrace new technologies. The demand for, and rapid uptake of, new technologies reflects a determination in rural areas both to take advantage of practical benefits of new technologies and to close the 'prestige gap'. The enthusiastic uptake reflects the ways in which social image shapes responses to technologies. It reflects a reluctance on the part of rural people to be seen as less sophisticated than their urban cousins. But it also reflects changes in development philosophy and policy, and specifically the

Millennium Development Goals programme that seeks to raise the quality of life of national populations and to eliminate rural–urban differentials. The current government and its development partners are committed to reducing town–village disparities by delivering better roads, water, electricity, health and education to villages beyond Apia.[7]

Rising incomes and uptake
The rapid uptake of new technologies also reflects income growth in Sāmoa over the last decade. Structural adjustment programmes, initiated in Sāmoa in the early 1990s, produced a period of sustained growth in both GDP and wages. Government employees have enjoyed significant increases in salaries, and this has been accompanied by parallel increases in private sector incomes. Both of these trends have resulted in the expansion of private credit and of the credit provision sector in Sāmoa. The uptake in rural areas also reflects growing incomes from commercial agriculture, commercial fishing, new forms of tourism such as beach *fale*[8] and, most significantly, the increased value of remittances. The expansion of the boundaries of villages, described in chapter 3, has effectively removed the earlier link between villages' factor endowments and the lifestyles of the villagers. The uptake is driven in part by competition within families and villages that leads families to adopt innovation for reasons that are as much to do with social status as they are to do with efficiency.

Migrant visits and uptake
Many gifts of technology are from expatriate rural villagers[9] who understand well how new technologies can transform the lives of their kin in the village. These gifts are often made during, or shortly after, visits when personal experiences remind visiting migrants how physically hard daily life can be in the village.

A visitor who collected ripe coconuts, *popo*, and carried them on a pole, *amo*, over his shoulder during a two-week stay went out and bought his family a steel wheelbarrow. Another visiting villager, who chopped wood for the family *umu* for a week and then carried it back to the village, returned to New Zealand and promptly sent his brother a chainsaw, two chains, two files and a petrol can. A young woman, concerned about the amount of food that was wasted because it could not be refrigerated, bought her family a refrigerator and a chilly bin. Another man worried about his elderly mother and aunty cooking outside in all weather in the *umu kuka* bought them a gas oven, cook top and gas bottle. These are, individually, small items but their combined impact can over time make significant differences to the lifestyle of their recipients. A two-stroke lawn mower that saved two hours of lawn-mowing time allowed its owner to spend two more hours fishing that, as he noted, was a lot more useful and interesting than cutting the grass with a bush-knife!

Rising awareness and uptake

The dispersal of the emigrant population and residents' regular overseas excursions have raised awareness of available technologies that has, in turn, increased demand for them in the village and has raised economic productivity. Fishermen, for instance, who have been abroad, have started to use compact, handheld GPS systems to fix the positions of productive fishing spots to which they can return quickly and reliably. As the fishermen note, the spots can be found by other means but it is faster, easier and less expensive to find and hold them with GPS. Long-line fishing has been transformed with the adoption of new quick-fix traces and hooks that make baiting more straightforward and fishing easier and quicker. Chainsaws were once regarded as a major advance over the axe, but now chainsaw mills, spotted at the New Zealand Farm Field Days by a village woman married to a New Zealand farmer, that can cut planks suitable for sale are now considered more valuable in the village. Similarly with agricultural spraying technology: at one time farmers were delighted to have hand-pumped backpack sprayers, but increasing awareness of the benefits of petrol-powered misting sprayers has now made these the benchmark for the aspiring farmer. The continuing dispersal of the Sāmoan population will increase the uptake of such technology by extending awareness of its uses and availability and by shortening the period between its becoming available and its adoption in the village.

A factor that may soon extend the availability of technologies is the growth of the service industry. This small but growing sector provides access to technologies to those with cash but not necessarily the equipment or the time to do the jobs themselves: urban wage-earners without, for instance, petrol-powered brush-cutters can and do hire others to cut grass on their property. Another significant new development that a couple is planning is the creation of an equipment hire business that would make technologies available to more people at a lower cost. Such businesses are likely to succeed because, as the would-be operators noted, everybody at some point needs wheelbarrows, concrete mixers, cement floats, scaffolding and ladders because 'building is going that way', and few except professionals are in a position to buy these items when their use of them is likely to be only occasional.

Government policy and uptake
For many years government pursued economic policies such as the imposition of high import tariffs that were designed to limit imports to preserve the country's hard currency reserves. The Sāmoan government, with encouragement from international financial agencies, has since formed the belief that an open economy may create productivity gains that can be taxed, thus producing more revenue for government than import licensing and taxes. Since the early 1990s, the government has, as part of a structural adjustment programme, reduced import duties on a range of goods that has eliminated the major impediments to technology transfer.

As part of this 'opening of the economy', the Sāmoan government has also removed constraints on the operation of local businesses, and new entrepreneurs have loosened the earlier grip of the commercial elite on commerce. Australian-based trading companies Burns Philp and Morris Hedstrom once stocked a small range of expensive homeware and appliances that were purchased mainly by expatriates and the part-Sāmoan elite. Now, as Chan Mow and Frankie's respectively, they stock a larger range of cheaper products sourced from China and India and aimed at the increasingly affluent Sāmoan market.[10] Some locally grown companies, such as Ah Liki, have become among the largest, most diverse and profitable companies in Sāmoa. These new entrepreneurs are sourcing up-to-the-minute technologies at lower prices from non-traditional markets including China and Korea.

As a consequence, new technologies are now available more cheaply than comparable products from traditional sources such as New Zealand and Australia. One neighbour, reflecting on the consequences of this transformation in retailing, recalled times when she –

> . . . had to go to Auckland to buy those sorts of things, and then you had to find someone in the customs department who you could 'tip' to get them through customs. It was so hard to get those things unless you lived in Apia and had friends in government who could sort these formalities out for you. Now you can tell the children overseas what you need and they can just send it. . . .

Policy shifts have produced price reductions that have brought a wider range of imports within reach of more people.

The government has done more than remove constraints: it has been an active agent in accelerating technological change. The government's Agriculture Store, which was once a division of a government department that sold only a limited range of hand tools and chemicals at subsidised prices, is now run as an unsubsidised commercial enterprise, the Agriculture Stores Corporation. It stocks and markets a much wider range of tools and products, and competes actively with other businesses to provide new technologies to Sāmoa's increasingly commercially oriented farmers.

More recently, the Sāmoan government determined that settlement and exploitation of underused land in the interior would occur if rates of private vehicle ownership increased and more people were able to access this land and travel easily to markets in town. The major obstacles to this vision were the limited availability, high price and poor quality of many used vehicles in Sāmoa, resulting from the fact that they could be sourced only from the US or American Sāmoa. In addition, these cars tended to be near the end of their lives and had to be paid for in American dollars. To raise levels of vehicle ownership, the government decided to encourage migrants to send cars and trucks to their families, and passed legislation requiring right-hand drive cars to be driven on the left-hand side of the road from September 2009, and then reduced import duties on these vehicles. This policy is designed to encourage migrants, living in countries where later model, right-hand drive, Japanese imports are readily available at lower prices and in better condition, to buy used vehicles to send to their families in Sāmoa.[11] It also ensures that migrant resources are harnessed for Sāmoa's economic growth.

Shipping services and uptake
The uptake of new technologies reflects the growing ease with which migrants can send new technology to Sāmoa. The increased availability of shipping, airfreight and courier services in expatriate population centres has made it easy to send all sorts of technology quickly and simply. At least ten sea and air freight and importing companies are now offering services to and from Sāmoa from the US, Japan, Australia and New Zealand. Courier services are also now being offered by some multinational courier companies. Sāmoan-owned freight forwarding companies can now deliver and uplift shipping crates, in a range of convenient sizes, from your home for shipping to Sāmoa. Company officials can assist exporters to fill in the required forms, thus eliminating for some the drama involved in completing documentation in English. Increasing competition for business in the sector has reduced the cost of getting freight to Sāmoa. These services have removed another impediment to the introduction of new technologies.

Social impacts of new technologies

The above factors explain why new technologies are becoming increasingly available in the village, but do not tell us how they are transforming the character of interaction in the village. To do this, we take five main technologies and show how each has, in different ways, re-shaped, or is re-shaping, elements of village life. Some of these, such as water reticulation, have already had a major impact on the lifestyle and social fabric of the village. Others, such as telecommunications, while already having made an impact, are likely to make an even greater one in the future. In addition, the growth of certain service industries is described, as an illustration of the expansion through the economy of the availability of technologies.

Water reticulation

The provision of reticulated water has altered the way people relate to one another within both villages and families. Before the arrival of piped water in the village, people went to a spring at the edge of the sea. These springs were exposed for one and a half hours before and after low tide, during which fresh water, filtered through sand, flowed from an aquifer into a series of linked pools dug in sand at the foreshore. The water in the upper pool was drawn for drinking. Water then flowed into a second larger pair of pools in which males and females bathed separately. Next, water flowed into a third pool in which clothes were washed. In some cases, these pools were developed into large and elaborate complexes, and became a symbol of the village's wealth and capacity to cooperate. The tide dominated the daily routine because it determined when families had to make their daily trips to the spring for water. Considerable attention was paid to the quality of the water and the communal activity that affected water quality. An eel resided in this particular pond and its health served as an indication of water quality. Considerable communal effort was invested in the maintenance of spring and pool systems. Representatives of various village committees managed conduct in these areas.

But the spring was more than a source of water: it was a source of information. Some very significant social interaction occurred around this pool in the three hours during which it was exposed. Information and gossip, which play an important role in governance and social control, were exchanged relatively efficiently during visits to the spring. In villages with only one spring, most of the population shared the pools and the information in the course of a single day. In the process, people also came to understand the finer points of social etiquette and the importance of considering the relationships of those present before sharing certain information. Children who accompanied their parents to these springs learned not only technical skills but also a range of valued social ones. In the conversations that occurred around these springs, relationships were reviewed and renewed, and key social values and norms reaffirmed.

When the water pipeline arrived in the village, a small number of standpipes were erected close to the main line throughout the village so that all families had access to piped water. This arrangement effectively divided the village as families went to the pipes closest to them and, because of the ways related households are clustered together within the village, ended up sharing these with kin. While the need to go to these standpipes to collect water for domestic use continued to bring people together, the new technology meant that representatives of all the village families no longer came together in any one place during the course of a day. The need to consider the social context of discussions and to understand the sensitivities of others was no longer necessitated by the simple task of accessing water.

This was further exacerbated when these pipes were extended so that many households had their own standpipe. More recently, the extension of water lines into houses has increased the fragmentation of village life and restricted the number of occasions on which individuals need to come together on a daily basis in the village. Furthermore, because indoor bathrooms have become a marker of wealth, they are now the standard to which people aspire, and this alone will almost certainly contribute to the further privatisation of more of village life.

The social impact of water reticulation has probably been exhausted. Indeed, its social impact is largely invisible to many people who have grown up since the spring was last in use. For them, piped water to the home is the only technology they have known. Its significance is now restricted to its new value as an indicator of relative wealth within the village. When the first household in the village mounted a highly visible solar water-heater on its roof, the discussion that followed was about its cost and the wealth of its owners.

Electrification
On the other hand, technologies such as electrification have ongoing social impacts. Electrification has altered and is altering the ways people relate

to one another, and provides power for technologies such as refrigeration, which changes life in the village, and television, which offers vicarious access to a world beyond the village. Before electricity, evenings were a time in which families gathered, said prayers and discussed the day's events by the light of benzene-powered lamps, *molī penesini*, or hurricane lamps, *molī matagi*.[12] People played cards and draughts and recounted cautionary tales, all of which confirmed the correctness of key social values and practices. A few families with battery-powered radios listened to the news from the government radio station and the evening farmers' programme. Children pretending to sleep in the shadows just beyond these discussions learned about everything from the consequences of adultery to the need to maintain even distant social relationships.

Some villages embraced the benefits of electrification early. Once its advantages were appreciated, groups of rural villages invested in small, cooperative diesel generation schemes funded by levies on users from the early 1960s to ensure that each home in the village had a single light bulb (Tuimaleaiʻifano 2000: 176). While the early impact of electrification was minimal because both power supply and the hours of operation were limited, electrification eventually extended the day in rural areas, making a range of 'acceptable' new evening activities possible. However, earlier usage was controlled by village committees who wielded their status as suppliers to ensure that 'appropriate use' was made of the technology. In 1965 in Palauli, Savaiʻi, a village *fono* that supplied power from a community-owned generator determined that some families were making 'inappropriate' use of the power and their light bulbs were confiscated. It was not so much the loss of light that hurt the families involved but the fact that the punishment was made so public: afterwards, they lived in lamp light while their neighbours enjoyed electric light.

In the 1990s, a government village electrification programme resulted in connection of 90 per cent of villages to the national grid; by 2000, 94 per cent of Sāmoans had access to reliable electricity. Since then, the system has been progressively extended and improved. Now access to and use of power are effectively limited only by a family's ability to pay. The ready availability of electricity has had a range of impacts on social organisation.

As government supply reached more villages and three-pin power plugs became more widely available, a whole range of new appliances started to find their way into family homes. Now, builders tell us, the owners of new houses are installing as many electrical power points as are found in homes in New Zealand. Throughout the village, the digital displays of microwave ovens, DVD players, large stereos, wide-screen television sets and computer screens glow eerily into the evening, signalling the wealth of the family inside and the generosity of their migrant kin, as well as the increasingly privatised lifestyles of families.

But some of the downstream technologies that have followed the introduction of electricity have had more significant effects on the social and economic life in the village. People now take many of these for granted: most have probably long since forgotten the ways in which they impacted on their own lives. When we were writing this book, we had to talk to others to reconstruct this earlier time, even though it was part of our own experience.

Refrigeration
A significant technology made possible by electrification is refrigeration, which has altered the ways in which people relate to one another. Before refrigeration, when a family received a large gift of meat or fish for a wedding, funeral or church opening, it could not be safely stored without cooking for more than a few hours. As a consequence, much food was divided up and redistributed among households within the village. Clear rules determined who received which cuts when pigs, fowl, turtles, bonito, shark and eel were divided (Hiroa 1930: 119–27). Not all distributions were so formal. When families caught, or were given, large numbers of fish, they would also redistribute these within their village networks. In some cases the formal rules were followed, in others distribution simply reflected personal relationships and alliances.

The food distributions acknowledged, and reaffirmed, social hierarchy. The first recipients of distributions were the chiefs or *matai* of the family, and these gifts confirmed donors' respect for, and obligations to, the *matai*. Another early recipient of distributions was the village pastor and these gifts acknowledged donors' respect for the pastor and the church. The remainder was distributed among kin and friends in ways that reflected relationships within individuals' personal networks. The redistributions were effectively 'public' and were closely watched: changes in the amount given to someone or, more significantly, the omission of a gift to a person who might have been expected to receive one, soon became matters of public discussion. People routinely hailed children carrying food, ostensibly to ask them where they were going but really to find out what they were taking and to whom.

Thus, redistributions reaffirmed, and occasionally redefined, the significance of relationships between kin and between friends. The distribution of goods outlined the boundaries of personal networks. The volumes and types of the gifts, and the order in which these were dispatched, signalled the importance of particular relationships within these networks. Changes in the amounts, or order, of distributions, or the omission of certain people, signalled shifts in the patterns of relationships and soon also became a matter of public discussion and speculation.

These redistributions were also a form of 'social insurance'. The effect of the redistribution was to settle old 'social debts' and to create new ones. The residual level of indebtedness between households was the 'social glue' of families and of the village. Distributions reaffirmed the importance of relationships between donors and recipients and ensured that this was known to all. Intra-family distributions bound households to the family and inter-family distributions bound families to one another within the village. The more widespread these networks of reciprocal obligation, the more cohesive families and villages tended to be and the better able they were to respond to crises.

The arrival of refrigeration in the village had an interesting effect on the pattern of production, distribution and redistribution of perishable commodities and on the clusters of relationships built on these distributions. Refrigerators freed some from the need to distribute food within social networks. Families with refrigerators could store incoming fresh food and were no longer compelled to redistribute it. The impact was limited initially because refrigerators were relatively small and inefficient and could freeze only a few items. Refrigeration did, however, extend the range of options to people and allowed them to send signals to those around them.

Not all who had refrigerators chose to suspend redistribution and effectively withdraw from the familiar exchange networks. Some sent token amounts of food to those around them to affirm these relationships symbolically, while retaining the bulk of the food for their household. Others used this option to draw attention to their generosity: the full gift made where people had the means and freedom to retain it for their own use reflected well on the generosity of the giver. Refrigerators also allowed some people to demonstrate their generosity by storing food for others and created new forms of social prestige and indebtedness. In addition, refrigerators allowed people in the village to extend their menus to include food items such as ice cream and cake, and to signal their wealth and their appreciation of foods that were once available only to urban elites.

Refrigeration has altered, and will continue to alter, the character of village life as more families gain access to larger and larger refrigerators and freezers.[13] As refrigeration becomes more widespread, it may well become the norm as a way to store food and in the process contribute further to the privatisation and individualisation of another area of Sāmoan social life. Even if families with refrigerators choose to maintain 'symbolic' distributions within their networks, in economic terms it would represent a significant departure from the economic redistribution that occurred routinely before the arrival of the refrigerator.

Radio

Electricity has provided access to media that have brought the world into the village, inevitably altering the ways people see both themselves and the village. Once, not so long ago, the excitement of radio was such that people listened spellbound to the government radio station, Radio 2AP, broadcasting church services, choral presentations, speeches made by nationally acclaimed orators, parliamentary sessions, advice to farmers and lists of recipients of money order telegrams. People listened for the names of relations and neighbours in the village who were about to receive money and resolved to pay them a visit the following day: not so soon that the connection between the telegram and their visit was too obvious, but not so late that the money had been spent or distributed by the time they arrived!

The proliferation of radio stations has increased the range of programming and made people more critical of what is broadcast. Throughout the day and night, people listen to radios: music, local news, talkback, the radio 'market', produce and fish market reports, church services, health education programmes, news broadcasts from affiliated radio stations in New Zealand and the US, and the ever popular Sāmoan parliament when it is in session. More, and more powerful, radio/stereos are left behind each year by departing migrants, and the volume of radios playing almost continuously seems to increase every year. It is now hard to walk through the village without being aware of the growing reach of radio and its impact on life in the village.

As the population density in the village increases, people live closer to one another and become more aware of the sound of radios. They complain that, while radios are convenient, they are too loud and disturb the silence of the village:

> Now, you know, people play their radios all day and all night. I think they must even play them while they are asleep. Some people play them during the time when people should be saying their prayers. I think those villages where the *fono* took stock of the situation and banned radios at certain times of day had the right idea. I'm not sure if our village *fono* could do that, but I wish it would.

Faced with greater choice in broadcasting, people have begun to select particular stations and to identify with particular forms of programming. In this segmentation of the audience, it is possible to see the beginning of a generation gap. Radio programming is a site where fundamental generational differences in taste are becoming apparent, with the young complaining that their parents, 'only listen to those religious stations which play hymns and Christian songs all day. With our grandmother being so deaf, the radio has to be played at full volume so she can conduct and sing along with the choirs. It's the same every day. We never get a chance to listen to our music.'

At the same time, parents complain about their children's taste in radio:

> You know they want to listen to all that black American music. I don't like it because it's all about gangs and it uses very bad language which people should not use on radio, or even in public for that matter. A lot of our young people who live overseas have got into trouble because of those gangs. I don't know why they want to listen to that music: it's not really music, it's just like talking loudly; the beat is always the same and they play it so loud. It's not part of our way of life.

Television

If radio provided the earliest links to the world beyond the village, these have been extended by the arrival of television. Some 40 years ago, only those with money could watch images of life in the world beyond the village. Some saw these in the picture theatres in Apia. Others saw them in the copra sheds of various trading companies in which they were screened by mobile projectors. In the villages especially, only films deemed suitable by the *fono* were shown, leading to incidents in which a *matai* who disapproved of particular content could stand up and direct the operator to stop the screening, much to the disappointment of the assembled audience.[14] Only 30 years ago, television programming came from Pagopago in American Sāmoa and comprised largely low quality material from a San Francisco television channel that included beauty contests, professional wrestling matches, sports quizzes, drag-racing competitions and cartoons, all of which were re-broadcast complete with advertisements for products for which bemused Sāmoan audiences could not imagine a use.

Since then, the Sāmoan government has become a television broadcaster and has, in turn, issued television broadcasting licenses to private entities. The proliferation of stations has resulted in expanded coverage, generating similar sorts of tensions between men and women and parents and children whose tastes are increasingly influenced by global trends. These issues surface in debates in households about who will decide who gets to watch what. Young people who are keen to extend their English comprehension and fluency are often more interested in English-language programming and music than parents and grandparents who prefer programmes in Sāmoan. Since older people generally make the final decisions, Sāmoan-language programming is favoured, for the meantime at least.

But setting aside the inter-generational differences in experience and taste that are revealed by these new media, the village is now much more connected with and exposed to the world beyond its boundaries. At one level, the screening of the weekly, 30-minute long, New Zealand magazine programme *Tangata Pasifika* shows village Sāmoa what their relatives are doing in New Zealand and airs debates about public issues that are sometimes a little way ahead of what is being shown in Sāmoa. At another level, the arrival of a Chinese English-language channel, CCTV, has increased the range and improved the quality of alternative programming and has brought a new tone to the debate. Several overseas religious organisations have also entered television broadcasting, further extending this exposure.

The DVD player
The government can control what is broadcast and retains effective control of what Sāmoans see of the world on television. The arrival of the inexpensive DVD player now provides an alternative form of entertainment and makes it possible to subvert Sāmoan government film censorship and its ability to determine what the Sāmoan population watches. When government was urged to prevent the public screening of the film *The Da Vinci Code*, on the grounds that it contained claims that contradict Catholic teachings and was disrespectful to the Roman Catholic Church, a copy of the DVD brought from New Zealand was soon circulating in the village. But not all DVDs that enter the country have a subversive effect. Many are records of family baptisms, weddings, university graduations and title-conferring ceremonies, in which Sāmoan 'tradition' is front and centre. The DVD player simply extends viewers' choices: people with players are no longer confined to what is shown on television or in the theatres. Viewer

choice is now limited only by what is in the DVD hire shop or what overseas relations can be persuaded to send or bring with them.

This expanding choice again throws up differences in what succeeding generations believe can and should be screened. Parents are happy to hire some wholesome Bollywood love stories complete with appropriate modesty and music, while their children may be more interested in an edgier film. Parents complain that their children want to watch Hollywood films in which people behave in frankly unbelievable ways: men swear in the presence of their sisters; women wear indecent clothes in front of their brothers; children assault their parents. These acts have no place in Sāmoan society. Parents reason that if children see these sorts of things, they may start to believe this conduct is acceptable and begin to behave in the same ways as 'those *papālagi*' people in the films. Children, on the other hand, are beginning to complain that their parents want to watch Bollywood films in which people act in frankly unbelievable ways: everything is always good, children always do what their parents ask them to do and love triumphs.

But the impact of the increased exposure is likely to have differential effects within the village.[15] While more people in the village now speak English, and more 'foreign' content is understood by more people, this is unevenly distributed. Younger people, whose English is frequently better, have a clearer understanding of what is happening in the global village. Their conversations cover a wider range of topics, and canvass ideas and possibilities that older people are reluctant to discuss. While younger people seem more willing to consider alternative worldviews and explanations, many older people who find programmes straying beyond their comfort zone simply turn off the television or DVD player and leave the global village. While they may be able to control what their households listen to and watch, and may be able to limit the influence of the global village for the meantime and in certain contexts, they cannot exclude it in others over which they have no control.

Telecommunications

Power has made available new telecommunications technologies that have increased the ease and reduced the cost of connecting with the world and have altered the ways in which people relate to one another in daily life. But there is an emerging digital divide in Sāmoa that separates those who have access to and can use these technologies, thereby gaining access to a world beyond the village; and those who cannot. At one time, those who had access to landline telephones had a significant advantage over those who did not. They could, technically at least, reach the world beyond the village, have private conversations, and seek advice and financial support.[16] But many of the lines were assigned to government offices and businesses and were not widely available to people beyond the Apia elite. Even in 1970 those without landlines who wished to call relatives overseas had to go to the central post office, pre-pay their call and then wait in long queues while operators attempted to connect overseas parties. The high cost and inconvenience of this meant that few people conducted other than urgent family business by telephone. In 1997 connection rates were around 4.93 lines per 100 population, and in 2005 the number of subscribers more than doubled to 10.89 lines per 100 population, but the relatively high connection costs and ongoing charges mean that landline telephones have not become a major feature of village life.

The really significant growth in reach and impact of telecommunications has occurred with the introduction of mobile telephone technology. It has resulted in an increase of teledensity from 6 per cent of the population in 2002 to 58 per cent in mid-2008 (Malielegaoi 2008: 67). From its introduction in 1997, subscription rates grew slowly from 0.45 subscribers per 100 people, to 8.99 per 100 in 2004, to 13.41 per 100 in 2005, to 23.59 subscribers per 100 people in 2006.[17] This translates into an increase from 12,500 subscribers in 2002 to 101,400 at the end of 2007 (Malielegaoi 2008: 67–68). Such exponential growth and falling real costs have been fuelled by government-promoted competition in the cellphone sector that has seen competing companies deliver ever cheaper call costs that continue to expand the reach of the villager.[18] The cheap and ubiquitous pre-pay cellphone, with its inexpensive SMS texting capacity and widely available small denomination phone cards, has reshaped communication among the young.

Their personal social networks are larger and more diverse than their parents might suspect. Cellphones allow them to form relationships and then to 'meet' and 'hang around' with people of whom their parents might not approve. They can express themselves more frankly and intimately in the world of text than they could in face-to-face encounters where sociolinguistic conventions prevail and limit what can be said. They can also conduct affairs of the heart more privately than was formerly possible where young women were under continuous surveillance by their families and siblings.[19] Furthermore, they can form and maintain these relations discreetly while apparently under the protection of the family and village.

The cellphone also connects young people in the village with the worlds of cousins and friends living beyond Sāmoa: in Los Angeles, Auckland and Sydney. It allows them to become part of a global 'virtual community' and to participate in activities and debates that are not occurring around them in the village. From the contents of 'inboxes' and 'outboxes' of young people's cellphones, it is clear that even young people in apparently remote villages can engage with a world of gangs that stretches from Los Angeles to Sydney. Cellphones also allow them to share, and seek support for, aspirations and ideas that may be unpopular in the village with people beyond the village who may be more sympathetic. Cellphones enable young people to express disappointment and anger over people and events in the village in terms, and with a force, that would be unacceptable in the village. The ability to find support for ideas that are unacceptable in the village may, in the process, hasten inter-generational differentiation and tension.

The digital divide may be limiting Sāmoan parents' and grandparents' abilities to be part of, and to influence, what happens in these spheres of their children's lives. Like parents everywhere, they often have little control over their children's social world. They complain that their children seem to be texting all the time and wonder what they are doing. At the same time, children are silently amused at their parents whom they say carry cellphones to send messages about their 'connectedness' but who do not know how to use the texting function or to listen to voice messages. For the meantime at least, children are free to engage with this 'other virtual community' without fear of interference.

TECHNOLOGY AND SOCIAL TRANSFORMATION

Computers and the internet
The availability of computers, and more particularly the internet, is increasing the digital divide, albeit with slightly different contours. Internet use statistics have shown significant increases. In 1997 there were only 0.17 users per 100 population, but this number grew by 2620 per cent over ten years to 4.46 users per 100 population in 2006.[20] This is, in part, a consequence of the growth in the number of private computers that have access to inexpensive dialup and, since 2008, more expensive wireless broadband; and access through a growing number of internet cafés and in tertiary training facilities. In 2009, Sāmoa had 11,307 hosts, 8000 users and a price basket cost of $NZ20.67 per month, derived from dialup plans of around $NZ11.50 per month through to wireless broadband contract prices of around $NZ75 per month.

A visit to any internet café reveals that the digital divide also presently lies along generational lines. Aside from visitors, the major users of the internet are school pupils and young adults who use internet cafés for around $NZ3 per hour to explore the world beyond the village for school projects and for social networking. Many adults who fund their children's internet use readily admit that they have do not know exactly what their children do on the internet, except that it has to do with 'school work' and that it is possible to communicate quickly with relatives who have computers using '*le i-meli*'. The introduction of Skype and the growth of social networking sites have further reduced the cost and extended the reach of the digitally attuned young people of Sāmoa.

But the digital divide also lies along the rural–urban divide. With the growth in usage comes the increasing number of public internet cafés and, most recently, activation of wireless broadband and of a high speed, wireless internet service around the Apia urban area. This, however, is a temporary divide. The government and its development partners are seeking to extend the internet access usage into rural areas to reduce the digital divide that was developing between urban and rural populations. Before wireless technology became available, this depended on the speed at which expensive landline-based networks could be extended. The pace at which this can occur has increased dramatically. This programme may eventually reduce the rural–urban digital divide but it is unlikely to eliminate the generational one. If the use of the cellphone is any indication, it may indeed extend it. The full social impact of this technology has yet to be felt in Sāmoa, but will occur sooner rather than later. Government and development partners are also looking to increase the amount of IT training available in schools that will extend the reach of those who enter school from now on and may further increase the digital divide by favouring those who remain in school longer.

It may also allow more Sāmoan young people to enter the increasingly active chat-room scene that is developing in the virtual world. There, the content, norms and forms of expression are not constrained, to anywhere near the same extent, by a concern for the reputation of one's *āiga*, or a sense of respect for the formal etiquette of communication. The anonymity of the internet chat-rooms allows participants to express their disappointments or frustrations frankly without the prospect of their feelings getting back to the world in which they live where they might be found unacceptable.

Building technologies

Not all of the technologies that are changing Sāmoa are based purely on new computer-based equipment or techniques. Some involve significant changes in much more mundane processes that are occurring silently such as the ways buildings are made.

In the recent past, many large buildings were constructed by a small elite corps of master builders known as *tufuga fau fale* or *tufuga fai fale* and their assistants (Handy and Handy 1924; Hiroa 1930: 84–90). The construction process was surrounded by a series of social activities that were designed to establish and maintain a set of social relationships between builder and client. These relationship-building activities preceded the formation of a 'contract' and marked the commencement of the 'contract', various milestones in the construction process, and the completion and formal handing over of the building. This accord was sought to ensure that the builder was satisfied with the relationship with his client and that he employed his talents to produce a solid, well-constructed and elegant building.

The process was expensive because it involved a series of 'gifts'[21] to the builder and his assistants that were over and above the cost of the materials and labour. These gifts were considered essential to signal respect for the builders and to establish the trust required for the successful completion of a project. Since neither the exact design specifications nor the various gifts and progress payments were agreed upon ahead of time, both builders and clients could, at various stages, become dissatisfied with the performance of the other. When dissatisfaction became apparent, projects were stopped while these matters were resolved. In all of these interactions, *tufuga* tended to hold all of the cards, and the client, reluctant to be seen to be mean, was liable to concede to the builder's demands, if only to avoid public speculation about the reasons for the suspension of activity. The best insurance in these cases was a good relationship (Hiroa 1930: 87–91).

The family or village usually supplied the labour for these projects. The labour was largely unskilled and had to be trained on the job and for the job. It also had to be fed for the duration of the job, a process that involved significant amounts of additional activity in the production and preparation of the food. The provision of food ensured that the best outcome was likely to be achieved. All of this activity generated a comprehensive set of social relationships, but it also added considerably to the amount of time and expense of many building projects and meant that their total cost was significantly higher than the actual cost of the construction component of the job.

The new contracting regime

More recently, a new set of contracting arrangements has become popular. Younger builders, many of whom had either trained or worked abroad, offered to construct larger, more complex buildings using new building technologies and new simplified contracting procedures.

One attraction was that new technologies such as laser levelling devices not only gave superior finishes, but could also be used to resolve concerns about quality. New technologies such as portable scaffolding increased speeds of construction and lowered costs; and use of new materials and technologies such as laminated beams offered greater strength and more design options and all at lower material and labour costs. Thus, buildings were able to achieve new design standards and a greater range of design options and to do so at lower costs.

The second attraction of these new contracts is that they are much less 'open-ended'. With smaller jobs, builders are increasingly prepared to cost materials and to provide quotes for material and estimates of labour costs. With larger projects, contracts are often documented and list design and material specifications, services and standards, parties' rights and obligations, and what is to be provided for a fixed price that is agreed upon in advance. This means that the clients gain more options and also more certainty about the process. The builder provides the required specialists, which shortens the amount of time spent in on-the-job training and reduces the potential for friction between builder and client. The contractor is responsible for feeding and paying them, which again eliminates significant non-building costs. Where local families billet the builder's crew, they recover some of the costs of the contract in the form of payments for accommodating the workforce.

The third attraction of these new arrangements is that it is in the builder's interests to complete the job as quickly as possible. There is now nothing to be gained, and much to be lost, by stringing out the job to assure themselves of accommodation, food and gifts as some *tufuga* have been known to do. Where the modern builder is paying his own assistants' wages from the contract price, the longer they take, the smaller the profit that is left at the end of the job. As one builder told us, he was anxious to complete our work because there was a growing demand for his services and a growing number of building firms that were moving to provide these new forms of service. In an increasingly competitive market with more sophisticated and demanding clients, builders are under pressure to complete contracts more quickly to win recommendations from satisfied clients.

While some of the elements of the former arrangements are retained, such as celebrations of particular points in the job and the retention of certain builder–client etiquettes and exchanges, these are often now symbolic: the reality is that new technologies and contracting arrangements are rapidly transforming the set of relations that once surrounded most public building projects.

The fate of traditional technologies

At the beginning of this chapter we mentioned several basic traditional skills that were being displaced by new technologies. We asked somewhat rhetorically whether traditional technologies and crafts were being discarded for ever. All we have argued so far would suggest that this is happening. But there are exceptions that suggest such a conclusion may be premature. Both involve the resurgence of traditional technologies, and each of these has made a comeback without subsidies or grants from museums wishing to protect older technological knowledges.

Traditional building technologies

The first is the resurgence of traditional house-building technologies, described so comprehensively by Te Rangi Hiroa (Hiroa 1930: 12ff) and Handy and Handy (1924), after a period in which traditional building technologies seemed likely to be progressively displaced by more modern building technologies. The recent resurgence is a consequence, ironically, of the growth of tourism that generated a demand for a more distinctive tourist experience. Tourism operators have realised that the air-conditioned, beige room in a resort hotel has limited appeal and is readily available and cheaper in Hawai'i and Fiji. To attract tourists to a more remote location, there is a need to produce a distinctively 'Sāmoan' as opposed to a 'Hilton' experience for discerning tourists. This has created a demand for a range of traditional buildings.

At one end of this trend are the large traditional buildings that have become centerpieces of big complexes. The earliest, and probably best known, of these is the large, beautifully detailed, *fale* at Aggie Grey's Hotel in Apia that sits in the centre of the complex and serves as both restaurant and the setting for traditional entertainment. This *fale*, built without nails, is linked to a series of other *fale* throughout the complex by walkways constructed in the traditional style. This project was followed by several big, highly detailed traditional buildings at the Kitano Tusitala Hotel in Apia that serve a similar purpose; and, in turn, by major buildings, accommodation and connecting walkways at the high-end Sinalei Reef Resort in Siumu. Several new buildings, including the Manumea Hotel, incorporating traditional design and building technologies as major architectural features, have recently been finished.

The Sāmoan government has begun to look to sponsor public buildings featuring traditional building technologies as assertions of national identity. The Sāmoan Consulate in Auckland includes a building in the traditional style known as Maota Sāmoa that is widely used for Sāmoan ceremonies that are lent moment by the 'authenticity' of the setting. The most prominent of the government's traditional buildings is the National University of Sāmoa's centre piece, its *fale tele*, or great house, which is the largest traditional building in existence and features traditional technologies throughout. It is significant too that this resurgence is seen beyond Sāmoa: the tallest traditional Sāmoan building, and one of the largest, is the Fale at the University of Auckland's Centre for Pacific Studies Complex in the heart of Auckland.

But the resurgence of the traditional construction technologies is not confined to high-end public buildings. It is also increasingly featured in villages with the break into the 'beach *fale* market' that involves the erection of smaller, open-sided buildings constructed on traditional patterns and with increasingly sophisticated traditional features such as decorative lashings, thatched roofs and woven blinds that are springing up all around the coasts of Sāmoan. Again, demand is driven by the interests of both tourists and some urban Sāmoans for a particularly 'Sāmoan' experience.

The fine mat or 'ie toga

Since this chapter commenced with a story about a mat, it is only fitting that it ends with one. The mat in this case is an elaborate and very finely woven mat, or *'ie toga*, that is an essential element of exchanges between families and villages on most significant occasions. These mats are still highly valued and, indeed, their value increased during the 1980s and 1990s as the women who once made them in weaving circles or *fale lalaga* stopped weaving them, at the same time as the demand for these mats in expatriate Sāmoan communities was growing.

In an attempt to produce a source of regular well-paid activity and to redistribute income to rural women, the Women in Business association started to provide instruction for women who wished to weave fine mats for sale. Agents of WIB moved around the country regularly, providing instruction and inspecting completed woven work. Women were paid on the spot for their production and, at the conclusion of the project, surrendered the completed mat to the organisation that then stocked and sold them from its Apia office. The result is a resurgence of fine mat weaving in outlying districts.

One could say that the project succeeded because Women in Business had identified a growing demand for new fine mats from both wealthier expatriate Sāmoans, and Tongans who had increasingly incorporated them into 'Tongan' ceremonial. However, the resurgence of both fine mats and traditional building technologies speaks to a growing confidence and a willingness to maintain and reclaim traditional technologies as symbols of personal and national identity.

A brief look into the future

What then of the impact of new technology on Sāmoan society? We should, perhaps, remind ourselves that technology is neutral: it embodies the potential to perform certain tasks in new ways and with different costs and benefits. There is nothing in the technology itself that makes its particular use inevitable. New technologies will not necessarily displace traditional ones, nor are they inevitably transformative.

Take the case of two portable sawmills. There are at least two operating around the district. Their impacts on social relations are, however, very different. The first was used by a man and his family to mill trees that had been felled as part of inland land clearance and to produce planks that could be sold for building. The man built a home in the village and used resources from the operation to serve his *matai*. He ran the mill until he had secured a reputation for enterprise and received his family's *matai* title. At this time he turned his attention to village and family matters. The mill is operated periodically to order by his sons to secure funds for the family's customary requirements. In this case, a new technology serves to strengthen and fund traditional activities. The second mill was operated by a man and his family in essentially the same way. They milled planks from large trees that they then sold to secure money to buy freehold land near Apia on which they built new homes. At that point, safe on their own land and beyond the reach of village obligations, they effectively removed themselves from village and district affairs and live a separate and private life. They continue to operate the mill on a commercial basis to maintain incomes needed to reside comfortably on family land. In this case, the technology provides its owners with a way of withdrawing from traditional obligations and activities and effectively undermines them by demonstrating that it is possible to live in Sāmoa but beyond the reach of the expectations of Sāmoan society.

Some traditional technologies may co-exist alongside new ones as they do in the case of construction. It may be that, in this case, the very scarcity of the skills necessary to construct and decorate traditional structures and their declining numbers will make them more valued and their builders more widely respected. They may become the preferred design choice for structures that are built to assert Sāmoan identity and may become icons of Sāmoan cultural expression. However, they will never replace the new building technologies that offer fresh design possibilities in a wider range of materials and at lower costs. So too with fine mats. While money may become an increasingly important element of ceremonial exchanges because of the high cost of staging them, cash cannot displace fine mats because they have a symbolic significance and iconic status within the culture. They will be made, not simply because people derive an income from their production, but because the mats and the production process have a profound cultural significance. At the same time, the advantages of imported mats for everyday use will ensure a decline in traditional and utilitarian mat weaving.

The danger of focusing on these comparatively resilient elements of tradition, however, is that it distracts attention from others that are nowhere near as secure: tradition itself may look unassailable when certain contemporary expressions of it are discussed, but it is clear that much has changed and much has gone forever. Whether it is traditional and in danger of being lost, or new and bound to introduce new capacities and dynamics, technology is likely always to have a significant impact on Sāmoan social organisation. It may even have the potential to undermine the sources of power of the traditional elites that have produced what appear to be enduring relationships. New electronic technologies, for instance, can bring new forms of highly valued cultural capital within the reach of more young people. This shift must have a potential impact in a gerontocracy like Sāmoa that presumes that age and wisdom are inevitably correlated. This technological shift can provide access to ideas that directly challenge values lying at the heart of Sāmoan worldview and lifestyle. But it can also provide access to virtual communities beyond Sāmoa that can support people who hold unpopular beliefs as they challenge tradition. These technologies can bring Sāmoan culture face to face with other cultures in ways that will challenge it as never before.

Beach fales are being built by villages to provide 'the village experience' for visitors and to increase rural incomes. The increasing role played by tourism in both the national and village economies will undoubtedly influence the aspirations of Sāmoans and the culture of Sāmoa.

Cruise ship in Apia Harbour. Ships periodically deposit 1500 passengers in Samoa for 12 hours and provide opportunities for taxi-drivers, merchants, handicraft makers and restaurateurs.

6.

Warm winds of change or gathering storm?

There is a widely held view among some Sāmoans that their commitment to Sāmoan culture and custom, *fa'asāmoa*, has protected Sāmoan society from the influences of external forces and that it will continue to do so. This conclusion rests on the fact that when one compares the extent of social change in Sāmoan society with that in other Pacific societies, Sāmoa has, in relative terms, changed rather less than other societies (Le Tagaloa 1992). Such analyses also hold that there may be something in the *fa'asāmoa* and the *fa'amatai* that is protective and has allowed the society to react deliberately to mitigate the impact of external forces and influences. This conclusion also rests on the view that Sāmoa has enjoyed significant and impressive political stability since its independence in 1962, which is in part attributable to the retention of fundamental elements of Sāmoan culture.

Some Sāmoan scholars, such as the anthropologist Unasa Dr Felise Va'a, place great significance on 'culture' as a stabilising social and political force and have argued that:

> ... Samoan culture is unique in the sense that it is the embodiment of thousands of years of language and cultural development.... It represents a solid core of knowledge and practice which has been largely responsible for the survival of the Samoan people into this third millennium. Therefore it is a treasure to be preserved and zealously guarded.... what we see in Samoa today is a re-invigorated cultural system, proof that despite the inroads in education and other social, political, economic and religious changes, Samoan society is essentially conservative. (Va'a 2006: 113)

Popular commitment to this 'solid core of cultural knowledge and practice' is both evidence and foundation of this cultural conservatism that provides Sāmoa, as Vaʻa asserts, with the will to resist inroads into tradition and culture. The will to resist, he argues, comes from commitment to the institutions in which the conservatism is embodied and expressed, and is 'characterised by attachment to the traditional lands of their *aiga* (family groups) and villages; to their churches and pastors; to their *matai* and *aiga*, to their language; to their wide array of ceremonials' (Vaʻa 2006: 114).

Popular commitment to this 'solid core of cultural knowledge and practice' also provides Sāmoans with the means to resist, he asserts, challenges to these institutions. The society is strengthened, rather than weakened, when faced with challenges because these focus attention on what is central to Sāmoan culture and heighten Sāmoans' sense of solidarity with and commitment to these institutions.

These analyses tend to focus on those elements of Sāmoan society that do not appear to have changed, and on social institutions and arrangements that limit the pace of change. Thus, Vaʻa notes that:

> True, there is always the odd individual who plays the role of 'heretic', who disagrees with everything that the *faʻa Samoa* stands for. But such an individual is the exception rather than the rule. And if such an individual should try to live in a Samoan community, he or she would eventually find himself or herself in all sorts of predicaments, simply because they would not be able to fit into the cultural life of their community. In Samoa there are many examples of such people trying to undermine the system usually ending unsuccessfully and often tragically. (Vaʻa 2006: 114)

Such analyses also acknowledge that the *faʻasāmoa* and the *faʻamatai* have come under pressure from external forces at various times, but argue that they have been incorporated into and managed by Sāmoan commitment to these institutional complexes. Thus, Aiono Dr Fanaʻafi Le Tagaloa argues that, 'Because the *faʻamatai* is the ideal social organisation, i.e. the most appropriate arrangement of social groupings within a culture, its ability to cope with change and the introduction of new ideas has been demonstrably successful in many different spheres' (Le Tagaloa 1992: 123).

Le Tagaloa goes on to argue that the *fa'amatai* had allowed Sāmoan society to incorporate Christianity in the 1800s, to resist the idea of monarchy that was promoted as an alternative to the Sāmoan polity through the 1800s, and to accept the introduction of health services into the Sāmoan community in the 1920s.

These analyses also acknowledge that while pressure from external influences have intensified, the *fa'amatai* has been able to resist them. Le Tagaloa, reflecting on changes in the electoral system in the 1990, contends that:

> It has been said in comparative terms that the political changes that the *fa'amatai* culture of the Samoan has had to sustain since 1990 have had the force of the tropical cyclones Ofa and Val combined. Many doubts have been expressed as to the ability of the *fa'amatai* to survive and to hang on there!
>
> But in the heartland of the *fa'amatai*, i.e. the *fono a le nu'u* and the social groupings of the *tamaitai, aumaga*, and *faletua ma tausi*, confidence in the ability of the *fa'amatai* to cope, to survive and to continue to maintain peace within each village, district, and island remains strong and persistent. (Le Tagaloa 1992: 132)

We do not deny that, in relative terms, Sāmoan society has retained significant elements of both *fa'amatai* and *fa'asāmoa* and that it is possible to trace continuities in key ideas and institutions. But rather than focusing on evidence of cultural conservatism in Sāmoan society, this book has chosen instead to concentrate on evidence of dynamism and its capacity for change. Our decision to adopt this approach arises from several issues that emerge from a preoccupation with evidence of the conservatism of Sāmoan society.

Our first concern with approaches that focus on continuity is that such analyses understate real changes that a careful reading of Sāmoan history shows have occurred. Our second concern with this view is that its emphasis on what appears to be constant in Sāmoan society leads its proponents to understate the dynamism evident in the society's engagement with challenges that it has faced in its exposure to global forces. Our third concern is that this view represents Sāmoan society as wholly committed to tradition and continuity, and does not reflect our experiences in the village where people are constantly thinking and talking about change. Our final concern is that periodic restatements of confidence in the resilience of Sāmoan culture, and in its ability to resist external challenges, lead people to postpone discussions about how to respond to processes that are producing significant changes and that deserve careful consideration and discussion. These concerns led us to explore and articulate another view, focused not on Sāmoan society's conservatism but on its dynamism, and the ways in which this had conditioned its responses to globalisation.

We contend instead that the observation that change is the only constant is as true for Sāmoan society as it was for Greek society when Heraclitus made his original observation about social change. The first part of the book reviewed some of the evidence of continuous change that commenced when the ancestors of contemporary Sāmoans arrived in the archipelago some 3000 years ago. Archaeologists and prehistorians are revealing more proof of early and significant transformation in Sāmoan social organisation and constructing possible explanations for these changes. As new evidence is located and the techniques employed in this search are refined, it is likely that we will come to understand more about the pace and scale of change during the period between the settlement of Sāmoa and the eighteenth century.

More is known about the pace and direction of change since the eighteenth century because this has been well-documented. In that time, Sāmoan society has engaged with three significant ideologies – Christianity, capitalism and colonialism – and a range of new technologies. Sāmoan society has not passively accepted all of the ideas or technologies that have become available as a consequence of increasing engagement with the world beyond its shores. The same histories that document the changes also document determined resistance to other ideas and technologies. A united Sāmoan political and religious leadership has been able to reject some incursions and to deny these traction. In the process Sāmoan leadership has 'managed' and refined each of these and has mitigated their impact on Sāmoan society.

But Sāmoan society has also selected and incorporated elements of these ideologies and technologies that its leadership has considered useful or beneficial. These decisions have resulted in significant changes that have been well-documented in historical accounts. While they may have been gradual and incremental, they are, nevertheless, important and have produced significant changes in key institutions in Sāmoan society. We have sought to document these transformations and to explain why people continue to underestimate and minimise the impacts of external forces and agencies in favour of a view that stresses stability and continuity.

But our major concern has been with the main vectors producing change in contemporary Sāmoa: movement of people, ideologies and technologies. We have sought to show that each of these has been altering the social, economic and political organisation of the family and village for at least 180 years and have suggested reasons why many Sāmoan people overlook evidence of significant historical social transformations and take a somewhat shallower view of the nature and extent of change. But our major interest has been with the ways in which these three forces are influencing contemporary Sāmoan society and social organisation. We have argued that Sāmoa confronts powerful new forms of each of these three forces and at a time when the traditional elites, who have so far 'managed' change, appear to be less able, and less willing, to agree on how to manage them.

We have argued that migration has created new, dispersed multi-nodal forms of the Sāmoan family and village that have become more dispersed and more complex than ever before. This is a trend that is likely to continue. In the process, influence within both family and village has also been somewhat dispersed. While the family and village in Sāmoa may remain the physical, symbolic and affective 'centre' of these multi-nodal families and villages, the 'centre' can no longer command the unquestioning allegiance and support of its migrant members because they do not derive income from the 'centre's' resources and their continuing participation is effectively voluntary. As a consequence, one could argue that the influence of the 'centre' on the family and village may well be declining.

At the same time, the significance of diasporic nodes of these dispersed formations, which arise from the wealth they generate and on which the

Sāmoan nodes depend, is growing. While their participation is required to support and fund the *fa'asāmoa* at the centre, it is not guaranteed. This growing dependence on diasporic nodes carries a risk for the solidarity of families and villages and for the *fa'asāmoa*. While some of their members who go abroad will remain committed to the *fa'asāmoa* and will continue to support their families and villages from abroad with remittances in cash and kind, others may use their leverage to bring about changes by supporting some activities and withholding support from others; still others will withdraw completely from participation in *fa'asāmoa*.

Since expatriate members of families and villages are free to send money when and to whom they choose, they may elect to send it to people and for causes that will consolidate *fa'asāmoa*. They may equally choose to send it to people and for causes that will effectively undermine *fa'asāmoa*. While some who receive remittances from abroad will use them to support their families' and villages' participation in Sāmoan custom, others may use them to secure freehold land so that they can move away from the family and village and avoid continuing demands for cash and resources to meet customary obligations.

Furthermore, the influence of families and villages at the centre may be continuing to decline. While the migrants who grew up in the 'centre' may have strong affective bonds with family and village in Sāmoa, their children who have grown up outside Sāmoa may have somewhat more attenuated ties to the centre, and their grandchildren may have only a limited knowledge of and nominal and symbolic commitment to the 'centre'. This is not to suggest that the migrants' children and grandchildren will not identify as 'Sāmoans' or that they will not commit to some form of Sāmoan culture, but rather that this is likely to be in new ways and their support will be for institutions with which they are more familiar and in which they are able to participate. Their Sāmoan identity and their Sāmoan society may be unique forms that are produced over many years in overseas Sāmoan enclaves.

Families and villages in the 'centre' that wish to maintain the commitment of their members in these increasingly influential diasporic communities will have to find new means of doing this. It will not be enough to insist to overseas-born Sāmoans that their parents or grandparents 'ate the family or village's sweat" and that they are thus bound to support their activities for all time. To maintain the support of their expatriate members, on which the centres have become dependent, the 'centre' may have to reconfigure itself in ways that make it easier to embrace or risk losing the very commitment on which its continued existence depends.

We have also argued that three ideologies have reshaped Sāmoan society over some 180 years. While the influence of elements of these has been considerable, powerful and united elites have been able to 'manage' the process by which these ideologies have been incorporated into Sāmoan society in ways that have limited their impact. The elite's influence in both religious and secular spheres has, until recently, ensured that change was gradual and incremental and that it benefited Sāmoan society and, in particular, the arrangements that secured its continued influence. The capacity of the elites to manage change in this way for much longer may be limited for a number of reasons.

Because the criteria for membership in these elites have shifted over time, membership of family and village elites is no longer as homogeneous as it once was. Whereas in the past, these entities tended to be united on contentious issues, today opinion is more varied and some members may be reluctant to follow a course of action simply because it has been done 'traditionally'. As debates over appropriate courses of action occur within what are now more socio-demographically diverse bodies, the energy consumed in and acrimony generated by these debates may further divide these formerly united elites.

This tension may be exacerbated by challenges from within families and villages as their members embrace new ideas that run counter to the collectivist ideologies on which their solidarity rests. Furthermore, these dissidents are able to invoke powerful constitutional rights to express their contrary views, and to voice their expectation that the nation's courts and government will protect and enforce these views, even where this may bring the state into conflict with traditional elites and the polities they control. Thus, increasingly the powers of traditional family and village elites may be contested both from within by the members on whom they depend for their authority, and from without by the government that is empowered to limit their authority and power and has shown an inclination to do so in a number of areas. Every time the decision of an elite is successfully contested, its authority and power appear that much less secure.

On this basis, one might argue that a weakened elite faces an increasingly energised collection of proponents and ideas that challenge arrangements it has traditionally supported and the ideologies that underpin them. The first such challenge may appear to come from the many well-funded NGOs that actively promulgate ideas derived from ideologies about human rights and social equity that justify the redistribution of opportunities among those who have been systematically excluded from power in the past. The second such challenge comes from international financial and development agencies and aid donors that have similar goals, and have leverage because they control resources that the Sāmoan government requires to pursue its development plans. Their ability to make development support contingent on the achievement of social goals that reflect a more inclusive and equitable society makes them a powerful force. The third challenge may come from a better educated youth population that has access to more knowledge from a wider range of sources and a vote that they are willing to exercise to bring about change. A fourth challenge may come from groups that are currently emerging around new axes of social identity, such as gender, sexual orientation and political philosophy, that, with support from allies beyond Sāmoa, could mobilise around these to pursue new social agendas. It may be that a more divided elite will confront an increasingly powerful set of forces promoting values that further undermine its power and authority. If the traditional elite is to survive a contest in which the odds may be running against it, its members may need to accept that they will have to concede some of their authority and power in order to retain any at all.

Finally, we have shown that over time Sāmoan society has been reshaped by new technologies. For the majority of Sāmoa's history, powerful and united religious and secular elites were able to 'manage' innovations by means that limited their impact on Sāmoan society and social organisation. Technologies that could be harnessed in ways that secured the power and influence of the elites tended to be accepted, while those that may have undermined this power were excluded. There is no doubt in our minds that the past management of technological change ensured a degree of stability and continuity in Sāmoan society that has served it well. There is, however, real doubt in our minds that it can do this again as effectively.

It is possible to argue that an increasingly heterogeneous elite, which is less able to reach a single view on matters of technology than ever before, confronts a set of technologies that are, by their very nature, more difficult to manage in the ways other earlier technologies have been. Telecommunications and internet costs are falling and they are becoming more readily available to more people. These make for an increasingly well-informed group who can access technology and a world of new ideas from within the family and village. Those who have access to these conduits can join communities and worlds and may become increasingly aware of the extent to which their lives and opportunities are constrained by elites. They may also become aware that in other places these constraints are contested and even illegal. Thus, while secular and religious elites may be able to control discourses within family and village, and may seem to have control of the public sphere, the new technologies may be silently and slowly undermining them in a private sphere.

To stem the loss of authority that can result from this trend, the elites may have to concede some of their power to retain a modicum of authority. They may, for instance, have to accept a more egalitarian form of social organisation that is designed to promote greater degrees of social equity. To refuse to do this is to provoke a confrontation that could cause considerable damage and be difficult to win.

The increasing movement of people, ideologies and technologies is currently converging in ways that will present a greater challenge to Sāmoan social institutions and social organisation than at any time in the past. One might be tempted to forecast that these winds of change are about to converge and to become a perfect storm that could be more devastating than ever before. This seems unlikely to us because, ironically, the very evidence of significant past change, which so many people seem so willing to overlook, may be the proof that Sāmoan society is sufficiently fluid and dynamic to allow significantly dramatic changes to occur without destroying the idea of Sāmoa in the process.

Notes

1 WARM WINDS OF CHANGE

1 This figure is from the 2006 Census. Estimates put the 2009 population at 220,000.
2 The 34 are: ACP, ADB, Commonwealth, FAO, G-77, IBRD, ICAO, ICCt, ICRM, IDA, IFAD, IFC, IFRCS, ILO, IMF, IMO, IOC, IPU, ITU, ITUC, MIGA, OPCW, PIF, SPARTECA, SPC, UN, UNCTAD, UNESCO, UPU, WCO, WHO, WIPO, WMO, WTO (as an observer).
3 These include conventions on Biodiversity, Climate Change, Climate Change–Kyoto Protocol, Desertification, Hazardous Wastes, Law of the Sea, Ozone Layer Protection, Ship Pollution and Wetlands.
4 This account is necessarily a summary of a relationship between two complex realities. Those seeking more detailed analyses are referred to Gilson 1970; Pitt 1970; Shore 1982; and Va'ai 1999.
5 Samoan kinship is complex, and those seeking a comprehensive discussion are referred to Va'ai 1999.
6 These include such 'traditional' bodies as the daughters of the village or *aualuma*, sons of the village or *aumāga*, council of chiefs or *fono a matai*, wives of chiefs and orators or *faletua ma tausi*, and more recent entities such as the women's committee or *komiti a le tumamā*, the session or *fono a tiakono*, and the youth club or *'au talavou*.
7 The *Samoa Observer* has in the last 15 years won a number of significant international awards for its independence. See, for instance, http://www.samoaobserver.ws/index.php?option=com_content&view=article&id=141&Itemid=79 (accessed 1 May 2009).

2 A BRIEF HISTORY OF SĀMOA'S ENGAGEMENT WITH GLOBAL FORCES

1 Sāmoa is considered one of two likely homelands for the Polynesian societies that developed in the east. Savai'i is regarded as a possible contender as the legendary Polynesian homeland Hawai'iki.
2 Gilson records this name as Roggewein (Gilson 1970: 65).
3 Recorded elsewhere as La Pérouse, see, Campbell 1989: 55.
4 Turner's mission was ended by the Methodist Church in 1838 and he left in 1839. Turner was replaced by Tongan missionaries under the guidance of Benjamin Latuselu who continued the mission until 1857 when the church again sent European missionaries to staff it.
5 The men were baptised in Wallis. Their original names are unknown but both were from Savai'i. See Hamilton 2005: 97.
6 The length of this vowel is not indicated in the original text.
7 It is not possible to give a detailed account of settlement here. For a comprehensive account of the development and character of the European settler community around Apia, see Gilson 1970: chapter 7.
8 It is not possible to give details of these machinations here. Those seeking a comprehensive discussion of the earlier period are referred to chapters 7 and 16, and to the conclusion, in Gilson 1970; and for the later period to Boyd 1969b and c.
9 Under the subsequent New Zealand military administration, in 1916, the recruitment of Chinese labour was again suspended because of concerns about 'racial purity', and a programme of repatriation was initiated. However, faced with a deteriorating domestic economy, New Zealand was forced to resume the programme in 1920.
10 The most comprehensive accounts of this period are those of Davidson (1967); and the historian Mary Boyd (1969a, 1969b and 1969c).

NOTES TO PAGES 52–79

11 Western Sāmoa became Sāmoa in 1997 by parliamentary act in what was arguably the last act of decolonisation.
12 See, for instance, the consequences of the contraction of the New Zealand income on the Sāmoan economy in 1992 (Macpherson 1992).
13 The first was the 'Western Sāmoa Economic Development Programme 1966–1970' that became known as the First Five Year Plan; these were replaced by shorter 'Statements of Economic Strategy' in 1996.
14 Some 99.5 per cent of Sāmoans are nominal Christians and the country's motto is *Fa'avae ile Atua Sāmoa*, Sāmoa is founded on God.

3 MIGRATION AND SOCIAL TRANSFORMATION

1 TEAL or Tasman Empire Airways Ltd was the New Zealand national airline. It pioneered the famous 'Coral Route' between New Zealand and the Pacific Islands using flying boats in the 1950s.
2 Television programmes received in what was then Western Sāmoa were broadcast from nearby American Sāmoa and were almost exclusively in English.
3 The first collection of plants was made in 1839 by botanists associated with the US Exploring Expedition and thereafter by amateur botanists between 1860 and 1893, and professional botanists between 1893 and 1920 (see Whistler 1980: 47–53).
4 These beetles, which burrow into trunks and leaf axils reducing productivity before eventually killing the tree, were causing coconut yields to drop by about 30 per cent in the 1930s. The beetles were controlled by an introduced virus from 1963 onwards (Stace 1956: 13–14), but have reappeared in many places as control efforts have flagged.
5 Neither of these claims can be confirmed, but there do seem to be reasons for thinking them correct as they were recounted independently by different people.
6 Sāmoans once used three native plants to poison fish. These were replaced by an import, Derris, that was introduced before 1929 (Whistler 2000: 137–8). Two varieties of Derris, *D. elliptica* and *D. malaccensis*, were routinely used before government banned their use.
7 For an account of the extent of 'European' settlement, see *Cyclopedia of Sāmoa* 1907; Davidson 1967; and Gilson 1970.
8 Sāmoans made an early distinction between themselves and the Melanesian peoples to the west of Sāmoa whom they referred to as *tagata meauli*, black people. This distinction was based only partly on skin colour: it was also linked to a biblical passage Sāmoans used to 'explain' the divine foundations of ethnic hierarchy.
9 This was also true in national politics in Sāmoa, and a number of Europeans aligned themselves, for a number of reasons, with Sāmoans against various colonial administrations.
10 This idea is often embodied in the saying *ua sui faiga ae lē suia fa'avae:* the practices may have changed but the foundations have not.
11 We will show in the following chapters that, in addition to news carried on these visits, developments in technology have also dramatically increased the amount of information that flows into the village.
12 This has become more common since the New Zealand pension was made 'portable', allowing Sāmoan pensioners to draw their New Zealand pensions while living in Sāmoa.
13 In following chapters we will explore the influence of the ideas and technologies that migrants bring to bear in both village and family organisation and activity in more detail.
14 New Zealanders of European descent are increasingly referred to as Pākehā to distinguish them from Māori New Zealanders. *Pālagi*, or more correctly, *papālagi*, is a term Sāmoans use to refer to Europeans.
15 Annual population growth rates in Western Sāmoa had risen from around 0.4 per cent per

NOTES TO PAGES 80–101

annum in 1911, to 3.35 per cent in 1936, to 3.72 per cent in 1951, giving it one of the highest rates in the world at that time (Stace 1956: 2).
16 Peace Corps volunteers installed a large number of simple but effective pit-seal toilets throughout the villages in the 1960s and 1970s that quickly improved the standard of village sanitation.
17 Cremation is not practised in Sāmoa and graves in many cases are on family land in the village.
18 This was not unusual and was reflected in national population growth rates that dropped from historical annual rates of around 3.7 per cent (Stace 1956: 2) to around 0.7 per cent (Minister of Finance 1978: Statistical Appendix 1, Table 1). Declining rates were evident first in urban and peri-urban villages, in which migration chains were established early, but over time, rates declined throughout the country as emigration gained momentum in rural villages.
19 Literally, the end of a village, referring to the emergence of a sub-village at the edges of an existing one that gained increasing political autonomy over time, while remaining under the latter's authority.
20 These rolls are constructed for fundraising activities known as *tusigā igoa* or censuses. Expatriate members are given warning of times, dates and locations of planned *tusigā igoa* and are invited to contribute. These events provide opportunities to contribute funds for the project and, in the process, to signal ongoing commitment to and membership of the village.
21 In a 2004 study of selected representative villages in both Upolu and Savai'i, all households in the village were receiving remittances from relatives abroad (Kerslake 2004: 1–15).
22 A comprehensive account of the history of this practice, and of the foundations of these exchanges, is provided by Schoeffel 1999.
23 Shankman (1976: 24–84) noted that remittances from expatriates were no longer controlled by family *matai*. Migrants were free to send remittances to untitled parents and siblings, which effectively redistributed access to technologies and their benefits within villages.
24 For information on Yazaki EDS Sāmoa, see http://www.australianarrow.com.au/Samoa.html (accessed 23 March 2009).
25 White Sunday, known as the *Lotu a Tamaiti*, falls on the second Sunday in October and celebrates the importance of children to their families. Many migrants send money and gifts to children in their families in Sāmoa.
26 MIRAB is an acronym for the four factors that distort the economies of these nations and societies: Migration, Remittances, Aid, Bureaucracy.
27 Albert Wendt's 1973 novel *Sons for the Return Home* explores this theme and captures the different responses of parents and their two sons who return to the village of their birth after living in Wellington.
28 These have included recommendations to limit the amount of cash donations, gifts of canned meat and fish, *pusa apa*, and the number and quality of fine mats, *'ie toga* presented at *fa'alavelave*.
29 The committee visited New Zealand for the first time in April 2009 to canvass this issue and to discuss ways of limiting the costs of ceremonial inflation with New Zealand-based Sāmoans.
30 See, for instance, the TALAVOU programme in the Ministry of Women, Community and Social Development (http://www.mwcsd.gov.ws/youth.htm) (accessed 26 April 2009).
31 In the past four years, various New Zealand companies have recruited bus drivers and process workers, and government departments have recruited prison officers.

4   IDEAS AND SOCIAL TRANSFORMATION

1 The most comprehensive accounts of these pre-contact theocracies were provided by missionaries such as Turner (1983) and later analysed by scholars such as Krämer (1994). They remain the best-regarded accounts but are, nevertheless, European accounts of a Sāmoan reality.
2 Tagaloa a Lagi, the being who created Sāmoa and then the other islands of the Pacific and their populations, was replaced by another God who created the earth and then the progenitors of

3   the human population. Furthermore, this new account replaced Sāmoa as the point of creation and centred on parts of the world to which few, if any, of those who accepted the new faith had been.
3   This changed, at least in one respect, as Sāmoan pastors and teachers were trained and began service in Sāmoan villages after Malua Theological College was opened on 24 September 1844 by the Reverends George Turner and Charles Hardie of the London Missionary Society. Sāmoan pastors were, despite their office, people whose first identity was Sāmoan.
4   Krämer (1994, volume 1: 11) holds that the fundamental features of governance and political organisation in Upolu and Savai'i were in place by around 1100 AD.
5   Even then, they could only employ force when a naval ship whose commander accepted the validity of the complaint was prepared to provide a show of force, so considerable amounts of time often elapsed between the 'breach' and the 'remedy', which exposed the impotence of the consuls and the Europeans in general.
6   This is particularly evident in the case of expansion of Sāmoan knowledge of the human condition in which a combination of circumstances combined to mask the real extent of the shift. This transition process, which initially confused us, is discussed in some detail in chapters 4–7 of our work on medical knowledge and practice (Macpherson and Macpherson 1990).
7   This is also known, less commonly, as *aso fa'apaupau* or heathen days.
8   A bird identified by Pratt (1911: 362) as *Rallus pectoralis*. Birds whose movements are watched at night may differ from village to village.
9   A parallel *feagaiga* relationship exists within an *āiga* between the descendants of its male ancestors or *tamatāne* and those of its female ancestors or *tamafafine*.
10 For a detailed account of the way in which a village polity can expel a respected and long-serving pastor for challenging the interests of powerful families, see Tuimaleali'ifano's account of affairs at Falelatai (Tuimaleai'ifano 2000: 176–81).
11 The permanent alienation of customary land, *fanua tau Sāmoa*, except to the state for public purposes, is now forbidden (Section 105 of the Sāmoan Constitution, University of the South Pacific 1988).
12 This is land confiscated from German nationals in 1914 and returned to the government at independence as the WSTEC estates. It is now the STEC estate and is administered by the Sāmoa Land Corporation.
13 This number is growing as government subdivides and sells land from the former reparation estates around the edge of Apia to provide land for the growing urban population.
14 In urban areas, where there is more freehold land and land is routinely bought and sold in a land market, people may be much more conscious of tenure, and far more willing to exercise rights that attach to freehold land.
15 The Household Income and Expenditure Study establishes these rates from a five-yearly survey of a random sample of 20 per cent of the Sāmoan population. These rates would be higher if those in formal education and those over 60 years of age were subtracted from the total adult population.
16 The 2006 Census listed some 24,000 people as being employed in some capacity in the informal sector and that if those employed in that sector were added to those in the formal one, this rate of participation in wage and salaried employment would be significantly higher. A recent study of women in Sāmoa's informal sector suggests that those in this sector are relatively well-paid (Taua'a 2008).
17 One can negotiate to 'pay', 'pay and feed' or 'pay, feed and supply food' to one's kin. Despite the relationship and a preference for paying and feeding a related 'employee', workers often opt for the payment option since they leave with more cash in hand. The basis of payment is hourly, daily or contract price, and, surprisingly, many opt for contract price because the money is needed urgently.
18 A new service industry has developed in Apia for urban people who need these commodities

but no longer have plantations on which to raise cattle and pigs, or time to secure fine mats from kin in the village. These stores provide all of the goods that may be needed for *fa'alavelave* and will trade goods from these events for cash.

19   Taxi drivers say their best days are pay days when they ferry wage and salary earners around town between their offices, the National Provident Fund office, banks and finance companies while they repay loans and various *fa'alavelave*-related bills.

20   Kerslake's 2004 study showed that minors and single workers continue to present their unopened wage packets to parents for their family's use.

21   This is truer of villages beyond the Apia area. In Apia, village social institutions are less evident and have less power. They are home to people who have come to Apia to work and simply rent or own property within the bounds of the former village but have no allegiance or obligation to the village.

22   The extent of this practice was first revealed in a crucial report by the Controller and Auditor-General (1994), and the 1994 Commission of Enquiry Report; ongoing evidence surfaces periodically in reports into matters in government offices and in prosecutions of officials.

23   G. B. Milner was Professor of Austronesian Studies at the School of Oriental and African Studies at the University of London.

24   For extended discussion of the formal structure of the *fa'amatai*, see the work of Asiata Saleimoa Va'ai 1999.

25   Gratton noted that where families became large and resided in several villages, they split into several semi-autonomous branches. Each branch, with the consent of the others, appointed its own titleholder to make governance possible (Gratton 1948: 12).

26   Titleholders were, 50 years ago, almost exclusively male. A small number of high titles were traditionally reserved for women. Women gained their influence in Sāmoan society through other institutions such as the *feagaiga* or covenant that balanced the power of brothers and sisters.

27   In Sāmoan, *o le ala i le pule o le tautua*.

28   In Sāmoan, *ua fa'aselu gaugau*.

29   In the 1945 Census, 5.6 per cent of the population held *matai* titles (Gratton 1948: 14).

30   A title that had been bestowed, only after long and heated discussions in both Sāmoa and New Zealand, on two people in 1980, was bestowed on 11 people in 2006. In an account of the ceremony, a *matai* explained to us, 'Your brother could have had the title. I explained to him that all he needed to do was to get you to send $SAT4,500 and he could have come with us and got a title.'

31   This term refers to the original holder of the title, who becomes the senior holder when the title is split (Gratton 1948: 20).

32   Those interested in these matters may find the following articles of interest: So'o 2000; Macpherson and Macpherson 2005; Macpherson and Macpherson 2006b.

33   For example, in a 2007 confrontation between police and villagers in Satapuala, the orators of the village negotiated with the police who withdrew from the village so that negotiations could continue, and confrontation between a large united village and a small police contingent was avoided. In an earlier confrontation, over a murder at Lona, the police, seriously outnumbered, withdrew and allowed the *fono* to identify and nominate the defendants who were subsequently presented to the police.

34   Huffer and Schuster's (2000) study identified four types of criticism of the churches' role in governance.

35   The full text of the letter can be found at the following URL: http://www.samoaobserver. ws/index.php?option=com_content&view=article&id=1846:conventionreligious-freedom-attacked-&catid=52:letters-to-the-editor&Itemid=61 (accessed 7 February 2009).

36   The advice related to the need for religious leaders to keep spiritual matters and financial matters separate, and is found in Mathew 22: 15–22; Mark 12: 13–17; and Luke 20: 20–26.

37 Similar views were reported in Huffer and Schuster 2000.
38 This is to be achieved by requiring candidates for national elections to have spent a significant qualifying period in the country, and by ruling out the possibility of establishing 'overseas' constituencies to represent emigrant populations.
39 Their ability and willingness to challenge the state are made possible in part by external funding that allows them access to human and financial resources that could not possibly be raised internally.
40 See, for instance, the current plan at the government website (http://www.mof.gov.ws/uploads/sds_2008_-_2012).
41 SUNGO (Samoa Umbrella Non-Governmental Organisation) was formed in November 1997 by 24 women's NGOs that later grew to around 72. It currently has 48 active NGOs on its register and has the ear of the Prime Minister.
42 These include the Small Business Enterprise Center (SBEC), Women in Business, the ADB-funded Small Business Development Project, South Pacific Board for Development (SPBD) and the EU-funded Micro Projects.
43 The recent establishment of the Samoan Victim Support Group, which works closely with the Sāmoan Police, signals public recognition of new forms of victimisation and of the need to provide more services for victims of such things as domestic violence and child abuse who were, in many cases, unable to find support for action against and protection from more powerful people.

5   TECHNOLOGY AND SOCIAL TRANSFORMATION

1   The material used is from the family *Pandanaceae* and has been identified by Hiroa as *Pandanus tectorius* (Hiroa 1930: 212). It is known in Sāmoan as *lau paogo*.
2   Yet, ironically, when a recent major social conflict occurred in Falelatai, it was over the use of sums of money collected to build and furnish a new church (Tuimaleai'ifano 2000: 176–80).
3   Also rendered as *e sui faiga ae tūmau fa'avae*.
4   Ironically, a load of *pāpā* from her shop would have said far more about our 'wealth' than a load of cheaper polypropylene mats could ever have done.
5   Sāmoa College and the Avele Agricultural College.
6   The Western Sāmoan Teachers' Training College and Trades Training Institute.
7   The earliest 'modernisation' development programmes contained recommendations to eliminate these differentials (see, for instance, Stace and Lauterbach 1963), but they rarely found the traction that they have under Human Rights Protection Party governments in the last two decades.
8   These small traditional houses are constructed by the sea and rented to tourists and people from Apia for modest daily fees that go to either villages or individual family owners.
9   A similar phenomenon occurred when liquour, which had been available only to elites and in urban areas, became available in rural areas. This was reported by Lima in his study of the history of alcohol use among Sāmoans (Lima 2004).
10 Chan Mow is owned and operated by the Ah Mow family; and Frankie's by a Chinese businessman, Frankie Cai.
11 This has generated new Sāmoan businesses in New Zealand that buy and prepare vehicles from Japan for export to Sāmoa.
12 Benzene and benzene-powered lamps were more expensive and were mostly found among the more affluent. Other families used cheaper kerosene fuel in hurricane lamps and still others used coconut oil lamps or *moli* or *moli popo*.
13 Lockable fridge-freezers that allow people to keep the contents of their fridges to themselves have, according to salespeople, become increasingly popular.

14 In Palauli, Savai'i, in the mid-1960s, several *matai* determined that a scene in *Blue Hawai'i* that saw Elvis Presley draw close to his co-star was a danger to the morality of the village. They directed the operator to cease screening the film and to show cartoons instead, much to the suppressed annoyance of the audience.
15 The village recently sprouted a video and DVD hire business that, despite some early scepticism, has become popular with the younger set that makes up most of its clientele.
16 For most, the telegram was the only alternative and replies, broadcast on radio, meant that their content was never private.
17 This data is from the UN Statistics Division's Millennium Development Goals Indicators at http://mdgs.un.org/unsd/mdg/SeriesDetail.aspx?srid=756&crid=882 (accessed 27 January 2009).
18 Competition between government-owned, but soon to be privatised, Sāmoa Tel and Digicel Sāmoa means that villagers can call New Zealand from Sāmoa at $NZ0.30 per minute using a stable GSM network with coverage of around 97 per cent of the country on a telephone purchased for around $NZ15 using $NZ3 pre-paid cards.
19 A stream of texts, sent accidentally to our cellphone on various occasions, drew our attention to the ways in which traditional sibling protection can be undermined and subverted by those with cellphones.
20 This data is from the UN Statistics Division's Millennium Development Goals Indicators at http://mdgs.un.org/unsd/mdg/SeriesDetail.aspx?srid=605&crid=882 (accessed 27 January 2009).
21 These were in fact more correctly described as payments since they were not, in practice, optional.

6 WARM WINDS OF CHANGE OR GATHERING STORM?

1 This metaphor expresses the debts that all owe to their family and village of origin whose 'sweat nourished them' and, in part, made them who they are.

Bibliography

Ahlburg, D., 1995, 'Migration, Remittances and the Distribution of Income: Evidence from the Pacific', *Asian and Pacific Migration Review*, 4 (2), pp. 157–68.
Ahlburg, D. A., 1991, *Remittances and their Impact: A Study of Tonga and Western Samoa*, National Centre for Development Studies, Research School of Pacific Studies, Australian National University, Canberra.
Anae, M., 1997, 'Towards a New Zealand-born Samoan Identity: Some Reflections on "Labels"', *Pacific Health Dialog*, 4 (2), pp. 128–37.
Anae, M., 1998, 'Fofoa i vaoese: Identity Journeys of New Zealand-born Samoans', PhD (Anthropology), University of Auckland, Auckland.
Australian Agency for International Development, 2008a, *Making Land Work: Case Studies on Customary Land and Development in the Pacific*, Australian Agency for International Development, Canberra.
Australian Agency for International Development, 2008b, *Making Land Work: Reconciling Customary Land and Development in the Pacific*, Australian Agency for International Development, Canberra.
Barnes, S. S. and R. C. Green, 2008, 'Who Built the Fort at Uliamoa?: Conjectures on Indigenous Technology Transfer in Early Historic Samoa', in D. J. Addison and C. Sand, *Recent Advances in the Archaeology of the Fiji/West Polynesia Region*, University of Otago Studies in Prehistoric Archaeology, No. 22, Dunedin, pp. 71–78.
Barnes, S. S. and T. L. Hunt, 2005, 'Samoa's Pre-contact Connections in West Polynesia and Beyond', *Journal of the Polynesian Society*, 114 (3), pp. 227–66.
Bedford, R. D., 2007, *Pasifika Mobility: Pathways, Circuits, and Challenges in the 21st Century*. Pasifika Papers Series, Institute of Policy Studies, Victoria University of Wellington.
Bertram, G. and R. F. Watters, 1985, 'The MIRAB Economy in Pacific Microstates', *Pacific Viewpoint*, 27 (3), pp. 497–512.
Bertram, G. and R. F. Watters, 1986, 'The MIRAB Process: Some Earlier Analysis and Context', *Pacific Viewpoint*, 27 (1), pp. 47–57.
Boyd, M., 1969a, 'The Decolonisation of Western Samoa', in P. Munz (ed.), *The Feel of Truth: Essays in New Zealand and Pacific History*, A. H. and A. W. Reed, Sydney, pp. 115–88.
Boyd, M., 1969b, 'The Record in Western Samoa to 1945', in A. Ross (ed.), *New Zealand's Record in the Pacific Islands in the Twentieth Century*, Longman Paul Ltd, Auckland, pp. 115–88.
Boyd, M., 1969c, 'The Record in Western Samoa Since 1945', in A. Ross (ed.), *New Zealand's Record in the Pacific Islands in the Twentieth Century*, Longman Paul Ltd, Auckland, pp. 189–270.
Buzacott, A., 1866, *Mission Life in the Islands of the Pacific. Being a Narrative of the Life and Labours of the Reverend A. Buzacott*, John Snow and Co., Paternoster Row, London.
Campbell, I. C., 1989, *A History of the Pacific Islands*, University of Canterbury Press, Christchurch.
Castells, M., 1996, *The Rise of the Network Society*, Blackwell Publishers, Oxford.
Central Bank of Sāmoa, *Annual Report for the Financial Year July 2007–June 2008*, Central Bank of Sāmoa, Apia.
Chan Mow, I. T., 2007, 'The Fa'amatai in the Face of the Winds of Change', in A. So'o (ed.), *Changes in the Matai System: O Suiga i le Fa'amatai*, Centre for Sāmoan Studies, National University of Sāmoa, Apia, pp. 119–37.
Clark, J. T., 1996, 'Samoan Prehistory in Review', in J. M. Davidson, G. Irwin, B. F. Leach, A. Pawley and D. Brown (eds), *Oceanic Cultural History: Essays in Honour of Roger Green*, New Zealand Archaeological Association, Dunedin, pp. 445–60.
Commission of Enquiry, 1994, *Report on Controller and Chief Auditor's Report to the Legislative Assembly. Period 1 January 1993–30 June 1994*, Parliament of Western Samoa, Apia.

BIBLIOGRAPHY

Connell, J. and R. P. C. Brown, 1995, 'Migration and Remittances in the South Pacific: Towards New Perspectives', *Asia Pacific Journal of Migration*, 4 (1), pp. 1–34.

Controller and Auditor-General, 1994, *Controller and Chief Auditor's Report to the Legislative Assembly: Period 1 January 1993–30 June 1994*, Controller and Auditor General, Government of Western Samoa, Apia.

Cyclopedia of Samoa, Tonga, Tahiti and the Cook Islands: A Complete Review of the History and Traditions and the Commercial Development of the Islands with Statistics and Data never before compiled in a single publication, 1907, McCarron, Stewart and Co., Sydney.

Davidson, J. W., 1967, *Samoa mo Samoa: The Emergence of the Independent State of Western Samoa*, Oxford University Press, London.

Douglas, N., 2005, '"Unto the Islands of the Sea": The Erratic Beginnings of Mormon Missions in Polynesia, 1844–1900', in P. Herda, M. Reilly and D. Hilliard (eds), *Vision and Reality in Pacific Religion. Essays in Honour of Niel Gunson*, Macmillan Brown Centre for Pacific Studies and Pandanus Press, Christchurch and Canberra, pp. 243–65.

Fairbairn, T. I. J., 1985, *Island Economies: Studies from the South Pacific*, Institute of Pacific Studies, University of the South Pacific, Suva.

Field, M., 2006, *Black Saturday: New Zealand's Tragic Blunders in Samoa*, Reed Publishing, Wellington.

Field, M. J., 1984, *Mau. Samoa's Struggle Against New Zealand Oppression*, A. H. and A. W. Reed, Wellington.

Fuataʻi, L. I., 2007, 'E Sui Faiga, ae Tumau Faʻavae: Practices Change but Foundations Remain', in A. Soʻo (ed.), *Changes in the Matai System: o Suiga i le Faʻamatai*, Centre for Pacific Studies, National University of Sāmoa, Apia, pp. 173–84.

Gilson, R. P., 1970, *Samoa 1830–1900: The Politics of a Multi-cultural Community*, Oxford University Press, Melbourne.

Gratton, F. J. H., 1948, *An Introduction to Samoan Custom*, R. McMillan, Papakura (Facsimile Edn).

Green, R. C., 2002a, 'Interpretations of Samoan Fortifications', *Archaeology in New Zealand*, 45 (2), pp. 309–24.

Green, R. C., 2002b, 'A Retrospective View of Settlement Pattern Studies in Samoa', in T. N. Ladefoged and M. W. Graves (eds), *Pacific Landscapes Archaeological Approaches*, Bearsville Press, Los Osos, California, pp. 125–52.

Green, R. C., 2007, 'Protohistoric Samoan Population', in P. V. Kirch and J.-L. Rallu (eds), *The Growth and Collapse of Pacific Island Societies*, University of Hawaiʻi Press, Honolulu, pp. 203–31.

Gunson, N., 1993, 'The Tonga–Samoa Connection, 1777–1845', *Journal of Pacific History*, 25, pp. 176–87.

Hamilton, A., 2005, 'God in Samoa and the Introduction of Catholicism', in P. Herda, M. Reilly and D. Hilliard (eds), *Vision and Reality in Pacific Religion. Essays in Honour of Niel Gunson*, Macmillan Brown Centre for Pacific Studies and Pandanus Press, Christchurch and Canberra, pp. 87–105.

Handy, E. S. C. and W. C. Handy, 1924, *Samoan House-building, Cooking and Tattooing*, Bernice P. Bishop Museum, Honolulu.

Hauʻofa, E., 1993, 'Our Sea of Islands', in E. Hauʻofa, E. Waddell and V. Naidu (eds), *A New Oceania: Rediscovering Our Sea of Islands*, University of the South Pacific, Suva, pp. 2–16.

Hauʻofa, E., 2000, 'The Sea in Us', in D. Hanlon and G. M. White (eds), *Voyaging Through the Contemporary Pacific*, Rowman and Littlefield Publishers, Lanham, pp. 113–34.

Hempenstall, P. and N. Rutherford, 1984, *Protest and Dissent in the Colonial Pacific*, Institute of Pacific Studies, University of the South Pacific, Suva.

Hiroa, Te Rangi, Sir Peter Buck, 1930, *Samoan Material Culture*, The Bishop Museum, Honolulu.

Hirsch, S., 1958, 'Social Organisation of an Urban Samoan Village', *Journal of the Polynesian Society*, 67, pp. 266–303.

Howe, K. R. (ed.), 2006, *Vaka Moana: Voyages of the Ancestors*, Auckland Museum/David Bateman, Auckland.

Huffer, E. and A. V. Schuster, 2000, 'Puleʻaga: Views of Governance in Samoa', in E. Huffer and A.

So'o (eds), *Governance in Samoa. Pulega i Samoa*, Asia Pacific Press and Institute of Pacific Studies, Canberra and Suva, pp. 41–66.
Irwin, Geoffrey, 2006, 'Voyaging and Settlement', in K. R. Howe (ed.), *Vaka Moana: Voyages of the Ancestors*, Auckland Museum/David Bateman, Auckland, pp. 54–99.
Kerslake, M. T., 2004, *Aspects which Contribute to the Creation of Wealth and Poverty within the Family Setting*, Research Committee, National University of Sāmoa, Apia.
Krämer, A., 1994, *The Samoa Islands*, The Polynesian Press, Auckland.
Kunitz, S. J., 1994, *Disease and Social Diversity: The European Impact on the Health of Non-Europeans*, Oxford University Press, Oxford.
Le Tagaloa, A. F., 1992, 'The Samoan Culture and Government', in R. G. Crocombe, U. Ne'emia, A. Ravuvu and W. Vom Busch (eds), *Culture and Democracy in the South Pacific*, Institute of Pacific Studies, University of the South Pacific, Suva, pp. 117–37.
Lima, Ieti, 2004, 'Tafesilafa'i: Exploring Sāmoan Alcohol Use and Health with the Framework of Fa'asāmoa', PhD (Sociology), University of Auckland.
Lockwood, B. A., 1971, *Samoan Village Economy*, Oxford University Press, Melbourne.
Lundie, G. A., 1846, *Missionary Life in Samoa*, Oliphant, Edinburgh.
Macpherson, C., 1974, 'Toward an Explanation of the Persistence of Extended Kinship Among Samoan Migrants in Urban New Zealand', DPhil (Sociology), University of Waikato, Hamilton.
Macpherson, C., 1978, 'The Polynesian Migrant Family: A Samoan Case Study', in P. Koopman-Boyden (ed.), *Families in New Zealand Society*, Methuen Ltd, Wellington, pp. 120–37.
Macpherson, C., 1988, 'The Road to Power is a Chainsaw: Villages and Innovation in Western Samoa', *Pacific Studies*, 11 (2), pp. 1–24.
Macpherson, C., 1992, 'Economic and Political Restructuring and the Sustainability of Migrant Remittances: The Case of Western Samoa', *The Contemporary Pacific*, 4 (1), pp. 109–35.
Macpherson, C., 1994, 'Changing Patterns of Commitment to Island Homelands: A Case Study of Western Samoa', *Pacific Studies*, 17 (3), pp. 83–116.
Macpherson, C., 1997, 'The Persistence of Chiefly Authority in Western Samoa', in G. M. White and L. L. Lindstrom (eds), *Chiefs Today: Traditional Pacific Leadership and the Postcolonial State*, Stanford University Press, Stanford, pp. 19–49.
Macpherson, C., 1999, 'Changing Contours of Kinship: The Impacts of Social and Economic Development on Kinship Organisation in the South Pacific', *Pacific Studies*, 22 (2), pp. 71–96.
Macpherson, C., 2004, 'Transnationalism and Transformation in Samoan Society', in V. S. Lockwood (ed.), *Globalisation and Culture Change in the Pacific Islands*, Pearson/ Prentice-Hall, New Jersey, pp. 165–81.
Macpherson, C. and L. Macpherson, 1987, 'Toward an Explanation of Recent Trends in Suicide in Western Samoa', *MAN (NS)*, 22 (2), pp. 305–30.
Macpherson, C. and L. Macpherson, 1990, *Samoan Medical Belief and Practice*, Auckland University Press, Auckland.
Macpherson C. and L. Macpherson, 1998, 'Creeping Paralysis: Dependency and Sovereignty in Peripheral Pacific States', in P. Larmour (ed.), *Governance and Reform in the South Pacific*, National Centre for Development Studies, Research School of Asian and Pacific Studies, Australian National University (Pacific Research Monograph Series), Canberra, pp. 74–98.
Macpherson C. and L. Macpherson, 1999, 'Changing Contours of Migrant Samoan Kinship', in R. King and J. Connell (eds), *Small Worlds Global Lives: Islands and Migration*, Cassell, London, pp. 277–95.
Macpherson C. and L. Macpherson, 2000, 'Where Theory Meets Practice: Cultural Constraints on the Governance Agenda in the Pacific', in E. Huffer and A. So'o (eds), *Governance in Samoa, Pulega i Samoa*, Asia Pacific Press and Institute of Pacific Studies, University of the South Pacific, Canberra and Suva, pp. 17–40.
Macpherson C. and L. Macpherson, 2001, 'Evangelical Religion Among Pacific Island Migrants: New Faiths or Brief Diversions?', *Journal of Ritual Studies*, 15 (2), pp. 27–37.

Macpherson, C. and L. Macpherson, 2005, 'The *Ifoga*: Establishing the Exchange Value of Social Honour in Contemporary Samoa', *Journal of the Polynesian Society*, 114 (2), pp. 109–34.
Macpherson C. and L. Macpherson, 2006a, 'Like Moths to a Light: Misunderstanding the Process of Pacific Labour Migration', *The New Pacific Review/La Nouvelle Revue Du Pacifique*, 3, pp. 65–83.
Macpherson, C. and L. Macpherson, 2006b, 'The Nature and Limits of Traditional Dispute Resolution in Contemporary Samoa', *Pacific Studies*, 29 (1/2), pp. 128–58.
Macpherson, C. and L. Macpherson, forthcoming 2009, '"It was not quite what I had expected": Some Samoan Returnees' Experiences of Samoa', in D. Conway and R. B. Potter (eds), *Return Migration of the Next Generations: 21st Century Transnational Mobility*, Ashgate, London.
Malielegaoi, Tuilaepa L. S., 2008, 'Keynote Statement: Pacific Telecommunications Conference', *Pacific Economic Bulletin*, 23 (3), pp. 66–68.
Martinsson-Wallin, H. (ed.), 2007, *Archaeology in Samoa: The Pulemelei Investigations*, Archaeology in Oceania, University of Sydney, Sydney.
McKay, C. G. R., 1957, 'An Introduction to Samoan Custom', *Journal of the Polynesian Society*, 66, pp. 36–43.
Meleisea, M., 1980, *O Tama Uli: Melanesians in Samoa*, Institute of Pacific Studies, University of the South Pacific, Suva.
Meleisea, M., 1987a, 'Ideology in Pacific Studies', in A. B. Hooper et al (ed.), *Class and Culture in the South Pacific*, Institute of Pacific Studies, University of the South Pacific and Centre for Pacific Studies, University of Auckland, Suva and Auckland, pp. 140–52.
Meleisea, M., 1987b, *The Making of Modern Samoa*, Institute of Pacific Studies, University of the South Pacific, Suva.
Meleisea, M., 1992, *Change and Adaptations in Western Samoa*, Macmillan Brown Centre for Pacific Studies, Christchurch.
Meleisea, M., 2000, 'Governance, Development and Leadership in Polynesia. A Micro-study from Samoa', in E. Huffer and A. So'o (eds), *Governance in Samoa. Pulega i Samoa*, Asia Pacific Press and Institute of Pacific Studies, Canberra and Suva, pp. 189–200.
Meleisea, M. and P. Schoeffel, 1983, 'Western Samoa: Like a Slippery Fish', in A. Ali and R. G. Crocombe (eds), *Politics in Polynesia*, University of the South Pacific, Suva, pp. 81–114.
Meleisea, M. and P. Schoeffel (eds), 1987, *Lagaga: A Short History of Western Samoa*, Institute of Pacific Studies, University of the South Pacific, Suva.
Milner G. B., 1966, *Samoan Dictionary: Samoan–English, English–Samoan*, Oxford University Press, London.
Minister of Finance, November 1978, *The 1979 Budget Statement*, Government of Western Samoa, Apia.
Ministry of Finance, 2008, *Strategy for the Development of Samoa 2008–2012: Ensuring Sustainable Economic and Social Progress*, Economic Policy and Planning Division, Ministry of Finance, Apia.
Moyle, R., 1984, *The Samoan Journals of John Williams 1830 and 1832*, Australian National University Press, Canberra.
Munro D. and S. Firth, 1990, 'Company Strategies – Colonial Policies', in C. Moore, J. Leckie and D. Munro (eds), *Labour in the South Pacific*, James Cook University, Townsville, pp. 3–29.
O'Connor, P. S., 1968, 'The Problem of Indentured Labour in Samoa under the Military Administration', *Political Science*, 20 (2), pp. 10–27.
O'Meara, J. T., 1987, 'Samoa: Customary Individualism', in R. G. Crocombe (ed.), *Land Tenure in the Pacific*, University of the South Pacific, Suva, pp. 74–113.
O'Meara, J. T., 1995, 'From Corporate to Individual Land Tenure in Western Samoa', in R. G. Ward and E. Kingdon (eds), *Land, Custom and Practice in the South Pacific*, Cambridge University Press, Cambridge, pp. 109–56.
Parham, B. E. V., 1972, *Plants of Samoa. A Guide to their Local and Scientific Names with Authorities;*

With Notes on their Uses, Domestic, Traditional and Economic, New Zealand Department of Scientific and Industrial Research, Wellington.

Pitt, D., 1970, *Tradition and Economic Progress in Samoa: A Case Study of the Role of Traditional Social Institutions in Economic Development in Western Samoa*, The Clarendon Press, Oxford.

Pitt, D. and C. Macpherson, 1974, *Emerging Pluralism: The Samoan Community in New Zealand*, Longman Paul, Auckland.

Powell, T., 1868, 'On Various Samoan Plants and their Vernacular Names', *Journal of Botany*, 6, pp. 278–85; 342–47; 355–70.

Powell, T., 1886, *O le Tala i Tino o Tagata ma Mea Ola Ese'ese e iai fo'i o tala i manu ua ta'ua i le Tusi Pa'ia*, Gresham Press, Chilworth.

Pratt, G., 1911, *Pratt's Grammar and Dictionary of the Samoan Language*, Malua Printing Press, Apia.

Pritchard, W. T., 1863–64, 'Notes on Certain Anthropological Matters Respecting the South Sea Islanders (the Samoans)', *Anthropological Society of London Memoirs*, 1, pp. 322–26.

Pritchard, W. T., 1866, *Polynesian Reminiscences, or Life in the South Sea Islands*, Chapman and Hall, London.

Rowe, N. A., 1930, *Under the Sailing Gods*, Putnam, New York.

Samoa Statistical Division, 2002, *Household Income and Expenditure Survey*, Samoa Department of Statistics, Apia.

Schmidt, K., 2005, 'The Gift of the Gods: The Sacred Chief, Priest and Supernatural Symbols in Traditional Samoa', in P. Herda, M. Reilly and D. Hilliard (eds), *Vision and Reality in Pacific Religion. Essays in Honour of Niel Gunson*, Macmillan Brown Centre for Pacific Studies and Pandanus Press, Christchurch and Canberra, pp. 42–65.

Schoeffel, P., 1999, 'Samoan Exchange and "Fine Mats": An Historical Reconsideration', *Journal of the Polynesian Society*, 108 (2), pp. 117–48.

Shankman, P., 1976, *Migration and Underdevelopment: The Case of Western Samoa*, Westview Press, Boulder.

Shannon, T. R., 1996, *An Introduction to the World-System Perspective*, Westview Press, Boulder.

Shore, Bradd, 1982, *Sala'ilua, a Samoan Mystery*, Columbia University Press, New York.

So'o, A., 1998, 'The Price of Election Campaigning in Samoa', in P. Larmour (ed.), *Governance and Reform in the South Pacific*, National Centre for Development Studies, Australian National University, Canberra, pp. 289–304.

So'o, A., 2000, 'Civil and Political Liberty: The Case of Samoa', in E. Huffer and A. So'o (eds), *Governance in Samoa: Pulega i Samoa*, Asia Pacific Press and Institute of Pacific Studies, Canberra and Suva, pp. 133–50.

So'o, A. (ed.), 2007, *Changes in the Matai System. O Suiga i le Fa'amatai*, Centre for Sāmoan Studies, National University of Sāmoa, Apia.

So'o, A., 2008, *Democracy and Custom in Samoa: The Uneasy Alliance*, Institute of Pacific Studies Publications, University of the South Pacific, Suva.

Stace, V. D., 1956, *Western Samoa – An Economic Survey*, Technical Paper 91, South Pacific Commission, Noumea.

Stace, V. D. and A. Lauterbach, 1963, *Economic Survey and Proposed Development Measures for Western Samoa*, Legislative Assembly of Western Samoa, Apia.

Stair, J. B., 1983, *Old Samoa or Flotsam and Jetsam from the Pacific Ocean*, R. McMillan, Papakura.

Steger, M. B., 2002, *Globalism: The New Market Ideology*, Rowman and Littlefield Publishers Inc., New York.

Stuebel, O., 1897, *Samoanische Texte. Unter Beihulfe von Eingeborenen Gessamelt und Ubersetzt*, Otto Elsner, Berlin.

Sutter, F. K., 1995, *The Samoans: A Global Family*, University of Hawaii Press, Honolulu.

Taua'a, S., 2008, *Women in the Informal Sector: The Sāmoan Experience*, National University of Sāmoa Research Reports, Apia.

Tcherkezoff, S., 2000, 'Are the Matai "out of time"? Tradition and Democracy', in E. Huffer and A.

BIBLIOGRAPHY

So'o (eds), *Governance in Samoa: Pulega i Samoa*, Asia Pacific Press, Australian National University and Institute of Pacific Studies, University of the South Pacific, Canberra and Suva, pp. 113–32.

Tcherkezoff, S., 2004, *'First Contacts' in Polynesia: The Samoan Case (1722–1848) Western Misunderstandings about Sexuality and Divinity*, Macmillan Brown Centre for Pacific Studies, The Journal of Pacific History, Christchurch.

Toleafoa, A. F., 2007, 'A Changing Fa'amatai and Implications for Governance', in A. So'o (ed.), *Changes in the Matai System: o Suiga i le Fa'amatai*, Centre for Sāmoan Studies, National University of Sāmoa, Apia, pp. 185–206.

Tomkins, S. M., 1992, 'The Influenza Epidemic of 1918–1919 in Western Samoa', *Journal of Pacific History*, 27 (2), pp. 181–97.

Tuimaleai'ifano, M., 1990, *Samoans in Fiji: Migration, Identity and Communication*, Institute of Pacific Studies, University of the South Pacific, Suva.

Tuimaleai'ifano, M., 2000, 'Talofa e aiga: ua 'ai e lago le tofa', in E. Huffer and A. So'o (eds), *Governance in Samoa: Pulega i Samoa*, Dunmore Press, Palmerston North, pp. 171–87.

Tuimaleai'ifano, M., 2006a, 'Matai Titles and Corruption in Modern Samoa: Costs, Expectations and Consequences for Families and Society', in S. Firth (ed.), *Globalisation and Governance in the Pacific Islands*, Australian National University Press, Canberra, pp. 363–71.

Tuimaleai'ifano, M., 2006b, *O Tama a Āiga: The Politics of Succession to Sāmoa's Paramount Titles*, Institute of Pacific Studies, University of the South Pacific, Suva.

Turner, G., 1983, *Samoa a Hundred Years Ago and Long Before*, R. McMillan, Papakura (Facsimile Edn).

University of the South Pacific, 1988, *Pacific Constitutions, Volume 1, Polynesia*, University of the South Pacific, Suva.

Va'a, L. U. F., 2006, 'The Fa'asamoa', in A. So'o (ed.), *Samoa National Human Development Report 2006*, Institute of Sāmoan Studies/United Nations Development Programme, Apia, pp. 113–35.

Va'a, U. F., 2000, 'Local Government in Samoa and the Search for Balance', in E. Huffer and A. So'o (eds), *Governance in Samoa. Pulega i Samoa*, Asia Pacific Press and Insitute of Pacific Studies, Canberra and Suva, pp. 151–69.

Va'ai, S., 1999, *Samoa Faamatai and the Rule of Law*, National University of Sāmoa, Apia.

Wallerstein, I., 1974, *The Modern World System: Capitalist Agriculture and the Origins of the European World Economy in the Sixteenth Century*, Academic Press, New York.

Wendt, A., 1973, *Sons for the Return Home*, Longman Paul, Auckland.

Wendt, A., 1974, *Flying Fox in a Freedom Tree*, Longman Paul, Auckland.

Wendt, A., 1977, *Pouliuli*, Longman Paul, Auckland.

Wendt, A., 1986, *The Birth and Death of the Miracle Man*, Penguin Books, Auckland.

Whistler, W. A., 1980, *The Vegetation of Eastern Samoa, Pacific Tropical Botanical Garden*, Lawai, Hawai'i.

Whistler, W. A., 2000, *Plants in Samoan Culture: The Ethnobotany of Samoa*, Isle Botanica, Honolulu.

Wilkes, C., 1845, *Narrative of the United States Exploring Expedition During the Years 1838,1839,1840,18 41,1842*, Lea and Blanchard, Philadelphia.

Willson, M., C. Moore and D. Munro (eds), 1990, 'Asian Workers in the Pacific', in C. Moore, J. Leckie and D. Munro, *Labour in the South Pacific*, James Cook University, Townsville, pp. 78–107.

Yamamoto, M., 1990, 'Transformation of Exchange Valuables in Samoa', *Man and Culture in Oceania*, 6, pp. 81–98.

Yamamoto, M., 1994, 'Urbanisation of the Chiefly System: Multiplication and Role Differentiation of Titles in Western Samoa', *Journal of the Polynesian Society*, 103 (2), pp. 171–202.

Index

Aggie Grey's Hotel, 179
agriculture, 3, 36, 71, 79, 88, 102, 158, 159, 161
Agriculture Store/Agriculture Stores Corporation, 161
Ah Chong, Su'a Rimoni, 115
Ah Liki, 160
Ahlburg, D., 146
aid, development, 54–55, 99, 143–6, 157; *see also*, Australia, and aid to Sāmoa; Europe, and aid; New Zealand, and aid and development; New Zealand Aid; USA, and aid to Sāmoa
air services, 25, 51, 60–61
Alaska, 74
alcohol: consumption rates of, 82; introduction of, 36, 37; payment in, 42
All Blacks, 3
American Sāmoa, 64, 119, 161, 170; Sāmoans in, 8, 60, 96, 126
An Introduction To Samoan Custom, 119
Anae, Melani, 93
Apia, 2, 19, 37, 38, 40, 42, 51, 66, 77, 110, 111, 112, 125, 126, 145, 150, 156, 157, 158, 161, 170, 173, 175, 179, 182
Apia–Auckland air travel, 60–61
Apolima, 48
archaeologists, in Sāmoa, 23, 24, 26–27, 188
Asian Development Bank, 143
Assembly of God Church, 140
Asu, 30
anthropologists, in Sāmoa, 24, 26–27, 45–46
Auckland, 151, 161; Sāmoans in, 60, 72, 75, 83, 84, 88, 89, 90, 174
Australia: and aid to Sāmoa, 55, 143, 144; and business with Sāmoa, 160–1; Sāmoans in, 86, 96–97, 126
Australians, in Sāmoa, 63, 64
Austronesians, 7, 26; language of, 26
authority, political and social, 13, 14, 39, 70, 103–4, 114, 121–3, 124, 128, 132–3, 142, 191–3; *see also*, chiefs, authority of

banana, 2, 49, 62–63, 66, 68
Bangladesh, 3
banks and banking, 8, 89; *see also*, loans, procurement of
baptisms, 73, 86, 112
Barnes, S. S., 23, 26

baskets, traditional, 151–2
BBC, 3
Bedford, Richard, 90
Berlin, 40, 67
Berlin Act 1889, 40–41, 44
Bertram, Geoff, 91
Bible, 36
birds, 64
Bismarck Islands, 42
'Black Saturday', 49
Bledisloe Cup, 3
botanists, missionary, 36
Bougainville, 42
Bougainville, Louis Antoine de, 30
Brazil, 62
breadfruit, 2, 66, 87, 138
Brisbane, Sāmoans in, 74, 75
Bro Town, 141
brother–sister relationships (*feagaiga*), 107
Brown, R. P. C., 146
Buck, Sir Peter (Te Rangi Hiroa), 45–46, 155, 179
building practices, 18–19, 64, 79–80, 99, 149, 153–4, 160, 176–80, 182; traditional, 154, 179–80, 181, 182
building projects: houses, 54, 79–80, 85, 89, 153–4; village, 14–15, 83, 84, 89, 99; *see also*, churches, building of; schools, building and renovation of
Burmeister, Augustus, 67
Burns Philp, 160

California, Sāmoans in, 72, 88
capitalism, 28–29, 30, 39, 57, 99, 101, 102–3, 108–13, 188
cash incomes, 111–13, 150, 160–1, 181, 182
cattle, 79, 112
CCTV, 3, 171
cellphones, 25, 173–4; *see also*, telecommunications; telephones
censorship and bans, 16, 23, 171, 172; *see also*, pornography, sanctions against
ceremonial exchanges, 94–95, 126–7
Chan Mow, 160
Chan Mow, I. T., 121
change: cultural, 119; economic, 4, 9, 57, 87, 189; political, 4, 57, 189; social, 4–5, 8–9, 15, 17,

207

INDEX

21, 24, 36–37, 55, 57–58, 59–60, 70, 77–78, 87, 99–104, 116–17, 120–1, 185, 187–8, 191
Changes in the Matai System: O Suiga i le Fa'amatai, 121
chiefs (*matai*), 13, 14, 16, 31–32, 54, 95, 110, 117, 166, 181, 186; authority of, 33, 34, 48, 55, 73, 83, 102, 103, 107, 121–31, 170; choice of, 121–3; suffrage of, 55; *see also*, authority, political
children, 2, 13, 93; *see also*, migrants, children of; young people
China: early empire of, 28; imports from, 2–3, 151, 160–1; *see also*, labourers, Chinese
Chinese–Sāmoans, 66, 67, 69
Christchurch, 90
Christianity, 29–30, 31, 56, 57, 99, 101–2, 105–8, 134, 140, 187–8; *see also*, churches; missionaries; pastors; religion
Christmas celebrations, 72, 89
church leadership, 134–42; *see also*, missionaries; pastors
Church of Jesus Christ of Latter-day Saints, 32, 138–9, 140
churches: as centre of village, 2, 14, 16, 56–57, 62, 100; building of, 14, 38, 39, 64, 89, 91; criticism of, 137–41; events centred on, 61, 72; *see also*, Assembly of God Church; Christianity; church leadership; Church of Jesus Christ of Latter-day Saints; Congregational Christian Church of Sāmoa; Council of Churches; donations, to churches; Methodist Church; missionaries; pastors; Roman Catholic Church; Seventh Day Adventist Church
Citizens' Committee, 51
Clark, J. T., 23, 26
climate change, 3
cocoa, 2, 150
coconut palms, 64–65, 93, 158
cold war, 54
colonialism, 28–30, 99, 101, 103–4, 108–13, 114–15, 188
Colorado, 63
commerce, 36, 37, 43–44, 47
competition, between families and villages, 86, 94–95, 112, 141, 158
computers, 25, 166, 175–6
Congregational Christian Church of Sāmoa (EFKS), 134, 138, 139, 140
Connell, J., 146
Constantin, 32
constitution, Sāmoan, 56, 57, 104, 131–4, 136, 191
consuls, 39–41, 104, 122; British, 40–41; Chinese, 43; German, 37, 40–41, 42; US, 40–41
Cook Islands, 31
copra, 3, 38, 43–44, 67, 150, 170
cost of living, 4
cotton, 38
Council of Churches, 134
courier services, 162
currency: exchange rates of, 4, 72; foreign, 4, 72, 102
customary obligations, 145, 190
Cyclone Ofa, 89, 187
Cyclone Valelia, 89, 139, 187

dance troupes, 92
decolonisation, 52
Deeken, Richard, 42
Denmark, 72
Department of Economic Development, 55
dependency ratios, 81–82
depopulation, 81–82
Deutsche Handels und Plantagens Gesellschaft der Südsee Inseln (DHPG), 42, 67
Deutsche Samoa–Gesellschaft, 42–43
development: assistance, 8, 54, 115, 143–6, 192; plans, 5, 55, 85, 157–8, 192
Dictionary of Samoan Language, 118–19
disabled people, 145, 146
discussion and criticism, of public events and figures, 142, 147, 171; *see also*, family, discussions in
disease: aetiology of, 116; spread of, 29, 30, 46–47, 48, 68–69; *see also*, filariasis; health; medical knowledge and practice
dispute resolution, traditional, 1, 114–15, 130–1
dogs, 64
donations, to churches, 72, 112, 138–9, 141, 145, 167
Dubai, 60
Duke of York Islands, 42
Dundee, 60
Dunedin, 60
DVDs, 141, 171–2

Easter, 89
economists, 24
Edinburgh, 72
education, 13, 14; standards of, 95–97, 158
elections, 86, 124, 130
Electoral Act 1963, 124
electricity, availability of, 2, 156, 158, 164–72

208

empires, *see*, imperialism
English language: learning and speaking of, 171, 172; *see also*, radio, English-language talkback
entrepreneurship, 85, 89, 160–1
environmental degradation, 82
equity, social, 120, 143–5, 192, 193
ethnic diversity, 1
ethnographic data, gathering of, 17
Europe, 28–29, 60; and aid, 55; Sāmoans in, 77–78
Europeans in Sāmoa, 30–31, 149; *see also*, settlers, European
European–Sāmoans, 66–67
expenses: court costs and fines, 112; medical, 112; school, 3, 112; *see also*, donations, to churches
explorers, 25–26, 30, 149

fa'asāmoa, 20, 52, 55, 56, 59–60, 71, 94–95, 99, 110, 112, 113, 117, 123, 131, 185, 186, 190
family (*āiga*), 19–20, 86, 91, 92, 121–3; and land, 38, 102, 103, 109, 128–9; and migration, 59, 72–75, 82–84, 189; discussions in, 15–17, 19–20, 73, 88, 127, 129; importance of, 12–13, 85, 176, 186, 189; power of, 44, 54
family planning, 10–11
Fasito'otai village, 125
Faueā, Chief, 31–32, 33, 118
Faumuinā, 49
fauna, 36, 64, 117–18, 149; *see also*, birds; cattle; dogs; pigs
Field, Michael, 50
fieldwork, in Sāmoa, 1
Fiji, 2, 26, 61, 179; Sāmoans in, 8, 72
filariasis, 118
finance companies and loans, 112
firearms, 31, 35, 37, 42
fishing, 2, 79, 93, 100, 159, 166; commercial, 158; techniques of, 65, 159; vessels for, 16, 85
flora, 36, 62–63, 64–65, 68, 71, 117–18, 149; *see also*, banana; breadfruit; cocoa; coconut palms; cotton; pandanus; papaya; talo
Fono a Faipule, 44
food: changes in, 2, 65–66, 168; distribution of, 166–8; imported, 2, 62–63, 65–66, 79, 95, 168; shortages, 3; staples, 4; traditional, 2, 65–66, 79, 86; *see also*, banana; breadfruit; cocoa; coconut palms; fishing; papaya; rice; talo
Frankie's, 160
freight services, 162
French Polynesia, 31

Fuata'i, L. I., 121
funerals, 61, 73, 84, 86, 90, 94, 112, 137, 166

gambling, 37
gender roles, 93
genealogy, 26
generation gap, 169–71
German: accounts of Sāmoa, 37; administration of Sāmoa, 41–44, 46, 47, 50, 66; *see also*, settlers, German
gerontocracy, 13, 47, 120, 183
Gilson, R. P., 25, 30–31, 33, 34, 41
globalisation, 1–2, 3–4, 7, 9, 10, 13, 15, 21, 25, 56, 57, 187; early phases of, 7, 24, 25–30, 61, 62–71, 75, 101; impact of, 25–26, 61–62, 92–94, 121, 187–8; linguistic markers of, 68–69; present phases of, 61, 71–91
goods, sent by relatives, 61, 85, 158–9
governance, 114–15, 116, 120
Gratton, F. J. H., 119
Great Britain, 3, 37; *see also*, settlers, British
Green, R. C., 23, 26
Gunson, N., 23
Gurr, E. W., 49

Handy, E. S. C., 179
Handy, W. C., 179
Hastings, 72
Hauo'fa, Professor Epeli, 91
Hawai'i, 63, 179; Sāmoans in, 8, 26
health, 36, 49, 79, 158, 187; scientific model of, 104, 115–16
historians, in Sāmoa, 23–24
Honolulu, 83
housing, village, 85, 153–5
human rights, 143–5, 147, 192
Hunt, T. L., 3, 26
hurricanes, 87

identity, social, 13, 92, 192
ideologies, introduced, 9, 99–104, 105–47, 189
ILO, 96
imperialism, 28–30
import prices, 79
import tariffs, 160
imported goods, 94, 151, 152, 160–2; *see also*, food, imported; goods, sent by relatives; India, imports from
income levels, 85, 87, 120, 156–7, 158
independence day celebrations, 22
India, imports from, 15, 160

INDEX

innovation, 9, 15, 16–17, 21, 36, 71, 149, 155, 158, 192; pre-European, 27
international agreements, 7
international organisations, 4, 5, 7, 11, 120, 143, 145, 192
internet, 10, 22, 25, 120, 175–6, 193
Invercargill, Sāmoans in, 89, 90
Iraq, 3, 72

Java, 62
Joachim, 32
Joint Sāmoa Program Strategy 2006–2010, 144

Kansas City, 90
kinship, 1, 57, 91; and labour, 110–11, 113; and land tenure, 109; connections and obligations, 39, 54, 99–100, 102, 111; importance of, 13, 100, 167; *see also*, family
Kitano Tusitala Hotel, 179
knowledge, traditional, 122–3
Korea, market with, 161
Krämer, Dr Augustin, 37

La Société Française de l'Océanie, 36
labour, 42, 51, 66–67, 96, 103, 115, commodification of, 37, 38–39, 103, 110–13, 116; communal, 81, 89, 99, 110–11; indentured, 43, 65; wage, 110–13
labour market, 87–89
labourers, Chinese, 43, 66, 67; Melanesian, 42; Sāmoan, 52–53; Solomon Islanders, 65, 66–67
land, agricultural, 15, 111; commodification of, 37–38, 39, 102, 108–9, 116; customary, 38, 56, 66, 69, 102, 108–9; freehold, 66, 67, 69, 85, 102, 108–9, 182, 190; pressure on, 79–82, 111; provision of for settlers, 41; reform, 45; tenure, 52, 66, 69, 108, 109; use, 79–82, 111, 116, 129, 161; *see also*, families, and land; kinship, and land tenure; villages, and land use in
Land and Titles Court, 73, 74, 83, 122, 128, 134
Lapérouse, Jean-François de Galaup de, 30
Lapita culture, 26, 27
law and order, 13, 14, 114–15, 116, 141; traditional forms of, 114, 130–4
Le Tagaloa, Aiono Dr Fana'afi, 186–7
leadership, 47, 57, 83, 91, 99, 104, 113, 121–32, 134, 188–9; *see also*, chiefs; church leadership
League of Nations, 44, 48
linguistic markers of globalisation, 68–69
literacy, 36
Logan, Captain Robert, 46, 48

London, Sāmoans in, 72, 74, 90
London Missionary Society, 31–32, 33, 35, 47
Los Angeles, 7; Sāmoans in, 74, 83, 174

Macmillan Brown Lecture series, 1
Macpherson, Cluny, 56
Macpherson, La'avasa, 56
Malaita, 42
Malaysia, 2
Malifa, Savea Sano, 135–6
Manono, 32
Manumea Hotel, 180
Maori, 52
Marianas, 44
Marists, 32, 36
Matāutu, 54
mats, 1, 112, 145–6, 149–51, 153, 180–1, 182; *see also*, weaving, mats
Mau movement, 44, 48–50
media, 58, 95, 120, 135, 136, 141–2, 147, 168
medical knowledge and practice, 1; traditional, 63, 71, 116, 118; *see also*, disease
Melanesia, 26
Melbourne, 88; Sāmoans in, 72, 89
Meleisea, Malama, 33, 42, 46, 54, 55, 56, 117, 121, 124
Methodist Church, 134, 138, 140
Methodist Mission, 31, 32, 33, 35
migrants: Sāmoan, 1, 7–8, 52–56, 72–75; children of, 1, 72–75, 76–77, 89–90, 92–93, 190–1
migration, 1, 4, 25, 83, 94–97, 99, 189; countries involved, 60, 72, 83, 86, 88, 89, 90, 111, 126, 130, 174; demography of, 79–82, 83–85; effects of, 23, 53, 58, 59–61, 76, 72–97, 158–9; Polynesian, 45–46, 66; return, 1, 72–73, 75–78, 79, 83, 90, 93–94; to New Zealand, 52–56, 94; to Sāmoa, 66; *see also*, family, and migration
Millennium Development Goals, 144, 158
Milner, George, 118
Ministry of Women, Community and Social Development, 95
MIRAB economy, 91
missionaries, 24, 33–35, 36, 118; power and influence of, 29, 31–37, 107, 117; Sāmoan, 34, 35, 63, 70, 72; *see also*, botanists, missionary; Sāmoan language, and missionaries
Missouri, 74
mobility, social, 88
money: impact of, 99; requests for, 77–78, 93–94, 111–12
Morris Hedstrom, 160

210

mosquitoes, 100, 155
Mulinu'u, 122
music, American, 170

Namulau'ulu Lauaki Mamoe, 43, 44
National Provident Fund, 112
National University of Samoa, 135, 180
natural disasters, 86, 87, 89, 139; *see also*, Cyclone Ofa; Cyclone Valelia; hurricanes
navigation techniques and practices, 26–27, 70, 149
Nelson, Taisi O. F., 47, 49, 50
New Zealand, 2, 3, 20, 26, 51, 52, 161, 169, 171, and administration of Sāmoa, 5, 44–50, 53, 79; and aid and development, 55, 143–4, 145; Sāmoans in, 1, 8, 53, 74, 83, 86, 90, 96, 111, 126, 130; visits to by Sāmoans, 20, 74–75, 76; *see also*, radio, New Zealand; television, New Zealand
New Zealand Aid, 146
New Zealand Farm Field Days, 159
New Zealand Recognised Seasonal Employment scheme (RSE), 96
NGOs, 5, 22, 142, 145–6, 147, 192
Niue, 26

O le Tala i Tino o Tagatama Mea Ola 'Ese'ese e iai fo'i o talai manu ua ta'au i le Tusi Pa'ai, 117
O Tama Uli: Melanesians in Samoa, 42
Obama, Barack, 3
Oloa Kamupani, 43
oral history, 26, 27, 102
oratory, 125

Pacific Ocean, 7, 26–27, 91
Pacific states, 5, 29, 54–55, 90
Pagopago, 72, 96, 170
Palauli village, 165
pandanus, 150
papaya, 151
Papua New Guinea, 42, 63, 70
Parham, B. E. V., 64–65
parliamentary debates, broadcast of, 21, 168, 169
partition, of Sāmoa, 41
pastors, 2, 16, 63, 107, 117, 134–9, 166–7, 186; conduct of, 134–42
patriarchy, 120
Peace Corps, 80
Peloux, Jacques, 32
Persia, 28
pigs, 79–80, 112, 138, 151

Pilitati family, 67
plantations, 14, 42, 65, 67, 71, 78; cocoa, 2; copra, 67; German, 65; work in, 42, 65, 67, 87
pluralism, social, 20, 22, 120
polygamy, 35, 101
Polynesia, 26, 155
Pomasa family, 67
pornography, sanctions against, 16
poverty, 95, 144–5
Powell, George, 36, 117–18
power, political and social, 13, 14, 39–40, 54, 103–4, 114, 133, 147, 191–2
Pratt, George, 36
priests, sacred, 35; *see also*, religion, indigenous
Prime Minister of Sāmoa, Lupesoliai Malielegaoi Tuilepa Sailele, 94–95, 139, 142
Pritchard family, 67
privacy, 154–5
prostitution, introduction of, 37
Pulemelei, 27
Pullack, 43

racism, 42, 45
radio, 21–22, 168–70; English-language talkback, 20; New Zealand, 169; reception, 157; Samoān-language talkback, 20–21; talkback, 20–21, 22, 169; US, 169; *see also*, parliamentary debates, broadcast of
Rapanui, 26
reciprocity, 13, 88, 109–10, 137–9
redistribution, 166–8
refrigerators, 51, 154, 157, 159, 165, 166–8
religion, 1, 2, 3, 22, 100; indigenous, 27, 32–35, 36, 57, 101, 105–7, 116, 118; material benefits of, 32–33; *see also*, Christianity; missionaries; pastors; priests, sacred
religious organisation, freedom of, 22, 132–3, 135–6
remittances, 3–4, 8, 54, 94, 146, 190; and economic growth, 162; and effects on families of, 54, 77–78, 97, 166; value of, 158
rice, 4, 65–66
roads, 14, 51, 89, 129, 157–8
Rodger, Victor, 92
Roggeveen, Jacob, 30
Roman Catholic Church, 31, 32, 36, 134, 171
Rome, 28
Rotumans, in Sāmoa, 65, 69
Roudaire, Gilbert, 32, 36
rural–urban divide, 156–8, 162, 175–6, 181

INDEX

sailors, Sāmoan, 72
Saipan, 44
Sala'ilua village, 95
salaries and wages, 110–11, 112–13
Sāmoa, ancient settlement of, 5, 7, 23–24, 26–27, 149, 188; culture of, 51, 55–56, 62; economic organisation of, 4, 8, 12, 13, 37, 39, 45, 51, 53, 58, 85–89, 96, 114, 158, 160; ethnic mix of, 66–68; Europeans in, 3, 37–38, 40; geography of, 7; independence of, 7, 8, 51–52, 66, 121, 124, 185; political organisation of, 4, 13, 39–40, 42, 44, 45, 46, 56–57, 58, 103–4, 105, 114–15, 131–4, 185, 187; population of, 7–8, 10, 43, 53, 56, 79–81, 85, 90–91, 147, 154–5; social organisation of, 4–5, 9, 13, 17, 25, 26, 35, 39, 45, 51, 54–55, 57, 58, 59, 62, 67, 70, 73, 85, 99, 114, 156, 165–8, 183, 185–8, 191–3; visits to, early, 25–27, 30; *see also*, change, cultural; change, economic; change, political; change, social
Samoa Observer, 22, 135–6
Samoan Broadcasting Service, 3
Samoan Constitution Order 1920, 48
Sāmoan Consulate, Auckland (Maota Sāmoa), 180
Sāmoan language, 26, 36, 118–19; formal, 20–21, 123, 127, 176; use and fluency of, 56–57, 92–93, 127; *see also*, missionaries, and Sāmoan language; radio, Sāmoan-language talkback; television, Sāmoan-language programmes
San Diego, Sāmoans in, 89, 90
San Francisco, 170
sanitation, 79
satire, 141
Saumae'afe, 106
Savai'i, 27, 32, 95, 157, 165
Sāvali, 22
sawmilling technology, 159, 181–2
Schoeffel, P., 117, 121, 124
schools, 3, 156; building and renovation of, 3, 13, 14, 83, 89, 91
Schultz, Dr Erich, 42
security, of houses, 154–5
service industry, growth of, 160, 163
settlers, 3, 32, 37, 39–40, 48, 66, 67, 70–71; British, 37, 66, 67; European, 30–31; German, 37, 67; US, 37
Seu Tia, 27
Seventh Day Adventist Church, 140
Shankman, P., 54, 146
shipping, 162
Sili village, 95

Sinalei Reef Resort, 179–80
Singapore, 86
Siumu village, 180
Smythe, A.G., 49
social development programmes, 144–5
social status and hierarchy, 35
Solf, Dr, 42–44
Solomon Islands, 42, 63, 65; *see also*, labourers, Solomon Islanders
Solomon Islands–Sāmoans, 66–67
Sons, 92
So'o, Asofou, 55, 56, 121
South Pacific Games, 15
sovereignty, 1
Spanish influenza, 46–47
sports teams, 3, 15, 89, 92
SS Talune, 46
standard of living, 79
Statements of Economic Strategy, 144
stores, 85–86
Strategy for the Development of Samoa: 2008–2012, 144
Stuebel, Dr Oscar, 37, 42
subsistence economy, 102, 111
suicide, reporting of, 11–12; youth, 1, 11, 82
SUNGO, 146
Suva, 7
Sydney, 3; Sāmoans in, 72, 74, 83, 88, 90, 174

Talamua, 22
talo, 2, 66, 151
Tangata Pasifika, 171
taxes, 40, 49
taxis, 86, 94
TEAL airways, 61
technology, 4, 16, 25, 58, 64–65, 71, 85, 87, 149–56, 158–9, 160–2, 177–8; spread and uptake of, 4, 23, 156–60, 181–3, 188–9, 192–3
telecommunications, 10, 20, 162–3, 172–4, 193
telephones, 3, 173–4; *see also*, cellphones; telecommunications
Telesā, 106
television, 3, 21, 61, 77, 100, 112, 170–1; availability of, 165, 166; effects of, 78; national, 139; New Zealand, 3, 171; Sāmoan-language programmes, 171
Teuila Festival, 22, 92
The Da Vinci Code, 171
The Samoan Islands, 37
theft, 154–5
timber milling, 16

title bestowals, 86, 112, 124–7
Tokelau, 68
Toleafoa, A.F., 121, 125
Tonga, 26, 27, 31, 41, 146, 181
tools, 65, 85, 87, 151, 154, 158–9, 161
tourism, 8, 92, 150, 158, 179–80
trade, 30, 36, 43, 67, 70, 72, 90
travel to and from Sāmoa, 8, 72–73, 74–78, 90, 94; *see also*, air services; Sāmoa, visits to, early
Tuimaleali'ifano, Morgan, 23, 49, 153
Tumua ma Pule, 46
tuna canneries, 60, 96
Tupua Tamasese Lealofi III, 49
Turner, Reverend Peter, 31, 32
Tuvalu, 26, 74

UN, 143–4
UN trusteeship, 44, 51
UN Universal Declaration of Human Rights, 143
UNDP Human Development Index, 144
unemployment rates, 87, 95
University of Auckland Centre for Pacific Studies Complex, 180
Upolu, 79, 110, 111
US Naval Expedition, 37
USA, 2, 37, 162; and aid to Sāmoa, 55; and influence on Sāmoa, 51–52, 68, 69; Sāmoans in, 8, 72, 83, 88, 89, 90, 174; *see also*, radio, US; settlers, US

Va'a, Unasa Dr Felise, 56, 185–6
Vailoa village, 27
Vaiinupö, Malietoa, 32
Vaitele-fou village, 145
vehicles, ownership of, 161–2
video players, banning of, 16
village councils (*fono*), 14, 16, 21, 34, 54, 89, 95, 103, 114, 122, 131–6, 163, 165, 169, 170
Village Fono Act 1990, 14, 114, 132
villages (*nu'u*), 17–20, 51, 69–72, 86–91, 92–94, 121, 189; and land use in, 64, 79–80; and migration, 59–61, 72–73, 75–78, 79–87, 189; and socialisation, 13–14; beautification programmes in, 14, 63, 89, 92; changes in, 1–5, 89–91, 100–1, 162–83; economy in, 85–89; gardens in, 79–80; importance of, 12–15; layout of, 14–15, 26–27; organisation of, 59–60, 73, 158; *see also*, housing, village; social organisation
violence, in Samoa, 82
Violette, Théodore, 32
voyaging in the Pacific, 26–27

Wales, 72
Wallis and Futuna, 31
warfare, Sāmoan, 31, 33–34, 41, 101, 105, 119
Washington, 74
water, availability of, 79, 80, 156, 158, 162, 163–4
Watters, Ray, 91
weaving: baskets, 151–2; mats, 145–6, 149–51, 180–1, 182
weddings, 59–61, 73, 86, 94, 112, 137, 166, 171
Wellington, Sāmoans in, 60, 72, 74, 75, 83
Western Sāmoa, 41–42, 44, 50, 52, 55, 119, 122
whalers, 70
White Sunday, 89, 141
Wilkes, Commodore, 37
Williams, Reverend John, 31–32, 33, 118
women, place and support of, 50, 93, 120, 130–1, 143–6, 147, 181
Women in Business, 145, 181
women's committees, 79, 150–1
World Bank, 4, 143, 144
World War I, 66
World War II, 25, 44, 50, 51–52, 60, 61, 63, 68, 79
world-systems theory, 28
writers, Sāmoan, 24

Yazaki plant, 88
YMCA, 145
young people, 93, 95–96, 120, 143–5, 147, 169–71, 172, 173–4, 175, 192; *see also*, suicide, youth

213